*The Earl and Edna Stice Lecture-Book Series in Social Science*

THE EARL AND EDNA STICE LECTURESHIP IN SOCIAL SCIENCE was established in the late 1980s at the University of Washington through a bequest of the Stices' son Glen. The goal of the lectureship is to bring outstanding scholars to the University of Washington to discuss issues dealing with the Bill of Rights, philosophy of law, philosophy of politics, privacy in an urban society, the concept of community, the purpose of government, and epistemology. The lectureship rotates among seven social science departments: Sociology, Geography, Political Science, Women Studies, Philosophy, Communications, and History. In 2002, the governing committee of the Stice Lectureship decided to start publishing a series of short, introductory books based on the Stice lectures.

*The Earl and Edna Stice Lecture-Book Series in Social Science*

GERALD BALDASTY, General Editor

*Intimate Citizenship: Private Decisions and Public Dialogues,*
by Ken Plummer

# Intimate Citizenship

Private Decisions and Public Dialogues

KEN PLUMMER

UNIVERSITY OF WASHINGTON PRESS

*Seattle & London*

The Stice Lectureship was established through a generous bequest of Glen Stice to honor his parents, Earl and Edna Stice.

University of Washington Press
PO Box 50096
Seattle, WA 98145
www.washington.edu/uwpress

Library of Congress Cataloging-in-Publication Data

Plummer, Kenneth.
    Intimate citizenship : private decisions and public debate / Ken Plummer.
        p. cm.— (The Earl and Edna Stice lecture-book series in social science)
    Includes bibliographical references and index.
    ISBN0-295-98331-0 (pbk. : alk. paper)
    1. Lifestyles.   2. Alternative lifestyles.   3. Intimacy (Psychology)
    I. Title.   II. Series.
HQ2042.P58    2003
303.4—dc21                                          2003046765

The paper used in this publication is acid-free and recycled from 10 percent post-consumer and at least 50 percent pre-consumer waste. It meets the minimum requirements of American National Standard for Information Sciences— Permanence of Paper for Printed Library Materials, ANSI z39.48–1984. ♾ ⊗

For Michael Schofield

# Contents

*At the end of this century it has for the first time become possible to see what a world may be like in which the past, including the past in the present, has lost its role, in which the old maps and charts which guided human beings, singly and collectively, through life no longer represent the landscape through which we move, the sea on which we sail. In which we do not know where our journey is taking us, or even ought to. . . . This is the situation with which a part of humanity must already come to terms at the end of the century, and more will have to in the new millennium.*

Eric Hobsbawn, Age of Extremes, 1994 (1995 paper): 16–17


*The choice is not between throwing away rules previously developed and sticking obstinately by them. The intelligent alternative is to revise, adapt, expand and alter them. The problem is one of continuous vital readaptation.*

John Dewey, Human Nature and Conduct, 1992: 239–40

# Preface and Acknowledgments

*The social does not "influence" the private; it dwells within it.*

Russell Jacoby, *Social Amnesia*, 1975

Some years ago, my very first undergraduate essay in sociology posed a beguiling question. It simply asked me to discuss the proposition that "sociology is not interested in people." I wrote my answer, attacking the claim, and soon learned that this was not what my tutors wanted to hear. Sociology, I was told, was concerned with social structures and social facts. It used the comparative method and examined the major patterns, transformations, and contrasts in social orders across time and space. As I got a lowish mark, so I learned my first lesson. And, of course, my tutors were right; these are indeed the grand claims of sociology. I should have known better than to believe that sociology was concerned with people. That was the concern of biology, psychology, the arts, maybe even humanism—but certainly not sociology.

Luckily, a few years on, as I struggled to use sociology to make sense of my own life as a young gay man, I encountered some books that told me this convention was really not the whole story. For there was, I discovered, a vibrant strand of thinking in sociology that traced social action, conversation, subjectivity, and biography, as well as the personal life, as valuable fields of inquiry—from Max Weber through C. Wright Mills and Peter Berger and on to modern feminist theorists. Recent widespread interest in such topics as "emotions," "auto / biography," "identity," and "bodies" continues to flag the fact that sociologists can fruitfully study worlds of personal life that have typically been seen as the domain of the psychologist and psychiatrist. Here, human lives become matters of social actions located in historical moments (time) and practices bound into specific places and "habitus" (space). Our very feelings, bodies, sexualities, and ways of thinking take on different patterns under different social conditions. Human nature is not a very human thing; it is indeed a very social thing.[1]

The personal life—its twists and turns—is hence an important part of sociology; a subfield might be called the "sociology of intimacy." The phrase embraces a myriad of arenas of personal life that were once perhaps taken for granted as "just personal matters" but no longer can be. Some of these arenas are well known and much studied, such as gender and families. Others have started to be studied, such as emotions and bodies. Still others

have hardly been noticed: most of the senses, for example—we have yet
to really ponder what the sociology of smells, sights, and sounds would
look like (although a sense of this can be found in Norbert Elias's *The
Civilizing Process*). For me, this is part of what might be called a critical
humanism.[2] A sociology of intimacy can show how these personal lives
assume different patterns under different social orders; can contextual-
ize them across life cycles; can show the ways in which all aspects of intimacy involve "doing things together"[3]—doing gender, doing sex, doing
relationships, doing bodies—and can show the links between intimacies and inequalities, such as class, ethnicity, gender, and age.

My own concern in this book lies with the seemingly rapid changes
that are taking place across the world in the personal life (from test tube
babies and cybersex to lesbian and gay marriages and families and single parenting) and the emerging arenas of public debate that are form-
ing around them. For many people in the late modern world, there are
decisions that can, and increasingly have to, be made about a life. I am
interested in how these personal decisions connect with public debates.
I am concerned with how our most intimate decisions are shaped by (and
in turn shape) our most public institutions: how the public may become
more personal and the personal become more public. This has long been
a concern of sociology, most famously perhaps with C. Wright Mills's
exhortation to connect "the personal troubles of milieu" with "the public issues of social structure,"[4] or what I prefer to see as personal sufferings and public problems.

The book follows a direct line; and as it builds an argument, it is not
a series of separate, disparate essays but an interconnected whole. It starts
by establishing the range of changes surrounding the personal life that
have been happening in the past few decades—most of which are leading to a sense of new intimate troubles and difficult choices. I do not want
to overstate the changes, but I do believe the force of evidence is enough
to suggest that something powerful is going on in our personal lives and
that future generations may well come to live in a very different world.
Indeed, just as my great-grandparents would find the world I now live
in to be one of truly amazing changes, so I suspect that upcoming generations will find the lives we are living now to be barely recognizable.
Change is in the air—as it has been for the last three hundred years or
so—and it is the backdrop to this book.[5]

Change brings fears, and we find many conflicts developing around
changes. Chapter 3 provides examples of the "culture wars." Some of the
conflicts outlined there seem to generate irreconcilable positions and lead

almost to tribal warfare. Both *conflict* and *change* hence form the back-drop to this book and provide the "problems" to which I want to respond.

Chapter 4 develops the core organizing concept to deal with such prob-lems: *intimate citizenship*. I suggest some of the major controversies sur-rounding the use of such a term and go on to claim that a newish form of *doing citizenship* is in the making.

Four themes provide the framework for the rest of the book, chap-ters 5 through 8. I look at how the public sphere is being radically redrawn in the twenty-first century. The phrase "intimate citizenship" senses the crucial role of pluralism and conflict along with the need for dialogue across opposing positions. I highlight the importance of stories of *method* grounded everyday moralities in resolving ethical dilemmas and search out the ways in which many of these issues now figure on a global stage.

My aim is simply to introduce a range of ideas about change, inti-macies, and politics—many of which are not in themselves new, but which have not been placed together like this before. Although the ideas have had a long gestation,[6] they remain provisional and will benefit from some refinement. A synoptical book like mine is a way of setting out the views in the debates.

## Acknowledgments

For their encouragement, I am grateful to the organizers of the Stice Lec-tures at the University of Washington, Judith Howard and Gerald Baldasty, and to the director of the University of Washington Press, Pat Soden; and I thank the Press's editor Pamela Holway for her careful and thoughtful reading of the manuscript. Two critical reviews—from Judith Howard and Jodi O'Brien—proved enormously helpful in refashioning a first draft.

Other groups who have heard versions of this talk and given valuable feedback have been at the Sociology Department, Trinity College, Dublin (special thanks to Hilary Tovey for inviting me); the International Sexuality Conference in Manchester, 1999 (special thanks to Gil Herdt, Gail Hawkes, and, as ever, Jeffrey Weeks, who shared an illuminating time); the Citizenship Conference organized in Leeds by Sasha Roseneil and others; the staff seminar at Thames Valley University (special thanks to my old school pal Malcolm Davies for arranging it); and to my own department at the University of Essex. The indefatigable Bryan Turner aroused my interest in citizenship during his stay as professor of sociol-ogy at Essex; as editor of the journal *Citizenship Studies*, he published a short version of this book. Students in my "Culture and Intimacy" course over the past few years at Essex University and the University of California at Santa Barbara have sometimes looked a little perplexed at what I have been trying to do, but they have always been bright and stimulating.

I also appreciate the support and encouragement of Harvey Molotch, Glenn Wharton, Chris Allen, Agnes Skamballis, Rob Stones, Peter Nardi, Beth Schneider, and Colin Samson, among others.

Along the way the Fuller Bequest Fund at Essex has played a helping hand. The merry band of Wivenhoe troupers enable me to live simultaneously in traditional, modern, and postmodern worlds! Once again, it took a sabbatical term in Santa Barbara for me to be able to finish the book, and I thank the university and the sociology department there for their continuing hospitality.

And, finally, I owe my biggest debt as usual to my own dear intimate partner of many years, Everard Longland.

*Ken Plummer*
*Wivenhoe and Santa Barbara*
*March 2003*

# Intimate Citizenship

Private Decisions and Public Dialogues

# 1

# Intimate Troubles

*When we decided it was time to make babies, I just thought it was the best sex in the world. I just thought it was more intimate, you throw away all the barriers; there was something about it that was just extra loving and special to me. And you lie back and think that a specially wonderful child was going to come out of it. And when it became apparent that there were problems and the first interventions are things like postcoital tests and timing intercourse, I remember going to the doctor. . . .*

*And then you get labeled with "hostile" mucus. That's just the tip of the iceberg. Your sex life is intruded on. . . . What happened with us, it was just taken away—the whole process was taken away. I felt horrible about it. We weren't even going to have sex to make a baby anymore. Mitch was going to do his own thing into a cup and he had trouble with it, the first time. He is very nearsighted, and it was just really uncomfortable for him. It was completely detached from what we were doing. You go to the doctor and he inseminates you, and he says, "I hope we got pregnant this time," and it is like you and the doctor are doing this thing, not your husband. My little brother asked me something about what it was like. And I said: "It is like a guy knocks you up and he doesn't even give you flowers."*

Michelle, quoted in Gay Becker, *The Elusive Embryo*

*Let there be no mistake: now, as before, individualization is a fate, not a choice; in the land of individual freedom of choice the option to escape individualization and to refuse to participate in the individualizing process is emphatically not on the agenda.*

Zygmunt Bauman, *The Individualized Society*

*We live in an age in which the social order of the national state, class, ethnicity and the traditional family is in decline. The ethics of individual self-fulfillment and achievement is the most powerful current in modern society. The choosing, deciding, shaping human being who aspires to be the author of his or her own life, the creator of an individual identity, is the central character of our time. It is the fundamental cause behind changes in the family and the global gender revolution in relation to work and politics. Any attempt to create a new sense of social cohesion has to start from the recognition that individualism, diversity and skepticism are written into Western Culture.*

Ulrich Beck, *"Living Your Own Life in a Runaway World"*

W<small>E ARE STILL</small>, it seems, living in a Dickensian "best of times and worst of times." If we are to believe the media pundits, every day brings its new "troubles." We are supposed to be living in an era that has witnessed the demoralization of society, the spread of urban decay, the rise of crime and brutal inequalities, and the decline of civility. Demon sex stalks the streets.

We are experiencing a war of men against women and the breakdown of family life; child abuse and violence toward women and the elderly are rampant everywhere, alongside a "crisis in masculinity." Ethnic cleansing has become almost common, as has tribalism. A culture of neglect, apathy, and alienation has been born. Children are out of control and under siege, while youth itself has become synonymous with trouble. Abortion signifies the loss of respect for human life that pervades society. Schools, streets, and communities are crumbling. An erotic pornscape has become the routine backdrop to much daily living. Films, from *Blue Velvet* to *American Beauty,* suggest simultaneously the hollowness of contemporary Western life and the violence, aggression, degradation, and sexual obsession that lurk not far from its surface. We live in an increasingly insecure world, characterized by global uncertainty and risk, along with tribal warfare and brutal exploitation, terrorism and the fear of terrorism, polarizing inequalities, and the dehumanization of billions of people.

And yet. At the same time, maybe as never before, the twenty-first century is inviting us to consider a plethora of new ways to live our lives. This is a world in which troubles have obliged us to confront a growing array of "choices" in our personal life—where for many both the troubles in and the options facing a life seem never to have been greater.[1] "Intimate troubles" can now bring with them seemingly major choices concerning families, gender, bodies, identities, and sexualities hitherto unknown in human history. The infertile can turn to assisted conception. Lesbians and gays can enter into registered partnerships and become parents. Younger people can be more experimental with their sexualities. Women have gained some measure of autonomy over their bodies and their lives. Older people are living longer—even into their centenarian years—and thus face decisions about whether and how to live alone. We are able to construct new sexual identities—from transgendered and queer to polyamorous and bisexual. Test-tube babies and "designer children," elective plastic surgery, cybersex and safer sex, along with transgender and bisexual politics—all these have become part of an "issues culture" of public debate that was largely unimaginable just fifty years ago.[2] And a larger number of people in Western cultures than ever before can make the choice to live their lives in real material comfort, global awareness, and democratic relationships.

To set some of the issues forth clearly at the outset—Who would have thought at the start of the twentieth century that by its end we would be seriously discussing such matters as:

*"Intimate troubles" and "choices" around new forms of publicly recognized "family life."* These include the value of single parenting; the legitimacy—moral and legal—of lesbian and gay partnerships, marriages, adoptions, and child rearing; the value of living alone and of adult friendships; and the widespread acceptance of divorce, out-of-wedlock conception, cohabitation, and remarriage. And with these come all kinds of new relationships among multiple stepfamilies, as well as new roles for an ever-expanding "gray" population. Old traditions still survive in the form of bride marriage, child marriage, arranged marriages, and forced marriages, but they increasingly meet with resistance from the participants, and alongside traditional marriages we find a proliferation of new "families of choice."

*"Intimate troubles" and "choices" around sexuality.* Not only have matters of so-called sexual orientation and sexual preference been placed firmly on the agenda by the lesbian and gay movement; so, too, have a string of concerns around non-procreative, non-penetrative, non-reproductive, "recreational," "safer" sexualities: telephone sex, cybersex, outercourse, masturbation, sadomasochism, "fist-fucking," and the fetish scene. These in turn raise concerns about teen sexuality and even about sexually active children.[3]

There is also the international commercialization of sex in which millions of men, women, and even children earn their living by performing live sex acts. And closely allied is the problem of what limits should be placed on "sexual representation" or "pornographic filth," as cybernet systems seem more and more to be clogged with sexual imagery of all kinds.

*"Intimate troubles" and "choices" around genders.* These include not only the frequent breakdown of traditionally conceived notions of the masculine and the feminine and hence new choices about different kinds of femininities and masculinities, but also the emergence of what some see as major "gender wars," as men and women seem increasingly incapable of living with each other and as sexual violence seems

to be on the increase. And side by side with this, newer concerns over bisexuality and polyamory,[4] gender benders and gender blenders, queers, lesbian daddies, dyke boys, drag kings, and transgender warriors are put on the agenda!

*"Intimate troubles" and "choices" around infertility, giving birth, and "designer babies"*—struggles over the new reproductive technologies or assisted conceptions. Here we enter into controversies around surrogate motherhood, test-tube babies, and the whole paraphernalia of in-vitro fertilization, egg donation, artificial insemination by donor, gamete and intra-fallopian transfer (or GIFT), the freezing of fetuses, embryo research, the commercial market in babies, and the decline of male fertility, coupled with fertility boosting. Moreover, we are only a few steps away from "cloning." Such concerns take us to the heart of key questions about intimacy: What is a mother? What is a child? Why have a child? What is a family? And there again, just what can it be like to be born the child of a 63-year-old mother?

*"Intimate troubles" and "choices" over the ever wider use of medical technologies and drugs to transform that most central organ of intimacy: the body.* These include implants, cosmetic surgeries, new medications like the impotency wonder drug Viagra and the miracle "morning-after" abortion pill, as well as disciplining machines like brain implants and electronic tagging that can now serve as direct adjuncts to our bodies, enter our bodies, replace our bodies. The body—even the fetus—is modified both internally and externally: it is a New World and language of people as "cyborgs," people as becoming "post-human." Just what does this mean—and do we really want to become post-human? At the same time, the sense of our bodies in time and space starts to become reconfigured as we are captured on the videos of a surveillance society.

*"Intimate troubles" and "choices" over how to deal with a growing array of unacceptable approaches to intimacy.* These range from the regulations that have appeared in most workplaces pertaining to courtship and sexual harassment to anxieties about serial sex murders to enormous fears surrounding the sexual abuse of children, together with concerns over sadomasochistic practices and calls for the registration of pedophiles.

*"Intimate troubles"* and *"choices"* over a whole gallery of new *"personal types"*—sex addicts and compulsives and PWAs (people with AIDS), surrogate mothers and "women who love too much," "Iron Johns" and "New Men," as well as those suffering from a whole new set of afflictions with labels like "post-traumatic stress disorder" and "false memory syndrome." Here we are witnessing the emergence of all sorts of new "private problems and public troubles" in a relentless flow of media events focusing on personal life. This includes books and films, television, and cyberworlds. To watch a TV talk show such as *Oprah* or *Jerry Springer* is to sense a proliferation of anxieties and a newfound fascination with the interior life.

Here in the public domain of television, day after day the personal problems of late modernity are enacted in myriad ways. Likewise, in cyberworlds, chat rooms can carry debates of the bisexual and the polyamorous life, and message boards can assist people in finding like-minded intimates.

This list could be extended. But it serves to flag both the *practices* of the new intimacy and the *discourses and debates* around these practices that are becoming increasingly common as we enter the twenty-first century.[5] These issues are here, and they are not very likely to go away.

Such issues threaten to overwhelm us as they lead more and more people to ask: *How do we live—and how should we live—our lives in an emerging late modern world?* (I use the terms *late modernity* and *postmodernity* almost interchangeably to characterize major changes of the sort discussed below. *Second modernity* is another such term.) From a great many sources come signs that at least *some* personal lives are being transformed. We could view them, as many do, in despair—as instances of decline, decay, or discipline. But we could also see these transformations as evidence of a desire for greater individualism and as an emerging pattern whereby we come to believe that we are gaining greater control over our lives. And, indeed, such gains are often real when compared with the limited choices of the past.

Of course, while some of these concerns do seem genuinely new—those linked to modern reproductive technologies or cybersex, for example—many of them have long and tangled roots in the past. The new is often not as new as we like to think. Sex work—or prostitution—may be "the oldest profession," same-sex marriages may have quite a long history, and families of the past were also governed by complex and varied relationships. And the panics and debates about moral and personal life have surely been recurrent themes at least of the modern world.[6] Indeed, conservative critic Gertrude Himmelfarb has tellingly suggested in *One Nation, Two Cultures* that much of the history of civilized societies "can be written as a continuing clash between a strict, austere system and a liberal or loose system"; while, in *Sexual Anarchy*, the more radical literary critic Elaine Showalter suggests that direct parallels exist between fin-de-siècle crises and those of today.[7] From concerns over sexual disease, the age of consent, and the arrival of "new women" to fears of homosexuality, the crisis of the body, and the appearance of a runaway Frankenstein world of technology, worries at the turn of the nineteenth century were not that different from the fears we face at the turn of the twentieth century. So we have to be careful about suggesting too much change and too radical a rupture.

But there surely is a difference. For many now argue that we are indeed moving into a radically new kind of social order. The titles of a spate of recent sociological studies soon give rise to a sense that something is afoot (apart from a publishing boom, perhaps). We have *The Transparent Society* (Vattimo), *Disorganized Capitalism* (Lasch and Scott), *Liquid Society* (Bauman), *The Individualized Society* (Bauman), *World Risk Society* (Beck), *Cosmopolitan Society* (Beck), *The Global Age* (Albrow), *The Information Age* (Castells), *The Planetary Society* (Melucci), *The Surveillance Society* (Lyon), *The McDonaldization of Society* (Ritzer), *The Exclusive Society* (Young), along with *global modernity* and *second modernity* (Beck), and *late modernity* (Giddens).[8] Indeed, Anthony Giddens, in the annual Reith lectures for the BBC, captured it all as a *Runaway World*: a world where traditions break down, where we actually find ourselves with less control over our lives, a world in which we need to democratize democracy. Recognized in these studies are a set of key social processes variously identified as "globalization," "detraditionalization," "mediazation," "digitalization," "reflexive modernization," "cosmopolitanism," "disorganized capitalism," "post-Fordism," "McDonaldization," and the "Third Way." It is also the world of the post-: post-feminism, post-history, post-identity, post-Marxism, post-colonialism, and post-modernism. All of this is, of course, the subject of much contentious debate, and we will return to it later.

Moreover, it is important to recognize that, at the twentieth century's end, across the globe, *most of us were and are probably living simultaneously in traditional, modern, and postmodern worlds.* But it must be stressed that we do this at manifestly different speeds, to differing degrees, and with differing levels of self-awareness. Those who are aging, for example, and most of the population of "developing / majority / Third-

World / low-income" societies may still lead lives guided largely by tradition. And some have yet even to enter the modern world. At the other
extreme, many younger people and richer nations may find the postmodern to be more and more congenial to the organization of their lives.[9]
Thus, *traditional intimacies* are still the norm in intense communities, in which people live surrounded by their families and neighbors and
participate in bonding rituals embedded in strongly patriarchal and / or
religious social orders.[10] For these people, for whom tradition lies at the
core of their lives, the relevance of new forms of sexualities and intimacies is minimal.

*Modern intimacies* have emerged over the past two hundred years or
so and have become enmeshed in the many features of modernity
already familiar to social scientists: capitalism, urbanism, anomie,
bureaucratization, commodification, surveillance, and individualization. As societies become more and more "modern," so do all these features rapidly multiply. There is an upside and a downside to all this. On
the one hand, intimate relations in modernity become a form of life
engaged in a search for authenticity, meaning, freedom: human relations
become individuated in a world of choices. There is a general democratization and informalization of everyday life, even as technological
growth speeds up. On the other hand, intimate relations become forms
of life increasingly trapped within wider bureaucratizing and commer-
cializing forces: human relations are subject to what has been called
McDonaldization and Disneyfication, at the mercy of the ever-harsher
demands of the world market. Lives become locked in financial relationships, in patterns of exploitation, framed by choices generated by
mass consumption and worldwide market structures. Intimacies in the
modern world are thus subject to contradictory tendencies.

*Late modern (or postmodern) intimacies* incorporate the latter stages
of the above, with newer possibilities grafted onto the old in a high-tech
global world. We are just "on the edge" of all this. Some people's lives
remain largely untouched by the postmodern world. But many lives are
affected—and increasingly so. Again, postmodernity has both positive
and negative dimensions, as Figure 1 suggests. Indeed, such disjunctions
are my primary focus in the pages that follow.

## Entering Cyberspace

To expand on just one example: the world of cyberspace and erotica /
pornography. Here we find a world of new problems that we have little

| The Dystopian View | The Utopian View |
|---|---|
| Widening disparities in levels of income, greater poverty world-wide | A higher standard of living for larger numbers of people |
| Social fragmentation and marginalization, the persistence of racism and sexism, balkanization | An emphasis on equality and an ethos of pluralization, in which differences are recognized and embraced |
| An atmosphere of impersonality and the loss of community | A sense of belonging to and participating in new social worlds |
| Narcissism, self-centeredness | Respect for other people's individuality |
| McDonaldization, standardization | A proliferation of choices |
| A dumbing-down of ethics and culture | A more sophisticated sense of self-awareness |
| Moral decline and a general lack of civility | Moral effervescence, global citizenship, and ethics |
| Entrenched hierarchies of exclusion | The democratization of personhood and relationships |
| Uncertainty, risk, chaos, a world out of control | The chance for a new world order and for global human rights |

FIGURE 1. *Utopian and Dystopian Worlds*

real idea how to handle but that have generated much talk over the past few years. Of course, in some ways the issue of pornography has been around for a long while.[11] Just as when photography was first introduced, it soon generated the pornographic photograph, so as soon as cyberworlds appeared, an erotic world appeared alongside them. And this is truly a new world: for the first time in history, unregulated erotica of all kinds are available at the touch of a computer key. And it is no small world, as anyone who explores a few Web sites can soon testify.

The cyberworld of erotica can even be credited with generating new forms of sex. Thus we have *cyberporn, cyber-stalking, cyber-rape, cyber-victims, cybersex, cyber-voyeurism, tele-operated compu-sex, sex chat rooms, sex news groups, sex bulletin boards, camcorder sex, virtual sex,* and even so-called *teledildonics.* This cybersexual smorgasbord has led to a major battle over the First Amendment, with those who support the freedom of the Web lining up against those who argue that the Web is destroying society. The Web can certainly foster talk, in chat rooms and the like, but it can under certain circumstances also work its way into private zones such as bedrooms, sex dungeons, and even toilets, thereby causing boundaries between the private and the public suddenly to crumble. Likewise, reality video is pumped live and uncensored into homes, and millions of chat rooms, with names like Club Love, Buddy Booth, and Couples Room, are available to anyone who cares to join. Consider some of the more specific questions posed by the arrival of cyberspace over the past few years:

> Do cyberspace interactions require the same rules as conventional mail? Can one remain anonymous? Is it acceptable to use pseudonyms? Can the choice of a fictive personality ("persona") do harm to other users? How decent is it to post a picture of your ex-partner on the Web? Can one gossip, lie, and deceive in the virtual world? Are you responsible for decisions taken by your personal digital assistant? What about "hacking," "spamming," and "flaming"? How well should one protect one's privacy? Should children's access to cyberspace be guarded? What dangers threaten your children when they surf the Internet? Should one arrange financial matters through cyberspace? Is software piracy the same as theft? Is digital surveillance of employees morally acceptable? What should we do if we want to protect free speech in cyberspace but also want to rid the Net of child pornography and racism? As more and more schools begin to use the Internet, questions come up such as: Should pupils be totally free in the use of the Internet? Can we design reasonable guidelines for children's use of cyberspace? Does cyberspace demand moral rules different from existing ethics? How adequate are the existing moral standards? Do we need a new morality for virtual reality?[12]

And this is just for openers. The ethical issues raised by cyberspace go on and on. And so, I suggest, it is for all of our changing intimacies as we enter a late modern world. As we move from "gay marriages" to the freezing of embryos for use in later life and on to euthanasia and sexual violence, we become saturated with moral problems. *New intimate troubles bring new ethical conflicts.*

## Doing Intimacies

What all these problems have in common is that they reside in what I will call the intimate sphere. This book is broadly concerned with intimacies, a term often heard these days. It does, however, mean many different things. According to the dictionary, the word first appeared around 1632; it is derived from late Latin and pertains to "the inmost," that is, our innermost thoughts or feelings. In *An Intimate History of Humanity,* Theodore Zeldin suggests that three kinds of intimacy have emerged over time. Initially, the notion of intimacy was linked to space and to objects—"an intimate room . . . into which one withdrew from the hubbub of relatives and neighbors," or intimate souvenirs and relics, such as a lock of hair, "which one cherished as though there was magic in them."[13] Later came a more romantic meaning, at the core of which was the union of two souls—most centrally through sexual intercourse. More recently still, Zeldin suggests, the term has come to signal a partnership in the search for truth, a union of minds.

It is in this last meaning that sociologist Lynn Jamieson sees the term at work today. For her, intimacy involves a very special "sort of knowing, loving and being close to another person" that depends upon a particular kind of "disclosure and disclosing." In this general sense, intimacy implies a close association between two people, a privileged knowledge of each other, and an overall attitude of "loving, sharing and caring." In the modern world, for Jamieson, there are four paradigmatic forms of intimacy: couple relationships, friend and kin relationships, parent-child relationships, and sexual relationships. We are dealing here with specific kinds of relationships, but also with a certain overarching ideal: people strive for intimacy—for good relationships. Novelist Hanif Kureishi's *Intimacy* deals with some of this, too—and yet by the time part of his novel became a film, the focus was more and more on the sex.

At the same time, some discussions of intimacy move us away from love and sexuality and into other areas. Elizabeth Stanko's work on women's experiences of male violence, for example, is called *Intimate Intrusions* (1985) and takes us into a very different sphere: rape and abuse, issues central to the women's movement across the world. But in a sense

Stanko's use of the term does connect back to its original meaning: rape is, after all, an inmost violation of the being and the body.

The term "intimate" thus has no unitary meaning but may be seen as a complex sphere of "inmost" relationships with self and others. Intimacies are not usually minor or incidental (although they may be transitory), and they usually touch the personal world very deeply. They are our closest relationships with friends, family, children, and lovers, but they are also the deep and important experiences we have with self (which are never entirely solitary): with our feelings, our bodies, our emotions, our identities. We *do* intimacies when we get close to all these feelings and emotions. Intimacy exists in the doing of sex and love, obviously, but also in the doing of families, marriages, and friendships, in child bearing and child rearing, and in caring for others. In these instances, intimacy is likely to have close links to particular kinds of gender, body projects, and feeling work.[14] Bodies, feelings, identities, relationships, interactions, even communities—all are central elements in doing intimacies.

## The Intimate Citizenship Project

Figure 2 lists the zones of intimacy and some principal questions linked to each. How are we to cope with these questions while living in a world of growing dissent where appropriate ethical blueprints no longer seem readily available? Our intimacies are now thoroughly contested. Can we find some sense of the universal, however provisional, on which we can agree in a time of such rapid change and, for some, social disintegration? Or does it even matter? In the following two chapters we will look at some potential areas of conflicts over ways of doing intimacy in the postmodern world. I will consider possible ways of finding "values in a godless world," or at least ways to appreciate the politics surrounding these new choices and changes.[15] I make no grand claims, but I do believe that a new language is evolving at the start of the twenty-first century—dim and inarticulate, but nevertheless audible. My task is to piece some of it together, to create a pastiche of fragments of new ways of living. In creating this pastiche, I will use the language of "intimate citizenship"—an idea I take to be a sensitizing concept, one that is not meant to be tight and operational, but open and suggestive.[16]

I use the notion of intimate citizenship to hint at worlds in the making, worlds in which a public language of "intimate troubles" is emerging around issues of intimacy in the private life of individuals. In a late

| Zone | Issue |
| --- | --- |
| Self | How to live comfortably with ourselves, how to be our own person |
| Relationships | Whom to choose as a partner, and how to live harmoniously together |
| Gender | How to live socially and culturally as a gendered being |
| Sexuality | How to construct our own sexualities, how to live happily and responsibly as a sexual person |
| The family | How best to care for children and for the elderly, how to preserve cherished values |
| The body | How to treat our bodies with respect, how to cope with illness |
| Emotional life | How to acknowledge and express what we feel |
| The senses | How to pay attention to tastes, smells, sights, sounds, and physical sensations |
| Identity | How to locate ourselves in our temporal and cultural milieu |
| Spirituality | How to feel connected to the environment, to the cosmos, to a higher power, or to God |

FIGURE 2. *Zones of Intimacies*

modern world, where we are so often confronted by escalating difficulties and a growing array of choices, the concept of intimate citizenship can help to suggest ways of doing the personal and intimate life. As I suggested in an earlier book, intimate citizenship looks at "the decisions people have to make over *the control (or not) over* one's body, feelings, relationships; *access (or not) to* representations, relationships, public spaces, etc.; and *socially grounded choices (or not) about* identities, gender experiences, erotic experiences. It does not imply one model, one pattern or one way."[17]

## Key Strands of Intimate Citizenship

In charting our course, we will first need to establish what is meant by "intimacies," a task I began above. (Figure 2 lists the main zones of intimacy that need to be explored.) Second, I will need to sketch the background of what concerns me: *the nature of social change and intimacies.* Of course, change is a feature of all societies, but I have been hinting that the changes the late modern world is experiencing are having striking consequences for the intimate life. The examples I provided at the start of this chapter to some extent illustrate this, but in Chapter 2 we will explore the subject of postmodern intimacies more fully.

Change brings with it dissent, and in Chapter 3 we will gain a sense of both "culture wars" and the contested nature of intimacies. Throughout the zones of intimacy, multiple voices are asserting strongly differing points of view. How will we survive in the future if there is no agreement—when we indeed live in a world of deep antagonism, tribal warfare, and ethnic genocide? Is a dialogue still possible, and if so what might it sound like?

One potential way into these problems is to take an old idea—that of citizenship—and re-dress it for postmodern times. The term "citizenship" must be viewed as problematic. Of course, it has a long history, one in which it has undergone many splits and turns of fortune. But if anything is clear it is that citizenship nearly always refers to the social, civic, public world, not to individual, intimate, or private worlds. So the very term "intimate citizenship" feels like an oxymoron: how can the world of the public be used to provide an "intimate citizen"? To answer this question, I focus in Chapter 4 on the many new meanings that have been given to the idea of citizenship in recent years.

But the concept of intimate citizenship also raises the issue of the links between the private and public spheres. Citizenship emerges in the public sphere(s); intimacy, in the private. If "intimate citizenship" seems an oxymoron, it also suggests a potential bridge between the personal and the political. Chapter 5 discusses the new shapes of the public sphere—which I see as multiple, hierarchically layered, and contested public spheres ("the black public sphere," the "gay public sphere," the "sex worker sphere," the "evangelical Christian sphere," and so on). Along with the classical (usually male) public spheres of political participation, several newish public spheres also require analysis. These include the new social movements, the mass media, and cyberspace.

Within such debates the issue of ethics and morality returns. How should we conduct our personal life in a late modern world, a life that can embrace aspects of tradition, the modern, and the postmodern? How can we find some sense of the universal, however limited, among all the pluralization, polyvocality, and difference? How will we live with a postmodern ethics that recognizes the importance of "freedom, justice, equality, care, recognition, minimal harm"? Part of the answer may lie in attending to the situatedness of moral debate, and this is best accomplished by listening to "stories" of all kinds rather than through abstract principles. It is concerned with *grounded or concrete moralities and with the function of narrative in public life*—its makings, its workings, and its uses. I turn to all this in Chapters 6 and 7.

And finally, since we can no longer function in isolated worlds, these issues need to be linked to issues of globalization, which I do in Chapter 8. Many of these debates can no longer be understood in terms of a specific country or nation but are engaged in on a wider scale and have much broader social ramifications. We may be starting to see the arrival of something like "global citizens," who raise issues of global intimacies through their many and varied experiences, whether these relate to international sex tourism or to new migrating families. At the heart of this discussion is the suggestion that we are on the brink of a new world order—either a dystopian one of fundamentalism, ravaging conflicts, and exploitation or a utopian one in which human-rights regimes will foster a wider order of world citizenship. Here we can start to look at the global public discourses around intimacies.

In this chapter I have established both the central problem of the book and the terrain to be covered. I have also, I hope, made clear that this is a very provisional quest. I know we will wind up with more questions than answers. But that is the nature of the task.

## 2

# Postmodern Intimacies:
## New Lives in a Late Modern World

"One Birth in 80 from a Test Tube"

*Guardian* headline, June 28, 2000

"Gay Couple's Twins Denied Access to UK"
*The babies were conceived after Barrie Drew and Tony Barlow[gay men] found a surrogate mother in California. But when they got back to Britain last week, immigration officials detained their babies and their parents were questioned for more than an hour.* *Guardian*, January 3, 2000

"Parents Create Baby to Save Sister"
*Doctors have used genetic screening to select a test-tube baby with precisely the right cells for him to act as a donor to his seriously ill older sister.*

*Guardian*, October 4, 2000

"Conceived, Delivered and Sold: A Baby for $6,000"
*A new trade, a sophisticated spin-off in people smuggling, has been spawned. Last July, Italian police recalled that up to three dozen prostitutes had been shipped to Germany to sell their children to wealthy western couples.*

*Guardian*, December 9, 2000

"Sale of Babies on Internet to Be Outlawed"
*The sale of babies on the internet is to be banned under new laws proposed this week. (Since www.adopting.org was set up four years ago it has been visited by 2.1 million. . . . Babies start with a fee of £5.000.)*

*Independent on Sunday*, June 17, 2001

"Internet Twins Belong in US, Judge Rules"
*The American twin girls at the center of an internet adoption row must be returned to their birthplace in St. Louis, Missouri, a London judge ruled yesterday. . . . A baby broker was paid £8,200 by Judith and Alan Kilshaw to arrange the adoption.* *Guardian*, April 10, 2001

"IVF to Give Woman a Baby by Brother"
*An infertile Frenchwoman is preparing to have her brother's child through artificial insemination at a British fertility clinic in an operation that will spark new debate about the ethics of IVF treatment. . . . The 47 year old woman used an egg from an anonymous donor and her brother's sperm.*

*Guardian*, August 27, 2001

*Wasn state judge rules in favor of gay marriage because no solid evidence of harm to children of gay parents - 8/4/03*

THE TALES OF "new reproduction" that introduce this chapter represent but a sprinkling of the new ways in which life itself is coming to be. Headlines like these were unthinkable just thirty years ago. It has been a quiet but almighty revolution whose implications are enormous and whose future is largely uncharted.[1]

Yet the new reproductive technologies are only one of many such sets of changes. The idea of "intimate citizenship" has been proposed to help us get a sense of precisely how intimacies may be changing and how they are being contested.In this and the following chapter, I seek to establish the need for such an idea and show how the notion of intimate citizenship speaks to a new public language of change and conflict.

## The Slow Collapse of the Grand Narrative of Intimacy

What I want to suggest here is that newly emerging intimacies reflect the slow death of any single "grand narrative" of personal life. Of course, no society has ever had just one narrative about how life is to be lived (as some postmodern social theorists seem mistakenly to imply). Societies have always been ambiguous, variable, conflictual, changing. But societies have typically sought to provide one overarching cultural paradigm that seems to plausibly hold together the world and its history—often by means of a God or gods. Christianity, Islam, and Hinduism, for example, have evolved into master narratives that stretch like canopies over whole cultures.[2] But just as they always have been, religious traditions are riddled with schisms, conflicts, disbelievers, and critics. These days, however, such conflicts are much more visible and public—and for many people this makes religious tradition less and less plausible as the source of the "one grand story" of the world. Yet, the very fragility of these traditions can ironically lead them to adopt stronger and stronger positions, to claim more and more authority, generating a powerful sense of tribal fundamentalisms over lives. Religious tradition is one—indeed, probably the major—source of conflict and tension around how to live life today. Most of the new intimacies, and the choices they make available, are vehemently opposed by religions of all kinds.

Despite this, people seem increasingly aware that this "one way" is visibly crumbling in the postmodern world. Our formerly strong conviction of unity, permanence, continuity—of one moral order under God—has started to collapse, and what we now find instead are fragmentations, pluralizations, multiplicities. Familiar notions of "the family," of what it really means to be "a man" or "a woman," of "the truth" of our sexuality, of what "the body" really is, of a core identity—all these ideas are being challenged. (And indeed some people, including myself, would argue that the world was never quite this simple anyway—though it has often been made to seem so.) A seemingly wider range of possibilities is now available. Whereas the traditional world was usually conceived of as a singular world, the postmodern world of intimacies is one of plurals. Thus, where we once spoke of "men and women," the postmodern speaks of masculinities, femininities, and, indeed, genders. There are now multiple ways of being gendered, even if there are dominant patterns.[3] Likewise, if we once spoke of "sexuality," we now recognize a plurality of "sexualities," as the recent appearance of academic journals with titles like *Genders* and *Sexualities* suggests. The family, too, has been replaced by postmodern families where "pluralism and flexibility [represents] a democratic opportunity in which individuals' shared capacities, desires, and convictions could govern the character of their gender, sexual and family relationships."[4] In each case, the idea of a unitary, "fixed" essence is deconstructed and delegitimated as a way of thinking about the world. Our language starts to become richer and more complex, allowing us to acknowledge a wider range of possible ways to be human.

Perhaps overoptimistically, in his epic account of late-twentieth-century social change, *The Information Age,* Manuel Castells suggests that we are moving into a "post-patriarchal world," one in which marriage, family, heterosexuality, and sexual desire—commonly viewed as a closely linked cluster in the past—are becoming increasingly separated from one another.[5] They are, indeed, becoming their own autonomous spheres. "Sex," for example, no longer works its once prime task of procreation: instead, it now serves a multiplicity of purposes, including pleasure, the establishing and defining of relationships, the communication of messages concerning attitudes and lifestyles, and the provision of a major mechanism for subjection, abuse, and violence. (In the perhaps unfortunate phrasing of Anthony Giddens, it may now be "plastic sexuality," a sexuality divorced from reproduction and thus much more "open.") Sexuality also probably now embraces a much wider range of routine sexual practices; in any event, options such as oral and anal sex are more openly acknowledged than in the past. In short, "sex" serves many ends, assumes many forms, is bound up with more things, and yet is becoming more autonomous, more a matter of individual choice.[6]

## The Social Flows of Late Modern Intimacies

This gradual shift from traditional unities to what may better be thought of as a pluralized pastiche is accompanied by many further-linked developments. Many, perhaps even most, of these developments are not wholly new: they are accelerations of past trends. Some years ago, Arjun Appadurai, writing about globalization, provided a striking image: he saw globalization as a series of *flows*—of media, people, ideas, finance, and technologies—across the world. As do many other things, late modern intimacies nest in these vast social and cultural flows. As they move across the globe, they leave their mark on the cultures they encounter, even as they are themselves subtly transformed. In part to suggest the scale of the change, I will briefly characterize eleven such cultural flows through which intimacies are shaped and disseminated.

### 1. *Intimacies and the Media*

Patterns of intimacy have become increasingly embedded in media and digital flows. This is true not just in the simple sense that most media provide endless stories and images of intimacy, along with debates over questions of intimacy. On television, for example, these range from the soap-opera tales of sex and family found in *Friends* (new ways of living together) and *Sex in the City* (New York sophisticates at sexual play) to the talk-show offerings of *Jerry Springer* or *Oprah* that flaunt the endless tragic possibilities of an individual life, to the "reality" shows such as *Big Brother* that expose relationships as they happen or show us how to live together for four weeks on a desert island! It is also true in a wider sense that much of our daily conversation is both about and informed by these media. Watching television and talking about it, for instance, has become a primary activity for families, lovers, and friends. The death of Princess Diana and her lover, the sexual antics of an Eminem, Madonna, or Michael Jackson, the romance and spectacle of the film *Titanic,* or the Clinton-Lewinsky "cigar capers," which were disseminated throughout the world on the Web—all these media-based images of sexuality start to infiltrate our most intimate talk and relationships. In the case of the Clinton-Lewinsky scandal, people began to ask exactly what constitutes sex—and indeed whether oral sex is really "sex." Terms that the average person had seldom if ever used suddenly became the province of all.

Let me clarify that I am not suggesting any straightforward cause-and-effect impact of these media on our intimate lives, such as the crude suggestion that pornography leads us to commit pornographic acts or that the media's portrayal of sex is generating moral decline (and both claims are common enough). Rather, I am suggesting that the very cultural air we breathe in a postmodern world is saturated with simulations from media. Many—especially the younger generations—live their intimacies through the media. From the first taste of breakfast TV as we wake up, through the constant companionship of our cell phone to the last check of our e-mail before we go to bed, our lives are immersed in media. We cannot get away from them: we make use of them at every turn and talk about them when we are not using them. Intimate lives are mediated lives.

## 2. The Digitalizing of Intimacies

Closely connected to media flows are the new intimacies being generated in cyberspace. It has been estimated that in 2002 there were roughly 600 million Internet users across the world, and that by 2005 there will be well over a billion.[7] Specific predictions are hazardous, but we are obviously talking about a lot. If we guess—perhaps rather modestly?—that between a quarter and third of Internet usage relates to intimacies, often sex, the scale of the issue becomes apparent.

To surf the Web is to explore a medium that is chock-a-block full of intimate words and images, from pages of information and advice about infertility (one of my little surfing sessions generated over a million sites on sperm banks) to images of the most "extreme" sexual fetishes ("Extreme" being the name given to one such fetish site that I discovered). Here we have new approaches to the body and emerging "techno-identities" and "techno-cultures." Although such new forms can result in people meeting in real space for "real sex," a vast amount of "virtual sex" is no doubt taking place in these virtual spaces. Much of this is little more than the dissemination of more and more specialized pornographic imagery suitable for private and usually solitary masturbation.[8] But sometimes it can involve the navigation of complex new relationships and new ways of communicating, such as the use of Web cams. I know many students who seem to spend all their spare time in "chat rooms" meeting new friends and creating new dates. A key issue is slowly becoming: just how are virtual relationships different from "reality" based ones, and what are the upsides and downsides of each?

## 3. The Technologizing of Intimacies

Another major way of approaching intimacies concerns the evolving technologies connected to them. Of course, we have long recognized the power of contraceptive technologies to transform the ways in which sexualities are engaged in and experienced. The dramatic fall in the birth rate in many countries, the use of condoms as a preventive device against AIDS, the pill, and the morning-after pill—all these shift the pattern of our intimacies. But perhaps most striking here has been the arrival, over the past thirty years or so, of the new reproductive technologies with their capacity for revolutionizing reproduction. The link between body and reproduction has been broken. Indeed, we have reached the ironic stage in history when much sexual activity—from masturbation and fetishism to sadomasochism to the "outercourse" advocated by many AIDS educators—has no reproductive potential whatsoever, while at the very same time much reproductive activity can be conducted in the absence of sexual intercourse. We have reached the age of assisted conception and the age of non-procreative sex. A time of "sexuality without reproduction and reproduction without sexuality."[9] Even a couple of decades ago, the idea of having babies at will, or of producing perfect "designer babies," or of cloning would have sounded like science fiction. In the end the implications of this must be quite staggering. Could it be that we are on the verge—indeed, have we already started to produce—a new kind of human being? We are just on the edge of having the ability to control the ways in which the species can be reproduced. We may actually be entering some kind of post-human age. If so, will this bring a post-human intimacy?[10] And what would this look like?

But we can go further than this. Scientific advances have wrought transformations not just around birth but also around death. We already have life-support systems that are able to prolong lives much longer than ever before, and now we have people placing their names on waiting lists for cryopreservation, cryogenics, and body freezing. They are queuing up to return to life in another century! This will surely bring a new form of intimacy, if people of today ever do come to interact with people of the future.

As I write this, I find myself chuckling. Can I really believe what I am writing? Maybe it's all a scientific hoax, or maybe I've been duped into apocalyptic thinking by the imaginative authors of science fiction. But the fact is that many serious-minded folk are now writing about and debating these practices, and I see no reason to wholly doubt what they have to say. Italian sociologist Alberto Melucci puts it very aptly:

> On the threshold of the twenty-first century, reproduction seems to have been stripped of even the last of its remaining natural roots and entirely converted into a social commodity. While reproduction above all

ensures the biological continuation of the species, the profound change in its "natural" status is marked symbolically by two phenomena which radically undermine the "naturalness" of human evolution: the threat of nuclear war and the manipulation of the genetic code. Both of these signal an irreversible shift in the direction of the species' evolutionary future: they tell us that our survival no longer depends on our reproductive capacity but rather on the choices we make between destruction, conservation or transformation—for both ourselves and other living species.[11]

## 4. The Globalizing of Intimacies

Globalization suggests "a runaway world becoming one place," and it has become one of the controversial cornerstones of contemporary social science debates.[12] Globalization has links not just to economic and market changes in liberal capitalism (usually associated with widening economic inequalities) but also to the spread of new media technologies, the homogenization of culture, and the weakening of the autonomous nation state. Intimacies are part of all this. For there are growing numbers of people who now conduct their personal relationships on a global scale. There are sexual partners, for instance, who no longer live together in the same country, let alone under the same roof. Colleagues of mine move around the world, stopping off in major cities, where they pick up their lives from when they were last there. I have many friends and acquaintances who live apart, at opposite ends of the globe, but who speak by phone and e-mail on a daily basis and fly to each other's arms very regularly.

But more than this: local cultures pick up, and usually transform, global elements of intimacies. There are major new markets in holiday travel, including but certainly not limited to sex tourism;[13] "intimate images" are disseminated throughout the world in films, TV programs, and videos, by pop culture, and in cyberspace. The women's movement and the lesbian and gay movement exist worldwide and carry on debates about intimacies; major international organizations have been established to fight HIV / AIDS; worldwide political organizations such as the United Nations discuss global human sexual and reproductive rights. I will return to all this in Chapter 8.

## 5. Intimacies and Individuation

Many traditional societies throughout history have little conception that human beings are individuals who have choices. But the notion of individual choice is a core feature of postmodernizing worlds. Indeed, what "modern" person could possibly disagree with the distinguished liberal philosopher Isaiah Berlin, who in a celebrated quote on freedom remarked:

> I wish my life and decisions to depend on myself, not on external forces of whatever kind. I wish to be the instrument of my own, not of other men's acts of will. I wish to be a subject, not an object; to be moved by reasons, by conscious purposes, which are my own, not by causes which affect me, as it were from outside. . . . I wish, above all, to be conscious of myself as a thinking, willing, active being, bearing responsibility for my choices and able to explain them by references to my own ideas and purposes.[14]

We surely must be allowed to choose whom (and if) to marry: the idea of arranged marriages or forced marriages is anathema to most "Western" minds. Likewise, we feel we should not be prevented from divorcing, provided any children will be adequately cared for. It is also surely now our right to have children: even if we are infertile or have no sexual partner, we can still choose to have a child through assisted conception. Indeed, we have the right to decide how many children we will have and even whether their prenatal life should be terminated through abortion. We also claim the right to choose the kind of erotic life we wish to lead, be it bisexual, homosexual, heterosexual, polysexual, polyamorous, or monosexual. Surely, too, we should be able to decide if we wish to modify our bodies in special ways—through transgender surgery or silicone implants. Again, if we are aging, we should have the right to choose how to live our lives in our later years. The list goes on. To suggest the opposite—that others can tell us whom to marry, when we can have children, what kind of sex we should have, or how to live in our old age—is to conjure up a world now rapidly in decline. Of course, such choices were not possible in the past and are not available in most countries in the world today, where arranged marriages and religious orthodoxies work to restrict choice. Indeed, in most societies throughout history and still across the world today, such choices would seem odd. But they are here with us, and part of the individuated world of choice.

Intimacy in the late modern world has thus been massively shaped by the development of a society ruled by an individualist ideology in which personal choices seem to proliferate—what Zygmunt Bauman calls the "individualized society" and Ulrich Beck "the individuated society." These are not "anything goes," wide open, "free" choices, but are themselves socially patterned: we cannot just choose anything. We are structured into a world of "choices" and "individuals." But as people are released from the roles, especially gender roles, that modern capitalist society prescribed, they are encouraged more and more "to build up a life of their own." All manner of relationships must now be "worked out, negotiated, arranged and justified in all the details of how, what, why or why not."[15] "For the sake of individual survival, individuals are compelled to make themselves the center of their own life plans and projects." Individualization entails "the disembedding of industrial society's ways of life" and the "re-embedding of new ones, in which individuals must produce, stage and cobble together their biographies themselves. . . . The individual is actor, designer, juggler and stage director of his own biography, identity, social networks, commitment and convictions."[16] This may be seen as what Giddens has called "the reflexive project of the self."[17] Although an increase in "self-consciousness" is common to both modernity and postmodernity, the newer order has seen a rapid spiral upward in this self-awareness. Choices proliferate, but they are socially patterned—often market-driven—"choices."

## 6. The Disclosing of Intimacies

Following from our growing preoccupation with self is another emerging characteristic of new-style relationships and intimacies: the desire to reflect upon them and to talk about them with partners. Whereas in earlier generations feelings were often regarded as something to be kept to oneself, there is now a trend, as Lynn Jamieson puts it, toward "disclosing intimacies," according to which it is increasingly important to talk to each other, to listen and understand.[18] Partners and lovers are encouraged to hold intimate conversations with each other; the distance between children and parents breaks down as children become confidantes to their parents and parents become "friends" to their children. Likewise, whether on "tell-it-all" talk shows or in detailed, biographical documentaries, the task is to speak the truth about one's intimate life: the more intimate, the better. And not only are couples expected to talk more to each other about their innermost desires, but their failure, even their reluctance, to do this may be taken as a sign that the relationship is not working. In this case, a whole army of "experts"—counselors, psychiatrists, social workers—may be called in to assist. And this will involve more and more disclosures and talk.

## 7. Intimacies and Equalization

The highlight of much of this self-reflective and self-reflexive talk about relationships is the claim that our intimacies should be equal, open, sharing, and trusting. Postmodern relationships often become an end in their own right: they are entered into as good in themselves and depend on the partners wanting to maintain them. In part this is linked to what has been called the "democratization of personhood."[19] Relationships between partners are meant to be characterized by self-fulfillment, flexible roles, open communication, and equality. These are the features of what Giddens calls a "pure relationship," which he views as implicitly democratic. Paralleling the ideal standards of political democracy, he suggests, there is an emerging "democracy of the emotions in everyday life." Hence a good relationship in the late modern world is:

- A relationship of equals, in which each party has equal rights and obligations;
- A relationship in which each person has respect for, and wants the best for, the other;
- A relationship based on open communication and dialogue between partners;
- A relationship in which trust has to be worked at and cannot be taken for granted;
- A relationship that is free of an arbitrary imbalance of power, coercion, or violence.[20]

This is only an ideal: most relationships still fall short of it. Nevertheless, until fairly recently marriages and other relationships were usually much more hierarchical, and a degree of authoritarianism was often built into the heart of the relationship. And this applies as much to child-parent relationships as it does to adult partnerships.

## 8. Intimacies and Insecurity

All this choice, freedom, and equality is not without its downside. The advantage of hierarchical and / or authoritarian relationships is that they establish a clear canopy of meaning that all can share. At least people know who they are and what they are expected to do. The confining of people to specified roles is most clearly visible in systems based on extreme inequality, such as the caste system and slavery. But support for the hierarchical distribution of power starts to crumble under the class conditions of late modernity. According to Bauman, another feature of the

postmodern world—or at least of the lives of the relatively affluent—
that is gathering momentum is *Unsicherheit,* a term that could variously
be translated as "uncertainty," "insecurity," or "unsafety."[21] *Unsicherheit*
is the combined experience of insecurity—about one's social position,
entitlements, and means of livelihood; uncertainty—as to their continuation and future stability; and unsafety—of one's body and one's sense
of self, along with the extensions of the self: possessions, neighborhood,
community. People become increasingly wary, and in their intimate lives
they become cautious: they are unsure of what to do, and they "lack the
courage to dare and the time to imagine alternative ways of living
together."[22] This is, of course, a very different picture from that painted
by those who applaud our expanding array of choices. Here choices are
frightening, and decisions taken are tacit and half-hearted; they float on
a sea of risk. When Bauman's vision of *Unsicherheit* is applied to sexualities, we find people who no longer know quite what it is they are
expected to do in their sexual lives—explore a bit, withdraw a bit, escape
a bit?[23] If the old stable structures are going, if much of the world is
becoming detraditionalized, what new, and unstable, forms are appearing in their place—and how unstable can we tolerate them being?

## 9. The Commodifying of Intimacies

Critical to all the processes we are talking about is the redistribution of
global capital. A major feature of this shifting economic landscape has
been the rise of the "logo society," with its goal of promoting more and
more consumption. As George Ritzer has remarked: "Consumption plays
an ever-expanding role in the lives of individuals around the world. To
some, consumption defines contemporary American society, as well as
much of the developed world. We consume many obvious things—fast
food, T-shirts, a day at Walt Disney World—and many others that are
not so obvious—a lecture, medical services, a day at the ballpark."[24] We
may speak of the commodification and consumption of intimacies—
the potential for our personal and intimate lives to become bound up
with sellable objects. The mammoth world of advertising, the entertain-
ment industry, and the sports world—all sell us images of the intimacies we should desire. Relationships become the subject of expensive
long-term therapy, and self-help books cover everything from how to
put more intimacy into our lives to the "Twelve Steps" for sex addicts.

But there is also an enormous world market in which intimacy is the
commodity on sale. Most obvious is the porn trade—from magazines
and videos to sex toys, underwear, dildos, vibrators, and various other

items of erotica.[25] But more than porn, intimacy is also deeply impli-
cated in clothing markets, music markets, magazine markets, book markets, health product markets (from contraception to Viagra), and the
massive industry on body work (health clubs, gyms, cosmetic surgery,
and the like). Then there are hundreds—thousands—of Web sites from
which one can purchase not only on-line dating services of any and every
sort but an astonishing array of sexual pleasures, all neatly coded and
organized in catalogues that put Krafft-Ebing's wilder taxonomies to
shame. (Find just what you want, order it on-line, pay for it on-line. In
fact, the cybersex industry meets all the criteria for McDonaldization—
it's rational, calculable, efficient, and predictable.) And on top of all that
are assorted "live sex acts," from Web-cam voyeurism and telephone sex
through numerous incarnations of real live sex.[26]

## 10. The Medicalizing of Intimacies

Medicine and medical technologies have long played their role in shaping intimacies. In the nineteenth century, doctors viewed same-sex relationships as a treatable disease; they patholologized women as "hysterical";
they invented all manner of devices designed to end the morbid existence of masturbation; and they concocted huge taxonomies of sexual
diseases with nightmare cures attached. Although hindsight might thus
suggest that medical insights are not always to be trusted, medical interventions into our personal life have continued throughout and past the
twentieth century, and at an accelerating pace, bringing more and more
facets of the personal life under the medical rubric. From the emergence
of sexology as a major medical subdiscipline and the rise of sex therapy, to drugs such as Viagra and the morning-after pill, to the pioneering
of transsexual surgery and the huge growth in the popularity of cosmetic surgery, and on to the new reproductive technologies, medical
science continues to transform the intimate worlds we live in. Just to
take one example: Viagra's sales in its first year topped $1 billion; by the
year 2000, some 200,000 prescriptions were being filled each week and
some 17 million people in the United States had taken it.[27] No doubt
the existence of all these drugs, therapies, and surgical procedures
increases our choices—but at a cost. Although our faith in the profession can make us reluctant to acknowledge the fact, these assorted new
drugs and medical procedures can have potentially serious side effects.[28]
Medicine can, moreover, adopt a coercive, sometimes even brutalizing, attitude toward our lives, turning our personal decisions into med-

ical ones and thereby delivering our power to choose into the hands of professionals.

## 11. The Destabilizing of Intimacies

According to the German sociologist Ulrich Beck, among others, we are entering the "risk society." Societies have always lived with risk, but the social, scientific, and technological developments of the late modern world have brought with them man-made risks. It is a manufactured uncertainty, and it brings unforeseen consequences. We see it in HIV / AIDS: a worldwide pandemic, with an estimated death toll at the end of 2000 of 21.8 million; and in 2001 a population of some 40 million living with HIV—hugely in sub-Saharan Africa (28,500,000) and Asia (6,600,000).[29] In China alone, 850,000 Chinese were living with HIV infection in 2001, with reported infections having risen by 67 percent in the first six months of that year. We see it in the new reproductive technologies: nobody can really predict the kinds of "designer babies," genetically modified animals, clones, or bizarre post-human creatures that conceivably could arrive on the planet in the not too distant future. But an atmosphere of risk can also be detected in the myriad smaller, more ordinary decisions of everyday life. As Anthony Giddens has pointed out:

> Consider marriage and family, for example. Up to even a generation ago, marriage was structured by established traditions. When people got married they knew, as it were, what they were doing. Marriage was formed to a large degree in terms of traditional expectations of gender, sexuality, and so forth. Now it is a much more open system, with new forms of risk. Everyone who gets married is conscious of the fact that divorce rates are high, that women demand greater equality than in the past. The very decision to get married is constitutively different from before. There has never been a high-divorce, high-marriage society before. No one knows, for example, what the consequences are for the future of the family, or the health of the children.[30]

"New families" now foster so many different kinds of relationships that the traditional kin diagrams of anthropologists can no longer make sense of them. No genealogical chart can readily accommodate the permutations of stepchildren, multiple grandparents, unmarried partners, surrogate children, and the like that have become almost commonplace. Perhaps more to the point, nobody can foresee quite what the implica-

tions of all these emerging clusters of "kin" relationships will be for society. "New families" bring new risks.

## Intimacies and the Persistence of Inequalities

Some of the ways I have just sketched out in which intimacies are being
reconfigured in a late modern world are manifestly new—digital, global,
and technologized intimacies, for instance. Others, such as the individualist ethic and the impact of medical knowledge on society, have roots
that go back much further.[31] At the same time, yet other flows exist—
usually to do with the structuring of inequalities—that also play major
roles in the shaping of intimacies, and these, too, have been around for
a long time. The world over, people continue to confront inequalities
that shape their most intimate lives: pronounced economic inequalities,
major imbalances of power between genders, social marginalization based
on ethnicity and race, age stratification, and the exclusion of all manner
of people who are disabled or otherwise perceived as "different."
Experiences of the intimate—loving, child rearing, sexualities, the body,
our feelings—need to be mapped onto these dimensions.

At their most apparent, across the globe, many intimacies have come
to inhabit worlds of victimization, harassment, abuse, violence, coercion,
hate, defilement, degradation, exclusion, and exploitation. Although men
are sometimes the objects of attack, the most common victims are
women, children, and sexual minorities. Ours is a world of female sexual slavery, sexual terrorism, woman-hating, homophobia, and hate
crimes. And, as has increasingly been documented, it is a world of genocide and genocidal rape. In parts of the world, even pregnancy can be a
death sentence. One out of every 48 women in developing countries dies
in childbirth.[32] According to one report on Rwanda, for example, 1 in 9
women dies in childbirth, and 1 in 10 children does not live a week.[33] Nor
do these problems exist only on a local scale.

To offer one illustration: according to a report released in 2000 by the
United Nations, "Around the world, at least one in every three women
has been beaten, coerced into sex, or abused in some way—most often
by someone she knows, including her husband or another male family
member; one woman in four has been abused during pregnancy."[34]
Specific figures vary across countries and for differing kinds of abuse,
but there can be no doubt that such abuse is widespread and frequently
condoned. This United Nations report, titled *The State of the World
Population: 2000,* concludes that:

- "In the United States, a woman is battered, usually by her sexual partner, every 15 seconds." (p. 26)
- "Across the world, at least one in every three women has been beaten, coerced into sex, or abused—most often by someone she knows." (p. 5)
- "As many as 5,000 women and girls are murdered each year by members of their own families in so-called honor killings—often because the woman was dishonored by being raped." (p. 29)
- "An estimated 4 million women and girls are bought and sold worldwide each year, into marriage, prostitution, or slavery." (p. 29)
- Worldwide, "some 130 million women have been forced to undergo female genital mutilation or cutting." (p. 26)
- "Each year women undergo an estimated 50 million abortions, 20 million of which are unsafe, and some 78,000 women die and millions suffer injuries and illness as a result." (p. 13)

Statistics can, of course, be misleading, and figures such as these require careful interpretation. It is nevertheless abundantly clear that violence against women continues to exist throughout the world, and on a tragic scale.

## Utopian Experiments in Living and Dystopian Risk

The changes I have been discussing may seem dramatic, but they must not be given too apocalyptic a reading. Change is and always has been ubiquitous, but at the same time changes often seem particularly momentous while we are immersed in them. Moreover, some of the changes with which I have been concerned are actually in the nature of "quiet revolutions" that have been taking place gradually, across multiple generations. They are to some extent governed by serendipity, and their consequences are uneven and unpredictable.

My account of these evolving developments, these social "flows," has not been exhaustive, nor have I made any attempt to prioritize them. At times, my account may have seemed quite upbeat. In the wake of all these postmodern choices, I like the research of the British sociologist Jeffrey Weeks, who rather cheerfully sees millions of little "life experiments" in everyday living.[35] This is not a world where people are trapped in their anxieties and insecurities, incapable of planning their lives. Rather, it is one in which more and more people are coming to enjoy new personal freedoms and an ever-expanding array of possibilities for the future. Late modern intimacies, for all their uncertainties, can give us a glimpse of utopia.

In other places, however, my account has suggested the darker side of late modernity. The Marxist in me wants to condemn the power of markets and the exploitation they encourage—the commodification of intimacies, the selling of sex in its most degraded and objectified forms. The radical feminist in me is outraged by the unfair distribution of power between the genders and the sexual violence that still invades so many lives. The humanist in me looks in shock and horror at the power of religions to destroy human life while talking benignly of tolerance and compassion. The sad fact is that human intimacies also dwell in a dystopia, and it seems at times almost obscene to debate the ethics of the new reproductive technologies or the legality of lesbian and gay marriages when so many of the world's intimacies are still subject to abject poverty, brutalizing power, and repressive religious traditions. These dystopian tensions will hover over this book. But they are not my main concern. Rightly or wrongly, my interests at present lie mainly with the relatively positive dimensions of expanding autonomy for intimate citizens. Postmodern troubles and postmodern choices do abound, and both may be signs of the future. They are worth looking at as long as the wider dystopian picture is not ignored. Major conflicts are everywhere, and I will return to this dark side of intimacies regularly.

# 3
# Culture Wars and Contested Intimacies

*They stick something up there and they can't even see what they're doing, they're just probing up you to suck the baby out of you. Now, to me that does not make one bit of sense, and in my opinion it's murder, because I've seen a movie called* The Silent Scream *and they stuck that tube up there and that baby was crying. And it was moving away from the object. The baby knew what was happening. And they say that's not murder.*

*[Young women facing unwanted pregnancies are in] a world of hurt. For them they need the choice of maybe being able to have an abortion. Because you're already struggling, you know, if you're a young girl and you're out there struggling your ass off to make ends meet, what's the burden of bringing another one into that struggle?*

Two women commenting on television programs about abortion
(quoted in Andrea Press and Elizabeth Cole, *Speaking of Abortion:
Television and Authority in the Lives of Women*)

*A society in which there was no opposition of interests would be sunk in a condition of hopeless lethargy.*

John Dewey, *Freedom and Culture*

*It is the great tragedy of social life that every extension of solidarity, from family to village, village to nation, presents also the opportunity of organizing hatred on a larger scale.*

Arthur Stinchcombe, *"Social Structure and Politics"*

*How can people who inhabit different and conflicting realities—worlds in which "the other" is discredited and demonized—sustain life together?*

Kenneth J. Gergen, *An Invitation to Social Construction*

CONFLICT IS UBIQUITOUS in social life. So it is not surprising to find contesting voices over the intimate life. From the "clash of civilizations" at a global level, through the "culture wars" and the new political alignments at the national level, to internal disagreements or schisms within smaller groups and social movements, and finally to ordinary arguments between friends and families, on a face-to-face daily level, conflicts are everywhere.[1] Much of this conflict, it must be recognized, is embedded in cultures of class and income, ethnicity and race, gender and sexual orientation, age group, and religion. These are the moral conflicts of our time, and they are everywhere.

Indeed, it is hard these days not to find a shrill cacophony of voices arguing about virtually every aspect of our personal lives and debating the ways in which other people "should" live. Some bemoan the loss of a simpler, more kindly past, some feel a sense of anxiety and insecurity—of *Unsicherheit*—at the rapidity of contemporary change, and some are seized with a terrible foreboding of moral collapse and the ultimate Armageddon. The changing intimacies of the late modern world, along with the ceaseless quest for more and more choices in one's personal life, have meant that many lives are now engulfed in moral wars around family politics, body politics, identity politics, gender politics, religious politics, technological politics, and, of course, sexual politics. This chapter looks at these and at the tensions they generate.

## Some Moral Conflicts of Our Times

Although some may say we live in amoral or immoral times, the fact is that issues of morality have rarely, if ever, been so prominent a part of everyday discussion. Bookshelves, the press, and television programs groan under the weight of bringing us the moral debates of our time—though we don't usually think of them as that. Thus, for instance, we discuss the future of the family every time we start talking about divorce rates increasing, about children being born out of wedlock, about the arrival of gay and lesbian partnerships, about who has the right to adoption or to abortion, about fatherless families and surrogate mothers who give birth for women in their sixties, about the need for the morning-after pill, about the increasing number of people who choose to be single, about cohabitation and serial monogamy, about infertility and its possible solutions, and so on. Likewise, we tackle the moral issue of how to live a sexual life the moment we talk about pornography and erotica, HIV and AIDS, sex tourism and the sex industry, fetish clothing, teenage chastity, Viagra and the morning-after pill, or cybersex, masturbation, sex chat rooms, and how strangers end up meeting. The lists of issues goes on and on, and a short book like this is not the place to get into the specifics of any one of these debates. And in any case that is not my point. I simply wish to highlight the sheer enormity, the range, and the probable escalation of these issues around our personal life. Figure 3 suggests but a few of these.

*Family Wars*
  Differing cultural family patterns
  Arranged marriages versus love marriages
  Ending marriages through divorce
  Single parenting
  Abuse and violence in families
  Lesbian, gay, bisexual families
  Alternatives to families: families of choice
  Generational issues: children, the elderly
*Gender Troubles*
  Democratization–polarization
  "Patriarchal domains"(e.g., in the workplace, at home,
    in political life)
  Violence
  "Iron Johns" and "New Men"
  Transgender warriors
*Erotic Wars*
  Lesbian, gay, bisexual, same-sex, queer rights: sexual, anti-
    discrimination, marriage, military, child custody
  The right to create sexually explicit images (Is it pornography,
    erotica, or art?)
  The feminist sex wars
  The politics of international sex work
  The pandemic of HIV / AIDS and safe-sex campaigns
  The sexual rights of young children, teenagers, and the elderly
  Polysexualities and the right to a wide range of sexual practices
  Cybersexualities: cybersex, including cyberstalking and cyber-rape
  International freedom from sexual violence: rape, abuse, genital
    mutilation, harassment, hate crimes, and other attacks on
    homosexuals
  Morning-after pills, Viagra, and other sex-related drugs
*Reproductive Politics*
  International debates on abortion: right to life vs. right of choice
  Contraception: morning-after pills, family size, the Catholic Church
  Test-tube babies: in vitro fertilization, surrogacy
*The Politics of the Body*
  The modification of human bodies: from plastic surgery to
    transgender surgery
  The Web enlisted in the reproduction process: reproductive politics
  The cloning issue
  Cryogenics

FIGURE 3. *Emerging Arenas of Intimate Conflict*

Granted, the shrillest of these debates probably take place among a relatively small but noisy bunch of extremists.[2] Nevertheless, the contemporary world does raise these dilemmas, which leads at least some people to think about them and wonder whether they can be resolved in the future. Simply put, my answer to this last is a probable no. In all likelihood, the future will bring partial solutions, but it will also be a world in which we have to live with constant moral contest. Take two key examples that essentially could not be found on the political agenda a short time back: "gay and lesbian rights" and "assisted conceptions."

## Gay and Lesbian Rights

For gays, a new culture of "variant sexuality issues" has emerged over the past thirty years.[3] As a result, debates can now rage openly about such matters as:

· A universal age of consent for gays and lesbians.
· The recognition of "hate crimes" that target lesbians and gays (as well as other groups) and the prevention of harassment.
· The acceptance of universal lesbian and gay rights, the inclusion of "sexual orientation" in charters of human rights and antidiscrimination laws, and mandatory training in "multiculturalism" and "gay affirmative action" in many workplaces.
· The importance of "domestic" or "registered" partnerships and marriage for lesbian and gays.
· The right of lesbians and gays to adopt or to have children, including the right of lesbians to undergo artificial insemination.
· The recognition of gays and lesbians in the military.
· The right to make available materials that speak positively about (or even "promote") homosexuality to exist in schools and in the workplace, as well as the championing of widespread gay and lesbian erotica in art and in the media.

Not that long ago such issues would have been greeted with outrage, or possibly with laughter—assuming they could even have been mentioned. Only relatively recently have such issues been allowed to appear openly on the agenda. But the closing years of the twentieth century have witnessed not only the fulfillment of some of the main demands of the original lesbian and gay movement. In some parts of the world, many of its wilder dreams are also becoming a reality. Of course, throughout the world pervasive forms of discrimination against lesbians and gays still survive, and in many countries no gains at all have been made.

Nevertheless, these issues are increasingly present, on the agenda, struggling to be heard.

Ironically, such issues thrive best where there is opposition. They need to be contested so that they become more visible, more focused, and ultimately more clearly argued. Contested issues help to build, structure, and transform the "interpretive communities" so often linked to social movements. It is within these newly emerging issues-cultures that what we might call "a struggle for dominant meaning" takes place. In the case of the gay and lesbian movement, opponents make arguments that then constrain the subsequent moves, debates, or options of the movement itself. Some kind of dialogic relationship, even if adversarial, is set up between movement and opponents. The pro-gays and anti-gays exist symbiotically, each helping to fashion the other's debates. In addition, certain key events and people appear that galvanize opinion and thus transform social worlds. In contrast to the near invisibility of gay issues some forty years ago, they have come to provide a major arena of public debate, in part because of cultures of opposition.

To create a public culture of ethical issues thus demands the presence of at least two sides. Arguments for gay rights depend on the simultaneous rise of anti-gay traditionalism. The role of evangelicalism in the United States cannot be lightly dismissed in all this; indeed, fundamentalism throughout the world may be viewed as a strategy, or set of strategies, whereby beleaguered believers attempt to preserve their distinctive identity as a people or a group. Boundaries, then, become imbued with massive symbolic significance, and their preservation becomes vital for life. It not just "gayness" that is the concern of these antagonistic but mutually necessary groups, but the whole apparatus of change. "Gays" and "lesbians" stand for the whole threatening order of change—changing women, changing families, changing bodies. For anti-gay elements, the new information classes—the "secular humanists"—come to embody "the enemy," as they are accused of promoting the slide into moral decay. In countering pro-gay opinions, anti-gay appeals rest upon a number of images and themes: they draw on "a lexicon in which homosexuality is 'sinful,' 'immoral,' 'criminal,' mentally disturbed, pathogenic, corruptive of the young, and socially disruptive."[4] The anti-gays fight the pro-gays in every available space. In the United States, for example, evangelists (like James Robinson and Anita Bryant, in her early days), academics (like psychologists Stanton Jones and E. L. Patullo or psychiatrist Charles Socarides), talk show hosts (like Dennis Praeger), as well as Norman Podhoretz, Jerry Falwell, and others, all work to galvanize anti-gay sentiment. At the same time, gay philosophers and political theorists like Mark Blasius, Richard Mohr, and Morris Kaplan, conservative journalists like Andrew Sullivan, and more radical critics such as Leo Bersani, Rosemary Henessay, Michael Warner, and Cindy Patton give momentum to the pro-gay position. The sides are lined up, symbiotically feeding on and amplifying each other. Far from being in decline, moral debate is most exhilaratingly on the agenda.

## Reproductive Technologies

Consider, too, the whole sphere of assisted conception and reproductive politics. Of course, contraception and birth regulation have been on the moral agenda for a long time now,[5] and abortion, adoption, and fostering children have continually raised issues about the right to have a child and the rights of the fetus. But only in the past thirty years or so have the politics of the new reproductive technologies and of assisted conception led to much more focused discussion of issues such as:

*and thus the right to sex.*

• *The rights and choice to reproduce (or not).* Thanks to the new reproductive technologies, infertility and other such problems no longer mean that people cannot have children.

• *The normative nature of motherhood.* The idea that women are meant to be mothers brings into focus the issue of women (and men) who remain childless and the pressures placed on people to "choose" to have children.

• *Issues of surrogacy.* The problems of one woman's body being used as a vehicle for the birth of another person's child.

• *The racialization of surrogacy.* Issues that arise when "racialized others" become the main "breeders" of other people's children.

• *Issues of "generation hopping."* By freezing and storing sperm, eggs, and even fetuses, children can now be conceived at a later time, even in a subsequent generation.

• *Issues around the rights and choice to have exactly the kind of child you want.* These range from choosing the sex of a baby, to avoiding illness and disabilities, to the use of cloning and / or gene therapy to produce "designer babies" or "perfect babies."

• *Issues around the commercialization of the fetus, infants, children, and even body parts.* International markets now exist for the purchase and sale of human life, including body parts. In some parts of the world—much of Europe, for example—such markets are outlawed; in other countries, such as the United States, they can be widespread.

· *Issues around embryo research,* including the use of stem cells and the status of the embryo as a living being, both key issues for bioethics.

· *Issues of parenting and the naming of new parental roles.* New approaches to parenting may come into being when we start distinguishing between gestational mothers (who provide a womb for the baby), genetic parents (who provide eggs and sperm), and parents as child raisers.

Ultimately, these conflicts go to the heart of what it means to be a human being. They raise questions about what it means to be born, to give birth, and to raise children—issues that cut to the core of intimacies. Conflicts arise over "the right" to have children—or indeed whether we have an obligation to do so, as some claim. They arise over concerns about gender roles, as women's wombs are now being taken over by (male?) technologies. They arise over issues such as pro-natalism, where parenthood is seen as the natural human condition, or normative motherhood—"the cultural expectation that all women should mother."[6] These attitudes in turn raise issues concerning those who remain outside the parent-child relationship. In the past such people were often stigmatized and devalued: they were "the childless" or "the infertile"; spinsters were thought to be frigid or suspected of being lesbian. The current cultural preoccupation with the nuclear family—two heterosexual parents raising their own biological children in intensive, private worlds—may well be historically rare. But even given this model family, controversies currently swirl over whether couples should have children or not, over who is best suited to parent the children and what parenting means, and over the best approaches to raising children.

Along with this come the complex debates over reproductive technologies. Symbolically at any rate, the idea of cloning is the most controversial of these emerging technologies, and it has brought with it significant political realignments. Most governments formally denounce and legislate against cloning, and in general thinkers on both the right and the left can find few grounds to support it. In the most traditional terms, cloning is said to be "against God's will" and "contrary to nature." What it brings—the severing of procreation from sex, love, and intimacy—is "inherently dehumanizing." If cloning were permitted, we would be led to ask, What will father, grandfather, aunt, cousin, and sister mean?[7] Others, such as the conservative thinker James Q. Wilson, believe that as long as the cloned child were loved and raised in a "proper" family of heterosexual parents, then cloning could be acceptable, although its practice would have to be governed by appropriate restrictions. Still others believe that cloning must be allowed in the name of freedom: in order for science to advance, for people to reproduce as they choose, to foster progress. Once again, an issues culture emerges, conflicts flourish, and new communities are shaped.

## The Enemy Within: Internal Schisms

Conflicts are everywhere, and this often means that they are local and endogenous—occurring within the same movement and among seemingly like-minded groups. As anyone who has ever been active in a social movement will almost certainly attest, such groups can experience almost as much tension and conflict from inside the group, among people who have the same broad goals, as ever they did from the enemy outside.

A classic example of this can be found in the women's movement, which for much of the 1970s and 1980s was split between radical feminists and libertarian feminists over such concerns as pornography, sadomasochism, and prostitution. These were the so-called sex wars, which still raise critical issues.[8] Women in the movement became polarized. Some claimed that sexuality was the central tool of women's subordination—from the manifest regulation of women's lives through the fear of rape and the existence of pornography, to the much more insidious nature of intercourse as itself a prime site for the subordination of women. Others, and they were deeply opposed, argued that women's oppression was multifaceted but that sexuality was a struggle in which women needed to find their own pleasure and desires, even if this means a pornography for women, or the pleasures of women in sadomasochistic practices.

The schisms remain, but often over newer targets such as global sex work or the new reproductive technologies. Sex work, for example, has (again) become a global problem for women, for it is linked to patriarchy and the exploitation of women, as well as to poverty, racism, and other inequalities. But there is little new again in some of these debates: sex work has a long history of contestation both within the women's movement and without. Thus in her work on the trafficking of women, Kathleen Barry builds a continuum of stages of patriarchal and economic development that ranges from "the pre-industrial and feudal . . . where women are excluded from the public sphere" to a post-industrial one where "women achieve the potential for economic independence." But Barry's work is not to the liking of some feminists. As Kamala Kempadoo comments:

[Barry] evokes an image of non-western women that various Third World feminists have identified as common to much western feminist theorizing. The Third World / non-western woman is positioned in this discourse as "ignorant, poor, uneducated, tradition-bound, domestic, family-oriented, victimized, " etc., and is conceptualized as living a "truncated sexual life." She is not yet a "whole or developed" person but instead resembles a minor needing guidance, assistance and help. The construct stands in opposition to that of the western woman, who is believed to have (or at least has the potential to have) control over her income, body and sexuality: the emancipated, postmodern woman. In true colonial fashion, Barry's mission is to rescue those who she considers to be incapable of self-determination.[9]

Schisms also appear over reproductive politics. Feminist stances range across a whole spectrum—for "motherhood" has traditionally been another area of contestation for feminists. Recall one of the earliest dictums from one of the first radical feminists, Shulamith Firestone: "Pregnancy is barbaric."[10] For Firestone, and for many other feminists, the source of female subordination lies in the strong connection of women to reproduction and mothering. Both these tasks help reinforce women's subordinate position under patriarchy, and the pattern can be broken only by women relinquishing their role—usually with men playing more of a part in parenting—or by the new reproductive technologies, which give women control over their own bodies.

But in stark contrast is the claim that such "womb robbing" or "womb leasing" is little more than an extension of prostitution. The womb now becomes something that can be extracted from the whole person. For Andrea Dworkin this heralds the arrival of a "farming model" of women, one that signals "the coming gynocide." The new reproductive technologies "will give conception, gestation and birth over to men— eventually, the whole process of the creation of life will be in their hands."[11] Likewise, Gena Corea writes that "The new reproductive technologies represent an escalation of violence against women, a violence camouflaged behind medical terms."[12] And Janice Raymond, in her book *Women as Wombs,* talks of all this as "reproductive abuse," as an aspect of "the spermatic economy of sex and breeding"—a "spermocracy." Critical of feminists who champion reproductive technologies, she links these new procedures to male medical technologies, to "normative mothering," to male sexuality (much of the technology involves male insemination of women's bodies, with men serving as ejaculation machines), and ultimately to the international trafficking of women, children, and body parts—where babies, brides, and surrogate mothers, overwhelmingly from poor countries, may be sold on markets across the world, largely to people in rich countries. In Raymond's account, these new technologies are truly counterfeminist.

So some feminists suggest that the new reproductive technologies will serve to liberate women from their bodies, while others take the opposite position—that these technologies will further the control and regulation of women's lives. Ultimately, this is all part of a broader debate over women's right to choose. For the radical feminists consent is not possible in a "unfree society." In Raymond's words, "feminists must go beyond choice and consent as a standard for women's freedom. Before consent, there must be self-determination so that consent does not simply amount to acquiescing to the available options."[13]

## The Trouble with "Normal"

The history of the lesbian and gay movement is likewise fraught with tension, in the case between assimilationists and radicals—and there is usually no love lost between them. It is a split between the "good guys" and the "bad boyz," between those who want to be responsible gay and lesbian citizens and those who argue that it is in the very nature of gay to be "outside"—to be transgressive, to be radical, to be a threat, to be queer. To become citizens is to become normalized, and hence to lose the very edge that gayness implies. Michael Bronski puts the radical case well:

> One of the persistent myths of the gay rights movement, and of liberal thinking, is that the dominant culture's fear of homosexuality and hatred of homosexuals is irrational. This is untrue: it is a completely rational fear. Homosexuality strikes at the heart of the organization of Western culture and societies because homosexuality, by its nature, is non-reproductive, it posits a sexuality that is justified by sexuality alone. This stands in stark and, for many people, frightening contrast to the entrenched belief that reproduction alone legitimates sexual activity. This belief is the foundation of society's limiting gender roles and the reason why marriage has been the only context recognized by society and the law for sexual relationships between men and women. It is the underpinning for the restrictive structure of the biological family unit and its status as the only sanctioned setting for raising children. It is the hidden logic determining many of our economic and work structures.

> In profound, often unarticulated ways, this imperative view of repro-
> ductive sexuality has shaped our world.[14]

For Bronski, homosexuals are the pleasure classes, and at the heart of
their experience is the celebration of sexual desire, of the hedonistic and
erotic in all its forms—a "seductive (and dangerous) vision of alternative possibilities." He continues:

> For decades, conservative psychoanalysts, religious leaders, and politi-
> cians have charged that homosexuality is about nothing more than hav-
> ing sex; that homosexuals are "obsessed" with sex; that homosexuality
> is a "flight" from the responsibilities of mature sexuality. And they are
> right.[15]

Bronski, and he speaks for many, celebrates the world of sadomasochism,
leather sex, the fetish scene, and the whole world of what we might call
"polysexualities."[16] Sex, sex, and more sex in all its forms is the name of
the game. And he is not alone. Various specific arguments are made, but
the key lies in the idea that some sexualities are queer and are simply not
meant to fit in: they are meant to pose challenges, create dangers, be a
menace, bring about radical changes. They are most decidedly not about
being "good citizens."

In contrast, a much more dominant strand of thinking wants lesbians
and gays to find their "place at the table," to be "virtually normal."[17] The
proponents of this position, who are often deeply personally opposed to
the radical stance articulated by Bronski, tend to be uneasy with anything
that would give gays or lesbians a bad name: from public sex and promiscuity to drugs, from radical marches to transgender politics, to anything
but so-called vanilla sex in private. Shunning the radical wing of the movement, they champion marriage and partnerships for lesbians and gays,
viewing the couple as the ideal form and seek gay rights as a way for gays
to fit in.

Nowhere is this schism clearer than in the debate over "queer family
values."[18] Throughout the world more and more lesbians and gays are
seeking some form of legal recognition as partners, and they are frequently
raising children. These families are different: they are "families of choice."
And these families are seen to be harbingers of a whole array of new experiments in living. There are also lots of them. As one commentator
remarked about the United States: "In 1976, there were between 300,000
and 500,000 gay and lesbian parents; today there are an estimated 1.5 mil-

lion to 5 million lesbian mothers, and between 1 million and 3 million gay fathers. Currently, between 6 million and 14 million children are being raised by at least one gay parent."[19] The figures may be approximate, but there is a clear suggestion here that raising children has become a much more common feature of gay life. Certainly, the idea of being a good parent and a good partner, and getting legal recognition for a partnership, has become one of the big stories of late-twentieth-century gay life. But it is a far cry from Bronski and the queer theorists. For them, the family is a profoundly conservative institution. Indeed, two of the biggest "gay battles" in recent times—that gays should be able to have families and that gays should be allowed to serve in the military—shock the radical wing to the core. In their view, the radicalism of gayness has been assimilated into the mainstream. The debate about marriage may have done much to normalize the gay movement, which may be a good thing for some. But for others, gay and lesbian marriage serves to reprivatize social life: it shuts down human possibilities; it reinforces heterocentric models of living together; it marginalizes the unmarried; and it upholds a particular conservative view of life which leads bit by bit to a serious loss of any broader political agenda. Worse: it allows some gays to continue in a state of erotophobia from which they can attack other gays and the eroticized experience.

Such conflicts are not in any way unique to the women's movement or the gay movement. Every social movement, including religious movements, appears to have them. Indeed, I have argued elsewhere that schisms often serve to energize social movements and give them momentum. Without internal schisms, they may indeed founder.[20]

## Hunter's Culture Wars: Positioning the Conflicts

In the middle of the twentieth century, H. G. Wells looked at the battle over that century as one between "Traditional or Authoritative Civilization" and "Creative and Progressive Civilization." The one declares, "Let man learn his duty and obey"; the other, "Let man know, and trust him."[21] By the end of the century, the distinction between tradition and progress was being strongly reiterated. The sociologist James Davison Hunter, talking in his influential book *Culture Wars* of the struggle to define American culture, detected a divide between the cultural conservatives or moral traditionalists and the cultural progressives or liberals.

The traditionalists, he says, reveal a commitment to "an external, definable, and transcendent authority . . . [defining] a consistent, unchangeable measure of value, purpose, goodness, and identity, both personal and collective. It tells us what is good, what is true, how we should live, and who we are. It is an authority that is sufficient for all time." By contrast, what is common to the progressivist view is "the tendency to symbolize historic faiths according to the prevailing assumptions of contemporary life. . . . Traditional sources of moral authority, whether scripture, papal pronouncements or Jewish law, no longer have an exclusive or even predominant binding power" over people's lives.[22] Whereas in the past the battle lines were drawn between religions or religious denominations— Protestant versus Catholic, Christian versus Jew—now the battle lines are being drawn between those who adhere to differing moral and political visions that cut across past schisms, suggesting new alignments. On one side are the forces of religious orthodoxy—Protestant, Jew, Catholic, Buddhist, Hindu, Muslim, or anything else—who continue to seek the truth from some sort of fixed authority, usually embodied in a canonical scripture or scriptures. On the other side are those who look to their own conscience—and engage more pragmatically to the shifts in the modern world—for clues as to how to live the new moral life.

In a later book, *Before the Shooting Begins,* Hunter takes his concerns further. He sees the United States as being torn apart by a series of moral conflicts, escalating step by step to the point that they are not mere culture wars but "shooting wars." The debates have become so acrimonious and bitter, with sides talking only at or way past each other, that the next step can only be bloodshed. Most of these conflicts center in one way or another on the body, as a key symbol of the wider social order, and the so-called abortion wars must be seen as their prime example. Here, indeed, are matters of life and death—and the notorious bombings of abortion clinics vividly demonstrate how culture wars may escalate into violence. Hunter finds advocates on all sides culpable for debasing public and democratic discussion; even those who claim to be neutral are in fact duplicitous, having their own ax to grind. His book is consequently devoted to clearing away some of this duplicity and moral outrage in an effort to find ways for us to speak together more constructively. In the end, he favors democratic dialogue—although his more recent pronouncements suggest that he is worried about people's ability to debate at all. In *The Death of Character,* Hunter argues that concepts such as character building, honor, or personal integrity no longer hold much meaning for Americans, a development that he blames largely on the educational system.

Traditional values surrounding personal life, then, are now severely

under threat from a multiplicity of conflicting voices. Will one drown
the others out? Can they coexist, and if so how? What are the possible
relationships of different positions to one another? The idea of intimate
citizenship must be worked out in the various arenas of contested moral
discourse that now exist. Ultimately, we enter here many of the classic
problems of contemporary political philosophy—for which issues of
democracy, freedom, community, participation, empowerment, equality, and justice have been paramount concerns in a theory of citizenship.
Looking at major divides, I would suggest that at least five broad kinds
of arguments are being made and positions taken.[23] *perceived* Briefly these are:

· *Traditionalism:* seeking a return to past values, usually based on a
religion. At its extreme, this position can become fundamentalist.

· *Progressivism:* recognizing the significance of contemporary change
and trying to make the world adjust to it.

· *Relativism:* adopting a "do your own thing" mentality and arguing
that anything goes that does not directly harm others.

· *Metacriticism:* transcending the whole society or system and offer-
ing critiques from beyond.

· *Dialogism:* rejecting one stance and a monologic position and trying to foster a mutuality of voices.

I can personally align myself with all but the first position, which is
the most difficult one to confront in a postmodern world. With varying
emphases, traditionalists see chaos around them and seek a return to an
older order in which a clear voice of authority and a firm moral structure held sway. The extreme version of this is fundamentalism, which
displays a number of major ideological features.[24] Fundamentalist arguments are concerned "with the erosion of religion and its proper role in
society": they react to what they sense to be its marginalization. Fundamentalists usually become highly selective in the issues they pick out and
in what they choose to ignore. They see the world as "uncompromisingly
divided into light, which is identified with the world of the spirit and the
good, and darkness, which is identified with matter and evil." For them,
there is an absolute (and usually literal) belief in the sacredness of key
texts. And finally, there is a belief in millennialism and messianism—"a
miraculous culmination. The good will triumph over evil, immortality
over mortality; the reign of external justice will terminate history." Fundamentalist groups tend to have a clear, chosen membership, sharp boundaries, an authoritarian organization, and strict definitions of acceptable

behavior. The issues they focus on are also usually very clear-cut: the rein-statement of "a unified faith, race, reason, gender duality, normal sex-uality, nation and or territory that never was secure."[25]

But, as William Connolly has suggested, fundamentalism may well go further than we think. In one sense fundamentalism is present almost everywhere. Even those who champion "difference" and "pluralization" may find that their own positions "rest upon fundamentals more or less protected from internal interrogation."[26] All positions, insofar as they are positions, must contain an element of foundational belief—and with that some weaker version of fundamentalism. We must thus be very care-ful, for we may all turn out to be closet fundamentalists at heart. How can we move beyond the limiting constraints of the various fundamen-talist assumptions that may lurk behind all our arguments? We are led back to the impossible question: Can we ever find a common ground? Can we ever just sit down and talk with our enemies? Is the whole thing hopeless, since fundamentalisms in different guises may be lurking everywhere? How can we create bridges, find connections, make links across divides? This last is indeed a key question of this book, and I return to it regularly.

Over the years, there have been attempts to do this from widely diver-gent backgrounds and positions. A leading American sociologist, Amitai Etzioni, targets moral conflict as a key issue in American culture and seeks to establish a New Golden Rule that will help us to move toward a dia-logic position: he sometime calls this position a "megalogue"—a society-wide dialogue that links communities.[27] Likewise, the German philosopher Jürgen Habermas seeks through his "discourse ethics" to establish ground rules that will foster the achievement of a consensus in "ideal speech sit-uations." Here a public sphere would be created in which free and unco-erced participant debate could occur. The aim of such debate would be to arrive at some kind of consensus.[28]

Others, such as James Davison Hunter, suggest that we look at the arenas of debate that may be weakening democratic action. For instance, special agenda organizations may play a vital, essential role in public life, but they can often lead to excesses and extreme and "distorted commu-nication." Ordinary public opinion may be undermined when we begin to recognize the ambivalence that most people experience about these serious issues. And the institutions of civil society—free press, schools, religions, and the like—that mediate between individuals and the state are often inadequate. Each of these arenas of public debate, he argues, need sustained and critical attention that seeks to unearth their excesses, their "distortions of rhetoric," their tendencies toward trivialization, and their unwillingness to seriously confront certain arguments.

Thus, discussion about ways to move ahead and build at least some bridges across our many differences is already taking place. In what follows I want to suggest three ideas: intimate citizenship, grounded moralities, and dialogue, which may all be of help in this task.

# 4

# The New Theories of Citizenship

*There has been an explosion of interest in the concept of citizenship. . . . In 1978, it could confidently be stated the "concept of citizenship has gone out of fashion." . . . Fifteen years later, citizenship has become the "buzz word" amongst thinkers on all points of the political spectrum.*

Will Kymlicka and Wayne Norman, *"Return of the Citizen"* in Beiner 1995

*I want to defend the strong thesis that doing without frameworks is utterly impossible for us; otherwise put, that the horizons within which we live our lives and which make sense of them have to include these strong qualitative discriminations. . . . The claim is that living within such strongly qualified horizons is constitutive of human agency, that stepping outside these limits would be tantamount to stepping outside what we would recognize as integral, that is undamaged, human personhood.*

Charles Taylor, *Sources of the Self*

*If the modern "problem of identity" was how to construct an identity and keep it solid and stable, the postmodern "problem of identity" is primarily how to avoid fixation and keep the options open.*

Zygmunt Bauman, *"From Pilgrim to Tourist"* in Hall and du Gay 1996

A S THE PRECEDING CHAPTERS have suggested, change and conflict are continuing to keep us in very uncertain times. Contemporary cultural flows of intimacies bring with them tensions, contradictions, anxieties, and contestations which some critics may see as signs of breakdown and moral chaos. They urge a return to the apparent safety of tradition, but for me this is a world now lost. There can be no turning back the clock. We are at a moment in history when the changes underway offer us the potential to create new ethical ways of living. There is no reason to believe that this will be easy, but it is surely worth a try.

How, then, are we to navigate our way through the tangled web of conflicts that now surround our personal lives? How can we live in a world of growing differences, contradictions, tensions, and confusions without finding a few slender threads of continuity to which we can cling? Can we indeed find some universals—however tenuous—on which we can agree in a time of such rapid change and, for some, social disintegration? A language of what I call "intimate citizenship" seems to be emerging, and it is the notion of citizenship that I will explore here. Although the concept arguably came into its own in modern Western democracies, the idea of citizenship is, of course, a very old—even a traditional—one. It may thus seem odd that I wish to graft this old idea onto postmodern thinking. What I suggest in this chapter, however, is that the very idea is being radically modified in the postmodern world.

## Citizenship and Identity

Two concepts, citizenship and identity, can aid us in establishing the problem and taking us to the heart of the matter: difference and unity. Citizenship is a term that signifies belonging to and participation in a group or community—something that brings with it certain rights and obligations. Identity refers, of course, to a sense of who one is and who one is not. Typically by constructing an individual history, identities suggest how this one particular individual differs from others and go on to suggest lines of activity into the future. In the context of intimacies, identities are expressed by statements such as "I am her husband," "I am gay," "I am the child of a surrogate mother," "I am transgendered." Both citizenship and identity highlight the idea that life is lived within certain boundaries and is guided by some sense of continuities, connections, and sameness. Both serve as group markers as well, with citizenship marking out one polity from another and identity marking out one group of individuals from another. Citizenship "carries legal weight," while identity "carries social and cultural weight."[1]

Many of the changes and conflicts I have been discussing speak to these political and group boundaries. It may be that new citizen identities will arise in connection with groups such as test-tube babies, lesbian and gay married couples and families, single parents, the polyamorous and the polysexual, the centegenarian population, the transgendered—and many others. These newly emerging groups of citizens already form part of the "issues culture" in which we now live and in which a new language of intimacies is being forged. At the same time, these groups provide their members with new personal identities, with a new sense of who they are: a single parent, a designer child, a lesbian father, a transsexual, and on to much more muddled identities such as that of the cybercitizen and the polyamorous, as well as the identities linked to new reproductive technologies.[2]

## The "New Citizenships"

The term *citizenship* is open to many different meanings and has been approached from a variety of theoretical positions.[3] It is hence what social scientists typically call a "contested concept." Three well-known models of citizenship are generally recognized. The first, strongly identified with liberalism, maintains a specific, even narrow, focus on the rights and obligations of citizens within a given state: it is the classic "rights and duties" model. The second, sometimes called the "town hall" model, emphasizes the participation of citizens in civil society and is closely linked to communitarianism and republicanism. The third, and vaguest, model views citizenship as founded on relatively radical communications that aim to prevent "state abuses and the greed of the market."[4]

Over roughly the past century three waves of interest in citizenship have been observed: an early wave before the First World War; a second in the 1950s and 1960s that had British sociologist T. H. Marshall as its principal spokesperson; and a third that has been with us since the early 1990s.[5] Leaving aside the first wave, the classic liberal formulation of citizenship is found in the work of T. H. Marshall, who defines citizenship as "a status bestowed on those who are full members of a community. All who possess the status are equal with respect to the rights and duties with which the status is endowed."[6] On the basis of this definition, Marshall distinguishes three clusters of citizen rights that have emerged chronologically over the past two centuries in response to concerns over civil, political, and social rights—clusters relating to justice under the law, to political representation, and to basic human welfare. Each cluster of rights is linked to key institutions: the civil and criminal courts, state governing bodies, such as Parliament or Congress, as well as local elective bodies, and educational and welfare services. What we can thus see is the emergence of communities that, in Marshall's own description, establish the "rights necessary for individual freedom": "liberty of the person; freedom of speech, thought and faith; the right to own property . . . and the right to justice"; the "right to participate in an exercise of political power"; and the "right to a modicum of economic welfare and security, the right to share to the full in the social heritage and to live the life of a civilized being according to the standards prevailing in the society."[7] This is an elegant and influential model that acknowledges the gradual expansion of the idea of citizens—and of civility—through each of these stages of modern society: civil-legal (mainly in the eighteenth century), political (mainly in the nineteenth century), and welfare (mainly in the twentieth century). People gain certain rights and the status of belonging as citizens as long as they live up to the expectations of their society—to work, for example, or to vote, or to respect the law.

Yet Marshall's view has had its critics. Some have accused his model of having an over-generalized "evolutionary tendency": it sees rights and citizenship unfolding in a specific order. Others object that it makes universal claims for an idea that is basically parochial, of relevance only to a limited number of (Anglo-American) countries. Yet others argue that Marshall's view of citizenship is too simplistic and thus obscures the true basis of inequalities: it divides the world into good citizens and deviant outcasts, who remain marginalized by the very concept of citizenship itself. And, closely linked to these critics, there are those who worry that Marshall's model is insufficiently concerned with how citizenship may be gendered or applied to a number of other "outside" groups. Indeed, Marshallian citizenship debates have been primarily concerned with matters of class and have generally ignored other sources of inequalities, such as racism. His approach cannot readily accommodate the very categories of difference and consequent inequalities and patterns of exclusion that have been the focus of so much recent thought: gender, ethnicity, age, physical disability, nationality, and sexuality hardly appear as issues. Even his treatment of class, which could suggest the creation of an underclass, is not quite adequate to the task.

One of the most telling problems of citizenship arguments in the past has been the way in which citizenship itself has been used to exclude certain groups—to render some people citizens by excluding others who are not. To be a citizen implies "the other" who is not a citizen. Even today, many books on citizenship are written by men and about the old issues.

Since the beginning of the 1990s some radical shifts in the debates over citizenship have occurred. British sociologist Nick Ellison, for instance, has suggested that both the state-centered, civic liberal model of citizenship (that associated with Marshall) and the civic republican (town hall) model have been largely discredited, at least in their fundamental forms. In reaction to the inadequacies of these two traditional models, a poststructuralist position has emerged that "posits the idea of a series of indeterminate subject positions fragmented amongst a range of constituting discourses" on a global stage.[8] Although the poststructuralist position goes some way toward recognizing the character of a changing, multivoiced, late-modern world, it also raises issues of fragmentation and lack of coherence that could make workable notions of citizenship very difficult to sustain. Still, the recognition of a plurality of groups living in a global world where notions of national citizenship are breaking down is surely becoming more common, and thus the poststructuralist approach is likely to be the most fruitful *starting point* for developing newer ideas of citizenship, such as the notion of intimate citizenship. It helps us get a hold on some of the most common problems of citizenship debates by keeping an eye on openness and fluidity while searching for boundaries and universals. In what follows I will look briefly at some of the debates that are slowly carving out a new sense of what it means to be a citizen.

## Boundaries and Exclusion

Citizenship debates have traditionally highlighted the boundaries and the margins of societies or groups. To be a citizen—whether as one who enjoys the status of a citizen or one who participates in one's society as a citizen—is to exist inside a particular frame. Accordingly, someone who is not a citizen exists outside that frame. This opposition—of insiders to outsiders—is, in fact, one of the major difficulties with the traditional concept of citizenship: the term *citizenship* typically implies a unitary group ("us") that defines itself in relation to those who are excluded ("them"). One of the standard criticisms of Marshall is that his citizens constitute an exclusive group—strongly identified with white males. To be a citizen means to work within a certain framework of values, typically that of the dominant group. As Iris Marion Young remarks:

> In a society where some groups are privileged while others are oppressed, insisting that as citizens persons should leave behind their particular affiliations and experiences to adopt a general point of view serves only to reinforce the privilege; for the perspectives and interests of the privileged will tend to dominate this unified public, marginalizing or silencing those of other groups.[9]

Feminists were among the first to notice this bias in Marshall's thought and to argue the need for a "feminist citizenship," but others have made similar arguments. In his influential book *Multicultural Citizenship*, Will Kymlicka makes a powerful argument for minority rights within a framework of citizenship. He is concerned less with individual rights (in contrast to classical liberal theory) than with group rights—with the growing clash of majorities and minorities within a given state over language rights, educational curricula, immigration policies, national symbols such as public holidays, and the like. Although in developing his theory of multicultural citizenship, Kymlicka is primarily concerned with the clash of ethnic groups with the dominant cultures of the world, his ideas can be extended to the situation of other minorities. Kymlicka's theory of citizenship represents a major development over classic liberalism, in that he attempts to find some universal common grounds while also recognizing the existence of differences. "Citizenship," he argues, "should be a forum where people transcend their differences and think about the common good."[10] But if this is the case, how can we deal with what falls outside? And indeed, must something fall outside? Extending his argument to the situation of women, who have traditionally been excluded from citizenship, Ruth Lister seeks what she calls a "differentiated universalism," that is, "a universalism that stands in a creative tension to diversity and difference and that challenges the divisions and exclusionary inequalities which stem from this diversity"—although, as she wisely remarks, the difficulties in this project "are not to be underestimated."[11]

In making the general claim that all women should be citizens, feminist critics quite appropriately use a general category (women) to make a general claim for citizenship. But when we start to think more seriously about the broader implications of gender, we have to confront the question, "Which women?"—and, for that matter, "Which genders?" Such questions may seem to some as straightforward as any other questions about boundaries. But they most certainly are not to the transgendered communities—to hermaphrodites, transsexuals, transvestites, drag kings and drag queens, effeminate boys, and butch girls. Even within the transgender movement itself, we find that some of its members celebrate the core features of gender (they do not see themselves as "trans": they *really are* the other gender), while others delight in the ambiguities of gender—of gender blending and gender performance. For them, gender is absolutely not a fixed identity and thus cannot have any citizenship rights attached to it, unless we regard gender as some kind of "trans-identity," with rights and obligations now attaching to shifting identities. As the radical gender activist Kate Bornstein quite bluntly puts it:

> I've said no to gender; and I am going to keep saying no to systems that would rein me in, classify me, pin me down, or keep me in my place. Nope. Not gonna play that game anymore. . . . [12]
>
> I am wondering if I could live without an identity, because that's the direction in which I seem to be moving.[13]

Such statements hint at a problem. How are we to deal with those who refuse categories, boundaries, and identities? How to deal with those who would transgress ideals of good citizenship? Transgressors do not want to fit in and be part of the civic order. They want to violate borders and boundaries. They do not wish to be "normal." Refusal to be called normal is not a problem of women's rights or women's citizenship, since such a refusal explicitly shuns the gender boundary that a reference to women would have to set. In discussing citizenships and identities, then, we need always to be aware of dissident (and diffident) citizens—those of shifting identities whose very social role seems to challenge boundaries.

We arrive, then, at the classic problem of universals and differences, or the "moral boundaries debate": who is inside and who is outside, who is included and who is excluded, both within and across social worlds. The process of setting boundaries often reveals strong patriarchal, racializing, nationalizing, and heterosexist elements, drawing boundaries that tacitly (and sometimes not so tacitly) exclude others on grounds of gender, ethnicity, nationality, sexuality, and so forth. The last decades of the twentieth century saw a lot of writing that attempted to demolish these boundaries and that celebrated a politics of difference. Quite rightly, much of this writing sought to discredit the notion of both universals and boundaries. Yet as the liberal sociological critic Alan Wolfe also quite rightly points out, "It is impossible to imagine a society without boundaries."[14]

> Inclusive democracy and exclusive group centeredness are necessary for a rich but just social life. Without particular groups with sharply defined boundaries, life in modern society would be unbearable. . . . Yet if the boundaries between particular groups are too rigid, we would have no general obligations. . . . We would live together with people exactly like ourselves, unexposed to the challenge of strangers, the lure of cosmopolitanism, and the expansion of moral possibility that comes with responsiveness to the generalized other.[15]

So the issue is really not just the *existence* of these boundaries (probably a social necessity) but the *nature* of these boundaries. The new citizenship debates live on the borders of this problem, and hence this issue will continually haunt us through this book. Maybe the task ahead is to develop further Lister's idea of a "differentiated universalism" whereby *boundaries remain present but shift and sway, are less permanently settled, less rigid and divisive, but rather become more porous, more archipelago-like, more open to change.* Boundaries are always being reworked. They become the recurrent site for debates about what is good and what is not: they display what Durkheim called "moral effervescence." These ongoing debates would lead to a recognition of the continuous need both for a drive toward

a common good and simultaneously for what has been called a "pluralization ethos."[16] And for recognition—the need to provide a location
somewhere for the voices that do not even want to be citizens.[17]

## "Natural Rights"

Another problem with the traditional discussions of citizenship centers
on rights and responsibilities, which have often been viewed as "natural" or "inalienable." But this is not the view of contemporary writers,
who instead argue that rights have to be invented through human activities and must be built into notions of community, citizenship, and identity. Rights and responsibilities depend upon communities to make them
plausible and possible. And, of course, rights change over time. The idea
of "gay rights," for instance, could not possibly have been on the agenda
in the eighteenth century: only as the identity of the modern gay was
fashioned did the idea that gays have rights emerge.[18] Rights accrue to
people whose identities flow out of communities made up of other members like themselves. Thus it was only as lesbian and gay communities
started to develop and women's movements gathered strength that a new
kind of citizenship—one that challenged the long-standing male bias of
the concept—became increasingly plausible. Likewise, cybercitizens can
only come into being and develop rights and duties alongside some par-
allel cybercommunity. Thus, the nature of our communities—the languages they use, the stories they preserve and harbor, the identities they
construct, the moral and political codes they champion—move to the
center stage of "rights" thinking.

"Citizenship," then, should not be seen as a necessary, evolutionary,
or essential concept, but rather as a sensitizing tool that can be used to
indicate a loose conglomerate of spheres of action in which communities are developed that in turn attribute certain "contestable" rights and
responsibilities to human beings in the arenas of law, politics, and social
welfare. For would-be citizens, telling personal stories about "their
rights" and establishing "communities of support" is a crucial part of
this process. There is hence nothing "inalienable" or "given" about such
a citizen's rights: they are, rather, heavily dependent upon the communities out of which they evolve. In turn, the stories such communities
create help to shape the rights that develop.

## State, Society, and Inequality

A related issue that also requires clarification pertains to the social arenas in which debates on citizenship take place. As we have seen, the con-

cept of citizenship can too easily imply the existence of "good" and "bad" citizens—the insiders and the outsiders—and often these are linked to specific groups nested inside a hierarchical social structure. One might well ask whether there can ever truly be *just citizenship in an unjust society*. Probably not, but, all the same, ideas of the "new citizenship" should always be mapped onto the overarching dimensions of class (income, status, power), ethnicity, age, gender, and other such attributes that can be used to manufacture inequality—to render certain groups inferior, or even to make them into the excluded "others." If, for example, we are talking about sexual citizenship rights as one domain of intimate citizenship, then the "sexual citizen" needs to be thought of as someone who occupies a classed, ethnicized, gendered, and age-grouped position in society. That is, not all sexual citizens will be treated equally, fairly, in the same way. And if we are talking about reproductive rights, it is apparent that these often work against the poor.[19] In order to gain a sense of who is most likely to be seen as the good citizen, and who may have a propensity to be marked out as the poorer citizen, we will need to take these dimensions of the overall social order on board.

Helpful here may be the well-known analysis and critique by the feminist political philosopher Iris Marion Young. Young has identified a number of key processes at work that help to organize inequality and domination. She urges us to examine social exclusion and marginalization. Which citizens are likely to be "expelled from useful participation in social life"? She asks, Who is likely to be most exploited; whose labor benefits another; and which of these groups are most likely to be seen as the good citizens? Who are the powerless; who "lack the authority, status, and sense of self that 'professionals' tend to have"? Who might be the objects of "cultural imperialism," in which "the universalization of a dominant group's experience and culture" establishes itself as the norm—the norm of the good citizen?[20] And, finally, she asks, who is more likely to experience hostility and violence directed at them simply because they belong to a given group?[21] Who, then, are excluded from citizenship, subject to exploitation, forced into powerlessness, victimized by cultural imperialism and violence? And how, above all, might the social exclusion of these groups be remedied?

## Obligations

Another common omission in many discussions of rights—and this includes many of the more recent ones—is the issue of obligations. These might include voting, paying taxes, and caring for others, such as chil-

dren. But it is a standard attack upon citizenship theory that it panders
to what might be called "the greedy citizen" who seeks only rights and
entitlements while attempting to ignore duties. Attacks of this kind come
from both the right and the left. Just what kind of obligations, then, are
we talking about?

Just as we might expect, the issue of obligations is contested and controversial, too. Thomas Janoski, for example, in a major attempt to construct a theory of obligations, has suggested a fourfold typology of
obligations, four broad types of obligations for the good citizen. These
are *legal obligations,* such as respecting the rights of others to liberty, freedom of speech, choice of religion, and so on; *political obligations,* such
as respecting democracy itself by voting in elections and protesting against
governments that violate rights; *social obligations,* such as tolerating social
diversity and helping the less fortunate; and *obligations relating to participation,* such as respecting all groups in the participatory process.[22]
Unfortunately, Janoski names a number of duties that many would find
unacceptable. For instance, he suggests a social obligation to "raise a loving family"—a duty that obviously poses a problem for those who prefer to be single. He also proposes that people should "pursue a career to
the benefit of society"—a duty that poses difficulties for those who do
not wish to be so involved in work. Any discussion of citizenship in the
late-modern world must recognize that just as rights are now contested
and plural, so too will be obligations.

## Identity

Finally, and taking us to the heart of the problem, there is also the matter of identity, which—though far from a new idea—has, like citizenship, become a buzzword of much social science lately.[23] The term, which
derives from the Latin *idem* ("same"), speaks metaphorically to a constant concern of the day: sameness, unity, similarity—as opposed to conflicts, differences, fragmentation.[24] By reason of its very terminology,
identity theory usually implies some sense of continuity and unity. If
never actually complete, the search is at least on for an identity—a project
aimed at learning who one is or what one's nation is. Identity is a concept that looks both *inward* and *outward.* On the one hand, it speaks to
the most microscopic of events—our inner world, how we feel about
ourselves, that slender thread of being that holds us together as a self, a
"me," a unity that offers a guide to who we "really" are. On the other hand,
identity also looks outward to the most macro of organizations—to the
nation-state and even to the global world. The titles of some recent books

are suggestive in this regard: *Catholic Identity* (Dillon), *Celtic Identity and the British Image* (Pittock), *Identity and Authenticity in the Middle East* (Meijer), *Global Identity* (Meyer), *Ethnic Identity in China* (Gladney), and *The Discursive Contradictions of National Identity*. Here we find identity allied with group solidarity, a belonging, and a recognition.[25]

Yet in between the inward- and the outward-looking approaches to identity is a whole array of communities bridging the gap between the personal and the cultural. People are searching for their identity *inside* (who am I?) by searching through their communities *outside*—gay, transgendered, female, ethnic, multicultural. Taken to an extreme this approach can yield a jingoistic, aggressive, even brazen self-definition: "I am a British, black, gay male." The categories underlying this statement of identity are often stridently clear: "I am what I am." At the opposite extreme, identities and the groups to which they are attached appear as so far dissolved and dissolving that identity itself is permanently unsettled, destabilized—always provisional, under construction, very much a project and never a thing. But even in this most extreme form the idea of identity has to recognize the need for, and the power of, categories and boundaries in the organization of the social world. It is just that what were taken as continuities and sameness have become so much more pluralized, so shifting and fragmented.

Now, to speak of citizenship usually also implies an identity—a person, a voice, a recognized type, a locus, a position, a subjectivity—from which the claim of citizenship can be made. And such identities bring with them pasts, presents, and futures: a sense of our past histories, a defining "other" different from us, and hints for future conduct based in part on this "otherness." Until fairly recently, these *identities of citizenship* usually were conceived of in terms of a universalized person (typically a privileged white male) and were made to seem rather solid, permanent, fixed, and essential. Citizenship generally accrued around identities based on nationality. Belonging to a specific nation conferred rights, obligations, and recognition. Citizenship told the story of a past national history, it viewed those who were not members as the enemy, and it suggested a future—often of bloodshed and war—to protect this identity. But the women's movement, lesbian and gay movement, and ethnic and postcolonial movements have raised a host of potential new identities that demand recognition and lay claim to rights and obligations.

Looking further afield, we also find a host of newer identities beginning to appear: new family citizens, stepchild citizens, surrogate-mother citizens, surrogate-children citizens, lesbian and gay partners citizens, children of lesbian and gay partners citizens, cybercitizens, transgendered citizens, sadomasochistic citizens, rape-victim citizens, and the like. Voices now speak from a multiplicity of shifting and unsettled positions. These voices are always in dialogic process, and people speaking from these positions may well find these have to shift further in the very processes of argumentation. But the voices cannot speak at all if they do not recognize the traditional categories, however humble and inadequate they may be. We need what might be called a *thin essentialism*. We need our essential sense of self, even as we change and modify it almost on a daily basis. That is surely part of the continuing politics of citizenship.

## Feminist Citizens and Sexual Citizens

Many of the rights that form the topic of current debates on personal life can be subsumed under Marshall's classic three areas—civil, political, and social—and certainly the intimate citizenship program demands for people individual freedom, political rights, and a promise that basic needs will be met; these may well be preconditions for citizenship of any sort. But largely as the result of the new social movements and the growth of the public media, hitherto unknown domains of social life have been created since Marshall's time, and these demand a new analysis.

A new way of approaching citizenship that can respond to changes, differences, and new claims has arisen, and with it comes a package of new terms—sexual citizenship, cultural citizenship, feminist citizenship, global citizenship, queer citizenship, flexible citizenship, diasporic citizenship, urban citizenship, technological citizenship, ecological citizenship, radical citizenship, and so forth.[26] (See Figure 4.) We seem to have reached a point where a thousand citizenships are ready to bloom. The idea of intimate citizenship builds upon, but certainly does not replace, at least two of these newer terms: *feminist citizenship* and *sexual citizenship*. Feminist citizenship debates have played a crucial role in the critique of classical models of citizenship by demonstrating just how gendered the process of citizenship usually is and how frequently women have been, and for the most part still are, second-class citizens. Feminists have thus put on the agenda a whole series of debates that were missing. David Evans's *Sexual Citizenship*, published in 1993, provided one further starting point for discussion. Evans is sharply critical of conventional views of citizenship. As he puts it: "The history of citizenship is a history of fundamental formal heterosexist patriarchal principles and practices ostensibly progressively 'liberalized' towards and through the rhetoric

| Identities | Rights |
|---|---|
| *Feminist* (e.g., Ruth Lister, Rian Voet, Sylvia Walby, Diane Richardson) | *Sexual:* (a) to various forms of sexual practice (participation in sexual activity; enjoyment of sexual pleasure; sexual and reproductive self-determination, including the right to say no); (b) to the development of sexual identities (sexual self-definition; self-expression, versus "don't ask, don't tell"; self-realization); (c) to rights within social institutions (consent within relationships; choice of sexual partners; public recognition of sexual relationships) |
| *Sexual* (e.g., David Evans, Diane Richardson, Jeffrey Weeks, Rosalind Petchesky) | *Lesbian and gay:* (a) to protection against violence and, more generally, to equal protection under the law; (b) to participation in consensual adult sexual relations without criminal penalty; (c) to nondiscrimination in housing, employment, and education; (d) to military service; (e) to marriage and / or its legal benefits (retaining custody of children; adopting children) |

*Erotic* (David Bell and Jon Binnie)
*Queer* (Steven Seidman)
*Cultural* (Bryan Turner)
*Deep* (Paul Clarke)
*Reflexive* (Nick Ellison)
*Dissident* (Holloway Sparks)
*Diasporic, multicultural* (Will Kymlicka, Michel Laguerre)
*Global* (Martin Albrow, Richard Falk)
*Flexible* (Aihwa Ong)
*Cyber / cyborg* (Tim Jordan; Chris Hables Gray)
*Transformative* (Jock Young)
*Cosmopolitan* (David Held, Manuel Castells, Ulrich Beck)
*Radical* (Engin Isin and Patricia Wood)
*Critical* (Pippa Norris)

SOURCES: For sexual rights, Diane Richardson, "Constructing Sexual Citizenship: Theorizing Sexual Rights," *Critical Social Policy* 20, no. 1 (2000): 105–35; for lesbian and gay rights, Martha Nussbaum, *Sex and Social Justice* (Oxford: Oxford University Press, 1999), chap. 7.

FIGURE 4. *Emerging Identities and Emerging Rights*

of 'equality' but in practice to effect unequal differentiation."[27] Accordingly, Evans introduces his own concept of sexual citizenship as a series of rights to certain sexualized life styles linked to markets.[28] Most of his book is given over to discussions of specific groups, mainly in Britain, but his principal example is gay rights and the "homosexual." Although Evans has little to say about lesbians, he also considers the sexual rights of women, bisexuals, transsexuals, and children. Crucial to sexual citizenship is the construction of subjects (or subjectivities) to which rights and obligations may be ascribed. Sometimes this can be controversial: in asking whether children are sexual citizens with sexual rights, Evans heads straight for a minefield of opinions regarding the boundaries of sexualities. But such issues needed surely to be placed on the agenda, along with the more accepted rights of a child. And can the concept of sexual citizenship be stretched even further to, say, the rights of the pedophile?

Two years later, a leading British sociologist of sex, Jeffrey Weeks, again questioned the prevailing notions of citizenship. In Weeks's view, citizenship has been a "major element of sexual politics since the 1970s, largely in the form of campaigns for rights."[29] But the concept of the "sexual citizen" is more recent and has served to render more formal and explicit the idea of sexual rights that had developed over the past thirty years in the context of the gay and lesbian movement. Weeks sees a new "sexual citizen" arriving, and he charts how this idea may help to advance political debates surrounding relationships between men and women, families, and the denaturalization of the sexual. Such debates need to balance the claims of different communities looking for ways to live life upholding both our diversity and our common humanity.[30]

Clearly influenced by both lesbian politics and women's rights, Diane Richardson has developed similar ideas. Like Weeks, she argues that "we live in an age when the politics of citizenship increasingly define 'sexual politics.'" According to Richardson:

> Globally, we are witnessing gay and lesbian movements (and sometimes bi-, sometimes transgender) that demand "equal rights" with heterosexuals in relation to age of consent laws, healthcare, and rights associated with social and legal recognition of domestic partnerships, including the right to marry, immigration rights, parenting rights, and so on. In a similar vein, there are groups campaigning for "transsexual rights" including the right to sex change treatment on the National Health Service, the legal right for birth certificate status to be changed, and, related to this, the right to marry legally. Recently there have been

attempts to place "sexual rights" on the agenda of disability movements, especially in relation to disabled people's rights to sexual expression. . . . We can even see some evidence of the language of citizenship being used in movements or campaigns whose politics are definitely not about seeking formal equality with heterosexuals. An example of this is the focus on prostitution as a human rights issue by some radical and revolutionary feminists.[31]

Richardson evaluates the classic models of citizenship in terms of their applicability to lesbian and gay rights, and she finds them severely lacking. Claims to citizenship status generally are not only guilty of a strong male bias, as many feminist writers have observed, but citizenship also privileges heterosexuality: "Within discourses on citizen's rights . . . the normal citizen has largely been constructed as male, and . . . as heterosexual."[32] Richardson goes on to identify three main areas in which the rights of sexual—as opposed to heterosexual—citizenship should be claimed. These are:

- Rights to various forms of *sexual practice* in personal relationships, including rights to sexual pleasure and to self-determination (the right not to be raped, for example, or the right to have children)
- Rights pertaining to *self-identity and self-definition,* such as the right to name the kind of sexual person one is and the right to self-realization
- Rights in connection with social institutions, such as the *public validation of a variety of sexual relationships,* including the right to choose partners and the right to public recognition of partnerships.

Richardson's arguments allow us to see that just as citizenship has been racialized and gendered, so has it been sexualized.

Another key study, *The Sexual Citizen,* by David Bell and Jon Binnie, examines the place of sexuality in both political and social theory and shows how the sexual is still—after all these years—routinely minimized, written out, "trashed" (even by those on the left, who often downplay sexuality as a matter of political correctness). But as the authors put it: "We consider all citizenship to be sexual citizenship, as citizenship is inseparable from identity, and sexuality is central to identity."[33] For them, sexual issues go to the heart of citizenship, and with that the theory of inequalities and the state. Their discussion highlights certain key areas in which the idea of sexual citizenship could prove especially fruitful. They look, for example, at the spaces of the city (in which both authors have a long-standing interest), envisaging global "queer cities" and the city as a network of love and friendships. They also take a critical look at the pink economy—or, as the authors put it, "the love that dares not speak its brand name." The language of the pink economy, they argue, is only so much homophobic hype ("Those rich faggots!") in a class-based world in which available and affordable options for the sexual citizen are unevenly distributed. The authors also discuss globalization and the problems raised by "transnational sexual citizenship," the importance of love and friendship, and the claims on the part of lesbians and gays to the right to marry and to serve in the military.

Running throughout the discussion is the idea that much of the citizenship debate "whitewashes" or "purifies" the issues raised by sexual liberation movements. The term *citizenship* (however much it may be stretched in ways I find valuable) inevitably seems to foreclose on certain ideas. In its standard interpretation, the notion of citizenship can lead to a world that is "privatized, deradicalized, de-eroticized and confined in all senses of the word: kept in place, policed, limited."[34] At the core of Bell and Binnie's book is the question of whether citizenship can ever allow for a radical or transgressive politics. (The authors like the idea of the "dissident citizen" proposed by Holloway Sparks.[35]) Bell and Binnie are concerned with the ways in which ideas of citizenship falter around issues of transgression and assimilation: how can someone be "queer and radical" and yet be a "good citizen"? Drawing on a now well-established literature about "good homosexuals," who seek normalizing and inclusion, as opposed to "bad queers," the authors worry that citizenship may well work against the "bad gays" and foster processes of social exclusion.

One drawback of the book, however, is that it focuses so predominantly on gay issues—what Bell and Binnie call the sexual citizen is really the queer (or bisexual) citizen. Little attention is paid to women's sexuality, to the problem of rape and violence, to abortion and reproduction, or to the debates over assisted conception, issues that are surely crucial not only to a feminist theory of citizenship but to any adequate concept of citizenship in the postmodern world. Indeed, the book tends to reinforce the divide between feminist and gay perspectives on citizenship. Interestingly, the book is written by two men.

Many feminists have also campaigned for the more general value of the idea at the United Nations. I think of the work of Rosalind Petchesky, who wrote perhaps the most prominent article in the field: for her the notion of sexual rights—"that new kid on the block," in her words—

reaches an international agenda. For it was only at the Fourth World Conference on Women in Beijing in 1995, and even then with huge controversy, that the term finally entered the international human rights vocabulary. We will return to this and her work in Chapter 8.

While the concept of sexual citizenship is clearly of value, my own preference is for a wider, more inclusive understanding of the personal life. Hence my preference for the notion of intimate citizenship, which embraces a broader spectrum of issues, including, of course, sexuality.

## Toward a New Understanding of Citizenship

As this chapter tries to show, a new citizenship is in the making. Traditionally, citizenship has meant being *recognized as belonging* and *participating* in a group where one is expected to do certain things, fulfill certain *obligations,* in return for certain *rights.* As more recent debates suggest, though, the concept of citizenship becomes much messier once we problematize the notions of boundaries, rights and duties, obligations, and identity—and proceed to place them all in a context of inequalities. Indeed, as the postmodern world experiences a growing loss of grand universals and categories become much less clearly demarcated, the very idea of citizenship increasingly poses problems around universals and exclusion: how to define who is and is not a member of a group and how to develop standards of inclusion. Working from the new and developing ideas about citizenship discussed above, let me now outline a workable— if tentative—account of the issues critical to the new citizenship.

- New areas of citizenship are developing, beyond the traditional ones of law, politics, and welfare, that draw on a wider range of political issues, including those of redistribution and recognition, and highlight a plurality of rights and responsibilities.[36]
- Two main components of citizenship—recognition and participation— which are now linked to a "differentiated universalism," raise the problems of universalism and differences and highlight the need to clarify moral boundaries.[37] In addition, dissident citizens—transgressors— also need to be taken into account.
- These new areas of citizenship are mapped out through participatory, differentiated social worlds and hence have a persistently contested status, with the result that pathways to resolving tensions need to be examined.
- Citizenship is contingent on the construction of recognized identities

around which rights and responsibilities develop. Rights may take the form of "individual rights" and/or "group rights," often connected to newly emerging social movements and communities.

• "Citizenship" must always be sensitive to the whole panoply of inequalities—of the problem of "just citizenship in an unjust society."

Intimate citizenship recognizes emerging "intimacy groups and identities," along with their rights, responsibilities, and need for recognition in emerging zones of conflict, and suggests new kinds of citizens in the making. Among these may be the cybercitizen, the new reproductive citizens (surrogate mothers, "lost fathers," "test-tube citizens," and the like), new family citizens, including post-divorce citizens, children and step-family citizens, grandparent citizens, single parent citizens, and elderly citizens, as well as the transgendered citizen, the fetishistic citizen, the sadomasochistic citizen, and, more controversial still, the pedophile citizen. Such a list may be a little tongue in cheek, but it does make us aware of who is "in" and who is "out" and aware of those whose rights and responsibilities require closer attention. Most people would probably agree, for instance, that the pedophile should not enjoy citizenship rights, and that may mark the far end of the boundaries of intimate citizenship that we can accept.[38] At the same time, even the pedophile may be a putative citizen whose very transgressions give voice to issues we would do well to debate in the public sphere. It is to these public discussions that I will now turn.

# 5
# Public Intimacies, Private Citizens:
Inequalities and the Pluralization of Public Spheres

*Our goal as activists, as gay people, is to get a message out there within the context of this mainstream media that controls it. So an opportunity to get on there [TV talk shows] and talk about gay issues is one that we're not likely to pass up. . . . I'm exploiting. I'm using the show. I'm using the talk show host, the producers, the air time, the network, whatever, to push my social agenda.*

Michelangelo Signorile, gay activist

*I wouldn't watch all this garbage. Who's sleeping with who, what's going on with this couple because they were two women living together, or whatever. . . . I think a lot of people have lost it. And . . . people are entitled to their private lives. It should be private. And anything that's put on display is just garbage. There's nothing wrong with having sexual topics on television. To put it on display is what's wrong. When it's private, you work with it, but when you put it on television live, it becomes dirt.*

Judith, fifty-five-year-old white teacher

*Talk shows are like giving Twinkies to a starving person. But I like pushing people's buttons. I think it is good to push people's buttons. I like shaking people up. I mean personally I get a thrill out of it. But the reason I get a thrill out of it is because I'm rebelling against something. I mean the personal is the political. When I go on these shows, when I come out of a dating game show, I always make it a point to kiss the guy if I can.*

Miss Understood, drag performer

*With all their silly profundity and profound superficiality, talk shows move power around.*

Josh Gamson

All quoted in Josh Gamson, Freaks Talk Back

*From classical Athens through revolutionary America or enlightenment Europe, the democratic public sphere has been marred by exclusionary tendencies. Not just slaves, but non-natives, aboriginal, propertyless men and all women have been excluded at various points from both direct political participation (e.g., vot-*

*ing ) and from participation in the discourse of the public sphere. . . . "The people"*
*have not all been citizens.*

                Craig Calhoun, *Social Theory and the Politics of Identity*

*The problems of private existence are to a certain degree absorbed by the public*
*sphere; although they are not resolved under the supervision of the publicist agen-*
*cies, they are certainly dragged into the open by them. On the other hand, the*
*consciousness of privacy is heightened precisely by such publication; by means of*
*it the sphere generated by the mass media has taken on the traits of a secondary*
*realm of intimacy.*

      Jürgen Habermas, *The Structural Transformation of the Public Sphere*

THE CONCEPT OF INTIMATE CITIZENSHIP flags a proliferation of debates about how to live a personal life in a late modern world. Such debates are usually conducted in what has come to be called the *public sphere,* the domain of civil society in which people deliberate, discuss, and even argue about life. The public sphere provides space for the day-to-day workings of a deep democracy. In this chapter, I look at this public sphere—how it has been characterized, how it is changing, how intimacies can be located within it, and who has access to it.

"Intimate citizenship"—as designating *public discourse on the personal life*—makes for a certain tension: it appears to be an oxymoron. Citizenship usually speaks to the public sphere and intimacy to the private. But, as this chapter argues, this very juxtapositioning sensitizes us to the important fact that the public and the private are no longer separate, autonomous spheres, if indeed they ever were. We need to move beyond the traditional dichotomy and instead establish links and connections. In proliferating and comingling, new public spheres and new private spheres put on the agenda a myriad of personal concerns. In the late modern world, the personal invades the public and the public invades the personal.

## Rethinking the Public and the Private

The division between the public and the private spheres, along with their evolution and continuing transformation, have been the focus of numerous commentators. Skirmishes have at times occurred over the very meaning of the terms. Many historians distinguish between the private spheres of home and family, usually considered a woman's sphere, and everything else, which is the public sphere, typically the domain of men. More generally, in the words of Jürgen Habermas: "We call events and occasions 'public' when they are open to all, in contrast to closed or exclusive affairs."[1]

The publication of Jürgen Habermas's *The Structural Transformation of the Public Sphere* (originally in German in 1962 and subsequently in English in 1989) generated much discussion and the book became for a time the most influential treatment of the subject. Habermas saw the modern bourgeois public sphere as emerging out of a feudal era that had denied open, public, and rational debate on issues of universal significance. Modeled implicitly on the polis of Athenian democracies, a critical public space appeared in the coffeehouses and salons, as well as the literary magazines, of the seventeenth and eighteenth centuries. This emerging space opened, ostensibly to all, the potential for rational deliberation in a public setting.

For Habermas, the public sphere begins to decline with the growth of the commercial press. Social life moves indoors, into private homes, and begins to focus more on private matters. A "refeudalization of the public sphere" takes place. The opinions of private men of letters give way to the mass media: whereas once men of letters formulated political opinions through dialogue, now the commercial mass media take over the function of shaping political opinion through such things as editorials. There is, he suggests, a serious decline in political debate, caused in part by the invasion of the public sphere by commercial elements, in part by the persuasiveness of the mass media, an essentially passive medium that induces a stupor of consumerism, and in part by the collapse of a clear distinction between the public and the private. But all this is by no means without its element of controversy. Habermas is describing the making of an elite world of rationality, argument, and criticism—a world that includes a relatively small group of men and excludes large numbers of other people.[2]

In many ways, feminist discussions seem to me to offer a much more promising entrée to these debates.[3] With a loose opening slogan of "the personal is political," feminist scholars have been particularly concerned with the value of the distinction from the first. The personal and the public cannot be so readily split up. While feminist critics do not dispute the existence of a private zone or the significance of personal experience, they do stress the ways in which personal lives are interconnected with the public and the political. They cannot be separated out so clearly, and they play a role in shaping each other. Thus, for instance, the family and the home—that "haven in a heartless world," that seemingly stubbornly "subversive" private sphere—lies deeply embedded within a matrix of power relations. Families, for all their privacies, are structured through laws and politics: they are the site for the reproduction of gender relations and indeed for the patterning of power relations between adults and children. The intimate zone is, through and through, socially produced, maintained, and transformed. And, in the same way, the seemingly distanced worlds of the public and the political are actually constituted through a network of passionate human beings engaging with each other, often in highly personal ways. The distinction is, then, in some ways a false one.

All this, of course, means that one cannot simply speak about an intimate zone that is cut off from the public, the social, and the political (any more than there can be a completely public zone cut off from any aspect of the personal). Intimate citizenship refers to all those areas of life that appear to be personal but that are in effect connected to, structured by, or regulated through the public sphere. They are rarely, if ever, simply a matter of the personal. This is true, for instance, of the most personal, even the most private, of family lives, which are ultimately engulfed in legislation regarding marriage, divorce, child care, and pensions, not to mention wider social ideologies of familism. It is true of much of gender relations, which are enmeshed in policies concerning equal opportunity, sex discrimination, and the like: gendering is often deeply patterned by ideas of the public (male) and private (female). This is true, too, of much of sexuality: sex laws, media stereotypes, heterosexism, patriarchies, and homonegativisms surround this "oh-so-personal" area of life. And it is likewise true of the regulations often placed on our bodies— through the existence, for example, of Britain's Human Embryo and Fertilisation Authority, which regulates the highly personal choices around fertility and assisted conception.

Again, what we are talking about here are public discourses on the choices that cluster around personal life, which are themselves not just personal but political and social. We are no longer talking about the separation of private and public spheres, but of continuums, pathways, and intersections between them.

Feminist scholars also suggest that Habermas's analysis of the public sphere was in any event a profoundly privileged one. The bourgeois public sphere of the past was never really *the* public sphere. As feminist political scientist Nancy Fraser points out: "Virtually contemporaneous with the bourgeois public there arose a host of competing counterpublics, including nationalist publics, popular peasant publics, elite women's publics, black publics and working-class publics. There were competing publics from the start."[4] Indeed, Habermas's conception of the public was, she claims, "bourgeois, masculinist, white supremacist." According to Fraser and others, we need to recognize numerous public spheres where there is the "proliferation of a multiplicity of competing publics." Some of these may even be "subaltern counterpublics"—subordinated groups whose debates take place away from, and indeed outside of, "the supervision of dominant groups." Thus, we need to specify an array of spheres and arenas—not just one—where public talk about the personal is possible. Nancy Fraser suggests that the most striking late-twentieth-century example of other public spheres may well be "the U.S. feminist subaltern counterpublic" with its

> variegated array of journals, bookstores, publishing companies, academic programs, conferences, conventions, festivals, and local meeting places. In this public sphere, Feminist women have invented new terms for describing social reality, including "sexism," "the double shift," "sexual harassment," and "marital, date, and acquaintance rape." Armed with such language, we have recast our needs and identities, thereby reducing, although not eliminating, the extent of our disadvantage in official public spheres.

Drawing on these ideas, I think the term "intimate citizenship" must learn from the outset to denote *a plurality of multiple public voices and positions*. We can no longer expect that pure, unifying positions will be found in the public sphere. The relationships between different voices and different spheres—some of which are clearly more powerful than others—must be placed on the agenda. It means recognizing, too, the very conflicts and contested areas we examined in Chapter 3: these may not only be omnipresent, but they may not even be capable of resolution. I have more to say on this in the coming chapters.

In addition, and admittedly with great difficulty, we must at least start to find ways of (minimally?) recognizing even those who claim to be beyond or outside citizenship—people who do not want to be part of the "normal order," those who wish to transgress, those who want to be "outsiders." These generate what we might call *the truly, truly subversive public cultures*, which, at their most radically difficult extremes, include groups like religious fundamentalists and revolutionary anarchistic terrorists. They do not want be citizens; they detest the status quo; they damn well do not want to be included.

What of queer groups who speak in public but deny any claim to citizen ship? They do not—to paraphrase the immortal words of Groucho Marx—"want to be a member of any club that would accept them." But it nevertheless behooves the critic and the analyst at least to consider where such groups stand and ask what role they could have in all this. We might want to consider them provisional or putative citizens—even dissident or transgressive citizens—who bear their own outsider discourses that, if given a hearing, could help the dominant discourse stretch its boundaries.[5]

Unlike earlier versions of citizenship, which often foundered by marginalizing or excluding certain groups, "intimate citizenship" cannot imply one voice, one way, or one model. On the contrary, it is a loose term that comes to designate an array of stories and a multiplicity of voices, in which different lives, different communities, and different politics dwell. It must allow for a constant stretching and pulling at boundaries, realizing they can never be fixed even as they must be present. It must embrace the existence of voices of the personal life that are in sharp—sometimes seemingly fatal—conflict. It must fit into the contemporary empirical reality of the ethos of pluralization.[6] It must recognize multiple, hierarchically layered, and contested public spheres such as the feminist public spheres, the black public spheres, the working-class public spheres, and the gay public spheres. To these must also be added the voices of those who often line up against such movements: an example might be what we could call the evangelical Christian public spheres.[7] And even within such a sphere are multiple voices that talk across them: the gay Christian public spheres, for example.

Public spheres are stratified by class, gender, age, ethnicity—and it is always wise to ask as well whose voices are not being heard. For public spheres may well perpetuate inequalities. We may also have to start to recognize that within these public spheres (the plural becomes important), voices may actually converse in different ways—that the model of pure and deliberative rational argument, as exemplified in the liberal critic and the public intellectual, may well have its limitations.[8] There should be room for more cooperative ways of talking—ways that are messier, less linear, and more emotional than the rationalist models championed in the past. We will need to become more aware of the distinction between the *forms* of talk and the *contents* of talk, and we will need to realize that certain groups can seriously discredit and/or discount others because they do not argue in the same tone, or use the same conceptual structures, or draw on the world of feelings in the same way. Carol Gilligan recognized this over two decades ago in connection with moral reasoning.[9] But examples reach further. "Black rap," for instance, is a language that many people find incomprehensible, even annoying or offensive. But it is often the vehicle of serious youthful critique and argument, and it can generate heated debate. Likewise, certain TV programs speak directly to class differences. Josh Gamson, whose book *Freaks Talk Back: Tabloid Talk Shows and Sexual Non-Conformity* provids the quotations that open this chapter, suggests how some talk shows bring to the screen working-class voices—voices low in status, unrespectable voices—that are usually excluded from public space. When they are heard, they cause controversy, outrage—revealing, perhaps, just how much their voices have indeed been excluded.

This multiplicity of voices leads me to suggest what I have come to call *the pluralization of the public spheres.* It returns us—as each chapter of this book does in one way or another—to the problem of living with specific differences in a context where some generalized other is still looked for.

## Pluralized Public Spheres and New Arenas of Debate

It might be helpful to go back to the drawing board for a while. At the start of this new century, we need to consider where we can find the public spheres of intimate citizenship. That is, where can we find generally accessible spaces where roughly "equal" voices can speak, debate, and deliberate in a fairly constructive, concerned, and public manner about what does go on, and indeed should go on, in personal life? Are these spaces everywhere? Where are they not to be found?

Those who argue that the public sphere has dwindled frequently also see the decline of political discussion everywhere—in the decline in voting, the growth of apathy, the collapse of community, and, at a greater extreme, in the trivialization of everyday life. If so, then we cannot find this active space of public debate anywhere, really. But even these critics have to acknowledge that the public spheres of deliberative debate may be shifting into new spaces and adopting forms that differ from those of the past. Thus, even though Robert Putnam, in his much discussed book *Bowling Alone,* is famed for documenting the decline of American community since the 1960s (there has been a shrinking access to the "social capital" of communities, as he puts it), he does suggest a number of trends that signal more active participation: the increased involvement of younger people in social and political issues, the spread of the Internet, the burgeoning of self-help groups, and grass-roots activities among evangelical conservatives.[10] Other researchers have suggested that an attitude of pessimism about decreased participation in the civic order and a decline of talk and concern about social matters may not be all that well founded.[11]

I would suggest instead that the public spheres of intimate debates exist in many places. A distinction may be needed here between the interactive and noninteractive public spheres. The noninteractive spheres—found in books, in the press, and on television programs—are available to the general public and they confine argument and debate within themselves: theirs is a one-way path of communication. And these have proliferated over the past century. The interactive spheres allow for direct and personal communication around public issues; we can find these in the active debates of social movements, in conferences, in schools and universities, and maybe more problematically on Web sites. People debate and discuss (and sometimes scream and shout) at each other. Often the interactive public sphere has links to and draws upon the noninteractive sphere: people read the newspaper and discuss the news in bars and pubs. Often the two forms merge: people debate an issue on a TV talk show or a reality program, while others simply watch. But those watching then take the issues and debate them at home, at work, even at play.

As I see it, then, such talk can in fact be heard in many places. Contemporary life may well be carried on against a ceaseless discussion about how to live life in the late modern world that is taking place in many different ways among many different groups in many different arenas. Some of this discussion may be subject to what critics call the trivialization or the "dumbing down" of our cultures: it is not serious enough, not elevated enough for them! (But is there any real evidence that public debate in the past was significantly more informed and more sophisticated? The notion of the local "town-hall" democracy in which everyone in the community participated as sober, thoughtful citizens is most surely a myth.) Perhaps because of the radical doubt, the "risk," that postmodernity brings in its wake, postmodern society may partially be characterized by constant public talk about how to live life in these troubled times. Thus, as the world of politicians and official political discourse has lost much credibility, so we find a world of "subpolitics" emerging wherein political issues becomes part of everyday life talk.[12]

To give just one striking example. It is estimated that 20,000 women from all over the world attended the Fourth World Conference on Women in Beijing, in September 1995, while a further 10,000 or so attended the Non-Governmental Organizations Forum on Women forty miles away in Huairou. Not only were these the sites of extensive, ground-breaking public talk about the plight of women across the world, the tentacles of these debates spread out across the globe as millions more participated through various media—especially through electronic networking and cyberspace relationships. Here we have a large visible public sphere in the form of an international conference, but it generates yet more networks of talk and discussion. As Dineh Davis has remarked:

> Thousands of women from hundreds of globally disparate nodes sent tens of thousands of messages, debated critical issues related to the Platform for Action, uploaded and downloaded volumes of official documents, made travel arrangements, exchanged suggestions for reading material and trip preparations, offered last-minute invitations and swaps on Huairou sites, and—post-conference—submitted summaries and opinions on the outcome. . . . These network activities were spawned in the peripheries of a very physical and global gathering of humans.[13]

This is a long way removed from Habermas's genteel drawing rooms; but if "public sphere" means anything at the start of the twenty-first century, it would surely have to include such forums. Similarly, it may well have to include international conferences of sex workers and international conferences of queers, who not only transform their debates into public issues but also into global ones.[14]

It may be helpful, then, to think of these pluralized public spheres as composed of a number of overlapping arenas and to sense that negotiation is required between and across them. In these arenas we find *different kinds of public debate*—from the highly deliberative and rational voices of the so-called "public intellectuals" to the more day-to-day voices of people telling moral stories. Some examples will clarify this.

First there are the *arenas of the new social movements.* From the women's movement and lesbian and gay movement to evangelical Christian movements, one of the main tasks of the new social movements has been to establish the rhetoric, the claims, and the arguments about their key concerns. Such movements were less in evidence during the period of "bourgeois" public spheres described by Habermas, but now they are everywhere. And from them arise "organic intellectuals" who participate actively in both political and practical life as organizers and spokespersons, not just as writers and thinkers; as well as "moral entrepreneurs" or "provocateurs" whose task it is to get emerging claims and issues of debate onto the public agenda.

Second are the *arenas of the new media.* Television, documentaries,

film, and the press are packed with debate and public talk about personal
life. From moral dramas and soap operas to talk shows, reality shows,
and of course "the news," the public discourses of the personal abound.
And as we watch people laying bare their personal lives through the media,
we incorporate much of this into our day-to-day living. The growing field
of audience research no longer simply asks people what they thought of
particular programs; it observes their daily lives in relation to it. Thus,
for instance, two feminist cultural theorists, Andrea Press and Elizabeth
Cole, have traced different responses to the presentation of abortion on
television. Looking at three specific programs (episodes of *Dallas* and of
*Cagney and Lacey* and a made-for-TV movie based on *Roe v. Wade*), they
analyzed women's reactions, showing how these were inflected by worldview and class position. As they comment:

> Today the mass media are active participants in our social conversations
> about political and cultural matters, influencing our ideas, opinions,
> and values. Individuals engage in public dialogue not only with other
> citizens but also with other mass media representations, and television
> plays a powerful role in these debates.[15]

Others have observed talk shows such as *Oprah* and *Jerry Springer* and
have suggested how they may be deliberately designed to generate controversy both on stage and off. Again, those who see such programs as a
"dumbing down," even as reactionary, claim they have no serious relation to dialogue in the public sphere. Instead, these endlessly chattering
voices are manipulated into degrading, sensationalistic situations in which
they are forced to expose their overvalued selves. Guests on such programs are often confronted with omniscient "experts" who can explain
to them the—usually psychological—"truth" of their lives. They find their
arguments structured into standard debates, and they react with the
antithesis of rational argumentation: clichés, inarticulate babble, even
violence and rage. They get sucked into speaking a debilitating, individualized psychobabble that encourages them to ignore what is going on
more widely. In their thoroughgoing preoccupation with self, they are
wholly lacking in any sense of a broader critique.[16]

Others, however, suggest that this is "the chatter of the dispossessed,"[17]
bringing hidden topics out into the open and giving the disenfranchised
a place to air their fragmented views. Even women and lower-class white
men can now have their say. This emerging discourse can be seen as a
"politicalization of the private." Indeed, it is "the vanguard of citizens
striving for social change."[18] Such uninhibited discussion fractures the

elite views and ways of speaking that dominate the media more generally. The participants "yell at each other, disagree with experts, come to no authoritative conclusions. . . . People who are usually invisible get to have their say and, often, are wholly disrespectful of their betters." Some see this as radical: new voices get heard and a new populism starts to appear.[19] There is also a tendency for such programs to generate a wider climate of acceptance and tolerance, where "normalizing the deviant" takes place. Television is, then, one instance of the reshaping of the public sphere; it provides an arena in which we can find the debating, discussing, and deliberating new citizen.

Third are the *growing electronic arenas.* Whatever discontents they may bring, the electronic media are swiftly expanding. As of March 2001, for instance, the equivalent of some 360,000 e-mail messages were sent every second in Britain, and access to the Internet had grown extensively in most countries.[20] Quite where the borders of this new space fall remains unclear. What is clear, though, is that almost every issue on which you might wish to find information, generate discussion or simply just talk with someone else exists on the Web.

Working on various projects over the past few days, I found major Web sites devoted to all sorts of things pertaining to intimate life: surrogacy, human fertilization, sex fetishes, the Human Genome Project, child neglect in China, transgender politics, and evangelical Christians, to name a few. When I entered the gay and lesbian evangelical Christians' pages, I found the site of the Metropolitan Community Church, founded by Troy Perry in 1968, which now claims a presence in nineteen countries (at www.ufmcc.com).[21] There are truly vast sites for women (such as WomensNet and Virtual Sisterhood): often these are in six or seven languages. Gays and lesbians likewise have massive networks: a home page on gay partnerships and couples (on www.buddybuddy.com, which is the Partners Task Force for Gay and Lesbian Couples, based in Seattle) overflows with bibliographies, histories, legal information, counseling tips, surveys, material about immigration, parenting, religion, marriage ceremonies, worldwide news clips, comparative tables concerning the world situation of homosexuals, and—a nice feature—the Committed Couples Photo Galleries, where music often invites you into couples' homes to get a glimpse of their lives. And all this is constantly updated and includes pages for chat.

We are still in an early stage of thinking about the Web in relation to the public sphere. It is clearly not an orthodox space—it lies somewhere out there in virtual reality, floating between the public and the private.

And because it is a space that one can enter and exit at will and on one's own, there is nothing to stop someone from simply ceasing to communicate with others who hold different views. Thus the Web could merely foster dialogue among the like-minded and hence work to generate computerized ghettoes. Moreover, nobody really needs to know who you are or where you are. It may be that the skills needed for sustained, socially responsible interaction will diminish as a result of electronic communication. I do think that digital communication is a new public sphere, but in its newness lie many issues.[22]

To these three examples we could add many more. These could include new educational arenas where, despite persistent talk of dumbing down, more and more people gain access to education through such things as the Open University, the University of the Third Age, on-line courses, and community colleges. There also seems to have been an increase in international publishing, journals, and conferences—made easier by the rise of the Internet—devoted to discussions of sexuality, reproduction, queer theory, the family, and the like. Likewise, there are "art worlds." Art has traditionally been housed in museums and galleries into which many people never venture. But nowadays we see almost endless public debate about what constitutes art—can popular novels, or rock and roll, or snapshots, or graffiti be "art"?—and the relation of art to taboo sexualities (witness the debates around Mapplethorpe or pornography). Then again there are what we might call "public courtroom dramas" (for example, the dramas involving Mike Tyson and O. J. Simpson), in which moral dramas pertaining to personal life are enacted—dilemmas about rape, race, violence, and so forth. In these and many other arenas of social life, the public and its debates are a growing presence.

## An Example: Gay and Lesbian Public Spheres

To illustrate these issues, let us look at the emergence of the gay public spheres (or perhaps more correctly, but certainly more clumsily, the gay/lesbian/bisexual/transgendered/queer public spheres). As Eric Clarke comments in his study of the gay public sphere, *Virtuous Vice,*

> homoeroticsm has gone public like never before. As an embodied identity for public persons and media characters and as a reference point in literary and visual culture, intellectual debates, and commercial activities, homoeroticism has become a staple, if conflicted, feature of the U. S. public sphere.[23]

Quite a significant series of studies now exist that chart the emergence of lesbian and gay cultures over the past century, but especially since the symbolic Stonewall rally in 1969. Just as with the feminist public spheres described by Nancy Fraser, we see here the growth of a distinctive public sphere—with its own highly developed media, its own professionals and spokespeople, and its truly enormous outpouring of written material on every aspect of gay life and from every theoretical discipline. There are thousands of specific interest groups—from Gay Rodeo Championships and Gay Ramblers to International Gay Choir Festivals and the International Gay Olympics. In Britain alone there are groups for the Welsh, Cypriots, blacks, Orientals, Asians, and Jews ("kosher gays"); gay groups for fans of badminton, squash, Lycra cycling, windsurfing, football, bridge, swimming, and sailing; and arts groups, groups for gay accountants and gay businessmen, for chamber choirs, for pagans and occultists, groups for teenage gays, groups for those "under 25" (Forbidden Fruits) as well as for the "over 40s" and the "over 50s." And in the midst of all this is a vast network of cyberqueers![24] There are self-help social worlds of counseling, help lines, HIV / AIDS and drug support, and scores of professional support groups— legal, medical, educational. A well-documented (and critiqued) gay, or pink, economy has developed. There are huge symbolic rallying events across the globe—the Mardi Gras in Sydney, Australia, for example, lasts for a month and is sponsored by major businesses. There is an *Ivory Closet of Lesbian and Gay Studies,* a social world that has gathered its own momentum through books and conferences.[25] Such intellectual work is crucial to the claims-making activities of any social movement. By the 1980s a solid band of gay and lesbian academics had begun to appear, holding their own conferences, writing their own library of books, starting their own courses, and producing academic journals—the *Journal of Homosexuality, GLQ,* the *Journal of Bisexuality,* the *Journal of Lesbian Studies, Queery, Sexualities,* the *Lesbian and Gay Review.* All in all, this is a textbook case of the creation of new public spheres. In short, hardly any aspect of social, political, cultural, or economic life has been left untouched by the megaculture of gayness, which has helped fashion the gay and lesbian issue into a major sphere of public life. Of course, it is an issue to some extent still surrounded by silences and hostilities, but that it has a place in the arenas of public debate in many countries is undeniable. And in these arenas is generated a lot of public, deliberative talk about the future of gay lives.

The gay and lesbian movement may thus be seen as (a) developing its own visible and positive culture, (b) leaking into broader public spheres and cultures, and (c) providing alternative, subaltern countercultures.[26]

In so doing it shifts the boundaries of the society at large. The visible culture of gayness has led to increasing recognition (coming out, finding a voice, making a space, creating a flow of texts), to increasing equality (in legal areas as well in equal opportunities and antidiscrimination programs), and to the emergence of more gay institutions (from political organizations to commercial networks identified with the "pink economy" to social welfare services such as AIDS support groups and help lines). Moreover, the gay public culture has created a language in which gay rights and gay citizenship can be discussed: terms such as "homophobia," "heterosexism," "sex panics," and "hate crimes" now capture very tangible phenomena that badly need to be addressed. They simply didn't exist some fifty years ago.[27]

But this visible culture is not hermetically sealed off. It also leaks into the wider culture. Thus, gay cultures have led to the gentrification of urban spaces, for example, in San Francisco, Los Angeles, and Manchester.[28] They have led to improved health care services through AIDS buddy schemes, AIDS support groups, health education, and the like. Gay cultures have even made some inroads in the rethinking of friendships and kinship—like the "families of choice" described by Kath Woodward and the solidarity of gay male friendships described by Peter Nardi—and they have also made contributions in the areas of fashion, music, art. Nor should we ever forget that the worldwide idea of "safer sex" was initiated by gay men in the early 1980s.[29]

All of this implies a necessary normalization process—bringing gay public spheres into the mainstream: it suggests some kind of assimilation. But many public spheres are comprised of more than simply different and subordinated voices. Rather, they contain people who do not wish to be co-opted into a dominant, even if pluralized, culture: they do not want rights; they do not want to be good citizens. They are outside society and want to stay that way. Indeed, they actively resist any plan for co-option: they wish to be forever radically opposed to the normal citizen. There is a perpetual culture of resistance, as the history of the gay movement clearly reveals. For some, homosexuality must always remain outside the mainstream.

## Identities, Communities, and the Construction of New Public Spheres

Public spheres are historical constructions that arise to help structure public debates over matters of concern. They are filled with people debating and discussing, and in democratic life they become vital. The gay public sphere discussed above is just one of many that have appeared in recent years, in which groups work to get their arguments and their stories onto the agenda. Pitted against counterpublics whose interests are antithetical to their own and who foster their own languages, worldviews, and stories, the new cultures recruit new members and connect to identities, emotions, and the doings of intimacies.

Elsewhere, I have suggested five generic processes through which new public spheres appear.[30] Although these processes may not be distinct or clearly articulated, they typically involve:

1. *Imagining, visualizing, empathizing.* This is the brave and crucial start: we have to imagine new kinds of citizens in the making (a task I began in Chapter 4). And there may well be blocks to this imagining: sometimes it may simply be hard to conceive of the issue—of what it means to be a test-tube baby, of what the new intimate concerns facing the old who live alone might be, of how children who have come to live their intimate lives more and more on-line experience the world. But without some sense of imagining these new ways of living, new citizens will not appear.

2. *Articulating, vocalizing, announcing.* Here words are eventually found to breathe a voice into what needs to be said, and the first signs of a debate can thus be heard. We will have to learn to speak a new language of registered gay partnerships, commercialized surrogacy, the sale of body organs across the world, the new global sex traffic, cybersex, and so forth.

3. *Inventing identities.* The words become stories, people become storytellers, and identities get attached to the stories. This is a politics of stories, through which new citizenship identities are created. Most apparent today are new stories of women, gays, and blacks and of an array of support groups such as abuse survivors or sex addicts. But there may be less apparent stories as well—of children of cyborgs, of grandparents of test-tube babies, of the old and alone.

4. *Creating social worlds and communities of support.* Here the language moves beyond any one individual and into a community, where identities in some ways become solidified. New communities thus emerge—communities of children of surrogate mothers, for example, or of cybersexed citizens, of global sex workers, of bisexual transgendered fetishists, of new families.

5. *Creating a culture of public problems.* Here the once unspoken and unimagined languages come to be turned into the public worlds of social movements, media, education, and the like, and a whole new world of

"public issues" is brought center stage. We begin to see the emergence of "public cultures" and "issues cultures" that develop around intimate lives. Issues cultures arise when people who are at odds with one another develop complex language strategies to assemble their cultures of difference and then proceed to frame debates that feed symbiotically on one another. Here the very debates and arguments themselves become social events that help to build, structure, and transform "interpretive communities" often linked to social movements.

Central to this process is the *politics of identity*. Here identities mark out categories of people who now seize on these categories as the basis for political change. Group identities come to perform key political functions. In one sense this is far from new: well over a hundred years ago, Marx's analysis of class, class consciousness, and class action conceived a shared collective identity as the basis for political change. But over the past thirty years or so—and largely through the rise of new social movements— identity politics has grown increasingly important. Focusing on specific interests—of women, or blacks, or gays (rather than on the universalist ones that were the hallmark of the Old Left)—such politics has signaled "the convergence of a cultural style, a form of logic, a badge of belonging, and a claim to insurgency."[31]

The politics of identity has led to a widespread recognition that groups, people with differences—from queers to the new reproductive folk to high-techies to the elderly, etc.—need to represent themselves in the political sphere. Such groups embrace their own personal category as a means of political action. This has sometimes been called "the ethnicity model," after what is perhaps the clearest case, that of ethnic groups who develop a political membership based on an identity as a prerequisite for political action. A conscious gay identity is likewise a prerequisite for any gay political action—it is vital for bringing people together.[32] For establishing citizen identities in the public sphere, a politics of identity seems crucial.

But at the same time, and as is now well known, such a politics can bring with it major problems. Much identity politics actually works to essentialize people and to create labels that suppress differences and create "others." Unless care is taken, identity politics can harden boundaries between groups and magnify their differences. It can generate fake uniformities and common histories that never really existed. It can stress the "naturalness," that is, the biological necessity, of these categories and identities, when they are in fact socially produced. It can put itself at odds with the process of change by reinforcing categorical, often binary, views—heterosexual/homosexual, mother/nonmother, man/woman, cyborg/human. Very often this can also mean that a politics of identity constructs the very terms through which those it identifies are excluded: it may indeed become its own worst enemy. Ultimately, then, essentialist identities can work to reduce individual choices and create false images of homogeneity.

So we are left with the problem of how to deconstruct essential identities in the public sphere and yet be able to have them available for political purposes. Suggestions include Shane Phelan's argument that "identity is a matter not only of ontology but also of strategy" and Gayatri Spivak's concept of "strategic essentialism." In other words, at times it becomes politically necessary to adopt the position that identities are more fixed, certain, and "essential" than we really believe them to be—a sort of ideological case of having one's cake and eating it too. At the same time, we start to look for better ways to articulate the idea that identities are *relational, hyphenated, fractured, fragmented, serial, diasporic, unsettled, hybridic.*[33]

Identities, as we saw above, are also part of belonging—of communities. Just as identities are fragmenting, so, too, are the communities that help shape them. Indeed, new terms also need to be found for community: the old communities may well have been too stable and stifling, too fixed in their boundaries, too likely to make people feel trapped. Old identities go with old communities. It may thus be more appropriate to start to talk of network communities, multiple belongings, reflexive communities, imagined communities. People are not born into such communities; rather, they throw themselves into them. These new, postmodern communities are not bounded in the same ways as in the past—which suggests new ways of thinking about space and time. They are "reflective": people think about how their communities originated, what made them necessary. They ponder their own histories and their need for reinvention. Communities are not just there and given. And they harbor resources for their own fashioning—they tell stories, generate rules and identities, create their own cultural and social capital.[34]

At the heart of these new communities lies the need for debate and discourse about where people are and where they should be going. Stories are told of partnerships formed, sex encountered, children born, friendships made, bodies modified, gender negotiated, identities refashioned, lives rearranged. These are the stories of intimacies that fling people into the moral controversies of our times. We will be returning to these everyday tales of morality in Chapter 7.

# 6
# Dialogic Citizenship

*We are pro-choice and pro-life supporters and other concerned citizens, who recognize that deep divisions exist on the issue of abortion but believe that this conflict provides an opportunity for dialogue and creative problem solving when we honor the humanity of those with whom we are in conflict and acknowledge that we need to come together, at times, to explore areas of common concern and the potential for joint action.*

*Our goal is to advance the concept and practice of common ground by responding to the real need being expressed at the grass-roots level for new approaches to the abortion conflict. . . .*

*We explore ways to address shared concerns such as teenage pregnancy and inadequate resources for women and children. Fundamental is that no one is ever asked to change his or her belief about the core issue of abortion.*

Common Ground (cited in Faye Ginsburg, *Contested Lives*)

*Some radically divergent ideas never meet at all, at least not in the experience of mortal beings. In other cases, meetings are staged repeatedly but never come off, ending only in mutual invisibility and inaudibility. Sometimes, however, meetings do occur, perhaps intensely conflictual and abrasive, but also in the long run, mutually transformative. Thus it may be that, at the end, on the real Judgement Day—if there is one—for which the philosophers are always preparing us, when all stories are told and the chips are in, counted and compared, we will be unable not only to say who finally won but even to tell which was which.*

Barbara Herrnstein Smith, *Belief and Resistance*

THE IDEA OF INTIMATE CITIZENSHIP emerges against a backdrop of debates in public spheres over appropriate ways of living life with others. In many ways it seeks to foster the civilizing of relations at a time when some people see only conflict, breakdown, fear, a dumbing down of society, or a general lack of civility in social life—the new barbarisms, as they have been called. At a time when a collapse of values and ethics is often said to be taking place, the concept of intimate citizenship can help show the way to new moralities and a new understanding of ethics.

In part looking back to various traditions of citizenship, and in part looking forward to an emerging postmodern world, the idea of intimate citizenship puts on the agenda a plurality of individual and collective rights and obligations around a wide-ranging, conflicting arena of intimacies. Whom to live with? How to have and raise children? How to honor the body? How to relate to others as a gendered being? How to be erotic? Intimate citizenship understands that such questions are bound up with membership in numerous complex groups and communities that bring with them their own inevitable tensions and schisms. It appreciates that this is all part of a widely differentiated social order in which deep divides exist between the "haves" and the "have nots," the racialized and the nonracialized, the included and the "other." It recognizes that the particular dwells within the shifting universals.

As we have seen in Chapter 3, all this means that we must learn to cope with constant and ubiquitous conflict—and there are no easy resolutions in sight. We are living the culture wars at every level of our lives—global, national, local, personal. And for some, the equivalent of moral warfare has started—the shooting has already begun. Locally, abortion clinics get bombed, gated communities appear, long-time residents rise up against "the strangers next door," pedophiles are driven out of town, while on television we can watch the melodrama of talk shows that routinely foster conversational street brawls, in which the participants are egged on by the audience, as a kind of grand climax to a televisual event. And then there are the intense battles waged within social movements themselves. It is a world of sex wars, AIDS wars, family wars, culture wars, moral wars.

Again, I must be clear: there is nothing new about such conflicts. Although the long catalogue of the horrors and death of the twentieth century (and now, as I write, of the twenty-first) must put an end to any simple or linear view of progress, some nevertheless argue that we have entered an age in which wars, for instance, are not the commonplace events of daily existence that they have been more or less throughout history.[1] Maybe what has happened, in effect, is that the world has become a place where disagreements are more visible and more open to "management." It may be that democratizing societies now generate a greater number of public spaces in which a wider range of people than ever before can engage in deliberative talk about the issues facing them. It may be.

In the next two chapters, I turn to some of the organizing principles of this deliberative talk that may help in the quest for intimate citizenship. Here I want to suggest that built into the heart of all contemporary ideas of citizenship must be the idea of dialogue. The capacity to discuss reasonably, to talk with opposing others—in short, to dialogue—is a sine qua non of being a citizen in the late modern world. In what follows I will look at some of the ways in which dialogic citizenship may be achieved; in Chapter 7, I continue this task but with an emphasis on ethics and stories.

## The Trouble with Dialogue

Imagine you are discussing abortion with someone who strongly disagrees with you. How can you sit down and talk about the subject reasonably? The stridency around the issue of abortion makes it a prime example here. The claims made by pro-lifers seem irrevocably at odds with pro-abortion or pro-choice activists. As one group views abortion as the killing of a living fetus, others—often of a different generation—tell another story: the right of women to choose. The stories of activists on both sides have been told many times, and they stand in stark contrast. The conflict is so well documented that one sometimes wonders whether any more can ever be written or said about it.[2] (Interestingly, though, it is primarily an American issue: in Britain—where about one in three women has had an abortion and 92 percent agree in general with the right to choose—the subject generates far fewer heated debates and receives much less attention in the press.)[3] And, as we saw in Chapter 3, the battle over abortion is only one of many such conflicts.

This chapter raises a core problem for new citizenship theories: how can we sit at the table with our enemies? In fact, we rarely do—and then only with great difficulty. When I have suggested this approach in public lectures, I have been accused of "going with the enemy," of pushing my liberalism too far. "We are not going to speak with our opponents" seems to be the underlying attitude: "How can you even think of talking with people who wish to see you and your lifestyle eliminated?" Indeed, it is very hard in this culture not to engage in polarized debates: this is more or less our routine way of doing things.

It *is* hard. Yet too often arguments grow needlessly polarized. Arguments tend to become firmly attached to individual people—to become part of them, be identified with them, belong to them. Thus, it is the person, rather than the argument, that is at stake in a debate. They cling tenaciously to their own argument, restating their own position. Blame, responsibility, honor, status—all these can result from the discussion and then accrue to the individual participants. So we blame or praise the individuals who take part in these debates, feel better ourselves, and keep our ears closed to the arguments themselves. Ironically, a lot of argument is not about the argument. It is about other things. Even among intellectuals I have often found this to be so.

## Conflict and the Search for Dialogue

I want to suggest, as many others have, the importance of dialogue for citizenship debates, even though some critics might view such an apparently simple idea as naive or even faintly utopian. All the same, my starting point is to suggest that we move away from the monologic view and adopt one that is more *intersubjective, interactive, interrelated, relational, dialogic, interpersonal, mutual, reciprocal.* As Charles Taylor comments:

> [There is] a crucial feature of the human condition that has been rendered almost invisible by the overwhelmingly monological bent of mainstream modern philosophy. . . . This crucial feature of human life is its fundamentally dialogical character. . . . The monological ideal seriously underestimates the place of the dialogical in human life.[4]

Rather than viewing debate in terms of two individuals, debates should be seen as relational—as a process of interdependent relations. Citizens then become dialogic: a good citizen does not speak in monologues but inhabits a world where people are interrelated and able to communicate with one another. With this in mind, let us consider what conflicts or debates across pluralized public spheres might now start to look like— what the dialogic citizen should do.

First, in a discussion you should *recognize the person you are talking with—neither denying nor degrading "the other."* This mutual recognition, or respect, is part of our basic humanity and is a precondition for discussion of any kind. Yet, as we saw in Chapter 4, the very idea of citizenship often constructs a person who is not a citizen, someone who stands outside and is denied a part in debate. We tend to speak of such marginalized others as stupid or evil; we dredge up some of the worst stereotypes that exist about this "other"; we stigmatize, degrade, and exclude. And the more we do this, the easier it is for us to sanction "evils" against them. So a precondition of dialogue must be to acknowledge that our enemies may be more like us than we would care to think and to accept our common humanity. Dialogic citizenship plays constantly with an awareness of otherness.

This suggests that we will also need to *rework a sense of the group, of solidarity, and whom we belong with.* We are never lone voices. We recognize that the "others" we engage with are at least partially members of the "we." Drawing on the work of George Herbert Mead on the social nature of the self and its dependence on others for its construction, Jodi Dean has recently introduced the idea of reflective solidarity to take on board the other who may be our enemy. She initially identifies two kinds of well-known solidarities: *affectional solidarity* is what we normally regard as love or friendship, in which we bond with the other; *conventional solidarity* grows out of common interests. Both of these can be rigid and exclusive. But, according to Dean, solidarity can also emerge from an intersubjective interaction involving at least three people. As she explains:

> I ask you to stand by me over and against a third. But rather than presuming the exclusion and opposition of the third, the ideal of *reflective solidarity* thematizes the voice of the third to reconstruct solidarity as an inclusionary ideal for the contemporary politics and societies. . . . It is a mutual expectation of a responsible orientation to relationship."[5]

This is ultimately a move to a new form of "we" that starts to incorporate the other. It may be difficult, but it is worth a try—broadening the range of significant others in our sphere of debate to incorporate our opponents.

A third suggestion is that we *strive to break down what has been called the "argument culture."* In a popular book of that name, social linguist Deborah Tannen has documented just how much our culture is dominated by "an adversarial frame of mind," where the best way to get anything done is to set about establishing, often quite aggressively, polarized positions. We see this in courtrooms, on talk shows, in politics, in teaching. There must always be "two sides to an argument," both must be presented as convincingly as possible, and may the best "man" win. It is interesting that expressions such as "culture wars" or "sex wars" or the "war over the family"[6] immediately present antagonistic sides. Now Tannen is not suggesting that we "just stop arguing and start being nice to each other." What she is opposed to are the ritualized elements of arguments. We do not have to presume there are two sides to every argument—there are often many more. We do not have to presume polarizations and dichotomies—there are often multiplicities and ambiguities. We should at least be suspicious of antagonistic responses—those that adopt a prepatterned and unthinking use of fighting to accomplish goals that do not necessarily require it. In her effort to discover constructive ways of approaching conflicts, Tannen finds lessons to be learned from other cultures, in which one may encounter different modes of discussion and debate. Thus, trying to avoid false dualities, avoiding false conflicts and polarities, being able to have victors without vanquished, using intermediaries to assist in debate, being aware of ritualized elements of debate—all these become possibilities.[7]

Next, our discussions should *appreciate that argumentative stances are not usually adopted in isolation from wider issues.* A number of studies, for example, on abortion, have shown that when people debate a specific issue such as abortion and take a "pro-life" or a "pro-choice" stand (themselves assuredly overly simplistic categorizations), the arguments they make are typically but a small part of a much broader worldview. Thus, opinions on abortion usually fit into a wider sense of what it is to be a woman, or how it feels to be part of an unequal society, or what it would mean to have a family at the current time. Conflict does not arise between isolated attitudes but rather attitudes embedded within entire worldviews. As James Davison Hunter comments in *Culture Wars:*

> Let it be clear, the principles and ideals that mark [these] competing systems of moral understanding are by no means trifling but always have the character of ultimacy to them. They are not merely attitudes that can change on a whim but basic commitments and beliefs that provide a source of identity, purpose, and togetherness for the people who live by them. It is precisely for this reason that political action rooted in these principles and ideals tends to be so passionate.[8]

If it is the case that people's arguments are bound up with deeper worldviews (and I think it usually is the case), then people do not simply argue about one issue: they engage with what they perceive as threats to whole ways of life. It is relatively easy to change our mind about one little idea; it is much harder to give up a whole way of life. We need to remember this when we find ourselves "arguing" in dialogues.

Closely connected is the need to *understand the emotional basis and history of much talk.* Many arguments go way beyond matters of simple opinion or reason.[9] The good citizen debating in the public sphere in a purely rational and impartial manner is a deeply inadequate description of many of these moral debates. For to hear people argue their opposed positions is to sense almost immediately that something much grander than reason is at stake: it often seems as if these people are fighting for their lives. Indeed, in "intimate debates" this may be true: many such debates are literally about life and death matters, and even when they are not, they are by definition about deeply felt personal issues. No wonder the arguments are often heated, passionate, drenched in rage and that opposing sides become noticeably agitated at the very idea of meeting up with each other. They will shake and sweat in the presence of their enemies, taking pains to avoid any kind of closer contact. Seemingly reasonable people can suddenly become apoplectic with rage. The desire to scream, weep, or become physically violent often lies just below the surface of these debates, and the language of loathing, of enemies, and of warfare soon takes over. Under such circumstances, any attempt at resolution or reconciliation cannot be pursued simply at the rational or intellectual level. The conflict goes much further than that. It may be shaped by deep prejudices and fears, by shame and anger, by moral indignation of all kinds, by authoritarianism, by a background of family and interpersonal experiences that open raw nerves.

Much conversation and argument, then, is not simply a matter of rational debate: it speaks to us from depths we do not understand—from our childhood experiences, our lifelong engagement with others, our personal life story. It would be odd indeed if our arguments were untouched by all this; yet we often speak as if they are not. And so we take this emotional baggage into our discussions. We need to be very aware that we do this and that the person we engage with is doing the same.[10] We need to avoid painfully emotive language that blocks discussion, but we also need to acknowledge the role of emotions in shaping arguments: the public sphere is rarely that hallowed site of neutrality, objectivity, and reason that some have claimed it to be. In contrast, dialogic citizens sense the emotional histories in arguments.

Sixth, discussion will require us to *develop new ways of approaching conflict.* Barnett Pearce and Stephen Littlejohn, in their study *Moral Conflict: When Social Worlds Collide,* suggest that a new sophistication has been developing around conflict—slowly appearing over the last century through the work of interventionist groups like the Red Cross and Amnesty International that focus on aid and problem solving. In the main, the authors note, we place great emphasis on the image of two diametrically opposed sides—you are with us or against us—and on the idea that only one side wins the argument. Compromises are viewed as signs of weakness. Such monologic conflicts are very common, and they assume that only one person can be right, that people should take sides, that the goal is to win the others over, and that the end justifies the means. Dialogic conflicts are, by contrast, much more open-ended and balanced. Understanding conflict is viewed as more important than knowing how to win. Indeed, it becomes crucial to recognize that conflict itself may often be a greater and more damaging problem that what is at stake in the conflict: wars well illustrate this, given the mighty devastation they can heap on people and the environment. Dialogic citizens understand that some ways of managing conflict are better than others—and ones built on good relationships may be the best.

Next, there is the major issue of *finding "common ground."* Most people can in fact find much to agree on, and dialogic citizens seek these points of agreement. In a sense this is the classic problem of contemporary moral theory, one that has been lurking throughout this book: how to find something in common—a sort of a universal—in a world where there seem to be only conflicts and differences. Many classical political theories (Rawls and his idea of "contract," for example, or Habermas and his "ideal speech") understandably incorporate a search for commonalties, for shared values. A corollary of this search for a common ground is what Bruce Ackerman has called "conversational restraint." As he suggests: "We should simply say nothing at all about disagreement and put the moral ideals that divide us off the conversational agenda."[11] In other words, we do all the dialoging we can about issues we can agree upon, and we leave aside, at least for the moment, those "dangerous areas" where we radically disagree. In the next chapter I turn to some of these possible common grounds in greater detail.

Finally, in all of this, we need to be constantly vigilant about the inequalities implicit in the dialogic voice. The search for nonconfrontational approaches to argument—for dialogue—is a worthy goal, but we need always to bear in mind that dialogues exist within frameworks of power. As I have repeatedly suggested, intimacies are located in worlds riven by inequalities and social divisions, wherein some people are marginalized, excluded, and colonized by others. And it is notoriously difficult for unequals to dialogue equally. To expect "conversational restraint" of those who are already restrained can simply perpetuate the existing inequalities. Some kind of recognition of this inequality needs to be part of the dialogic process.

## Looking Ahead: New Experiments in Dialogue

None of this is at all easy. Whenever I have raised the above issues in seminars, it always provokes at least someone to say: "Why should I listen to people who want to deny *my* every right but who won't listen to *me?*" Or to say: "I can listen and talk with anyone but fundamentalists because they won't grant *me* any space of my own." Or even to shout at me: "Your universal values are just the bourgeois values of the West!" All I can say is that it will not be easy. After all, for the greater part of history learning to talk with our enemies and to seek common ground has probably not even been a goal. Authoritarianism, of whatever kind, has no need of tolerance, empathy, or dialogue. But if we do not learn to have dialogues and at least momentarily realize that we share some common values, then there may be little hope for a future.[12]

Still, adopting some of these suggestions *could* lead us to talk more productively about issues of intimacy and citizenship. Conflicts may not always be resolved, but at least the discussion—and indeed the living— around them can be conducted in a less acerbic mood. We may learn more about how other people think and why they might hold such diametrically opposed views, to arrive at an understanding of why we hold onto our own views so tenaciously. We may even discover that we can agree on some common values, even as others remain mutually anathema.

One quick illustration can be found in the networking that took place during the Fourth World Conference on Women in Beijing in 1995. Dineh Davis showed that while the women at the conference disagreed about a wide range of issues, they could usually do so with tolerance. She writes:

> Every imaginable subject within the general bounds of "human rights" was discussed. These topics ranged from the legal rights of prostitutes to the Vatican's stand on the rights of the fetus; from domestic concerns in an African, European, or Asian country to international policies and politics; from lesbian and gay rights to domestic violence, rape as a war crime, and the plight of the girl child. . . . Though opposing views were aired, very few met with overtly intolerant responses. Even then, the reprimands were "gentle."[13]

That women from all walks of life and social backgrounds could get together and talk across divisions and boundaries is indeed a hopeful outcome.

There is now evidence from a number of "dialogic projects" that a certain change could be in the air and that dialogue is a possibility, even as we accept the inevitability of conflict in social life. In the United States, for example, the National Issues Forum, the Public Conversations Project, and the Public Dialogue Consortium have all carried out experiments in dialoguing.[14] In each case, opposing groups are brought together in a comfortable environment and then each member's background is explored so that there is an opportunity for "getting to know you." Only when an atmosphere of togetherness and mutual respect has been established do key issues begin to be discussed.

Another excellent example of the dialogic approach can be found in the Common Ground Network for Life and Choice—a wide-ranging network that brings together pro-choice and pro-life activists. The task is to de-escalate tensions and search for common grounds, even though ultimately disagreements may prevail on the issue of abortion itself. In a typical scenario, participants move through five phases.[15] Members introduce themselves, exchange biographical information, and in so doing probably discover that each "side" is composed of a more diverse array of people than they might have thought. They then tell their life stories and show how they came to their respective views. Discussions follow on matters on which both sides can agree, and this leads to working out more ways to improve communication, find common ground, and develop some kind of common politics. Finally, groups work together on achieving these goals. In dialogue-oriented groups that focus specifically on abortion, what often moves center stage are the issue of adoption and the attempt to reduce sexual activity among teenagers. As one participant commented: "It was shockingly easy to identify issues we agree on, like the need for aid to pregnant women who are addicted to drugs, the need for better prenatal care, and the need to reduce unwanted pregnancy."

## The Positive Face of Conflict

Abortion is a heated topic, and it is very encouraging to see what a dialogic approach can accomplish. In other areas, however—such as the debate over gay rights or over pornography—finding common grounds may be much less easy. What I have nevertheless tried to do in this chapter is sketch some of the general conditions for doing just this.

I am not, of course, suggesting that we should aim to eliminate all social conflicts. Not only are conflicts endemic to social life, but they indeed play positive roles. They can serve to clarify issues, mark out boundaries, and promote social change. In the absence of some sort of opposition, we may not be able to see our way to key issues. Sometimes, extremes of opposition—even fundamentalisms and tribalisms—can be useful in revealing the absurdities of arguments carried too far while also sharpening our understanding of the issues that need to be confronted. There are positive functions to conflict.[16] Nor should language always be weakened or neutral, as my argument above might seem to suggest. As Benjamin Barber has observed: "It is neutrality that destroys dialogue, for the power of political talk lies in its creativity, its variety, its openness and flexibility, its inventiveness, its capacity for discovery, its subtlety and complexity, its empathetic and affective expression—in other words, in its deeply paradoxical, some would say dialectical, character."[17]

There is, then, an important role for conflict to play in all this dialogue: but dialogue should be the goal of intimate citizenship.

# 7

# Stories and the Grounded Moralities of Everyday Life

*Virtue is a social construction. People make morality when they construct narratives of virtuous people.*

George Noblit et al., *The Social Construction of Virtue*

*What becomes of traditional moral matters when the grand narrative of the self devolves into multiple stories, pared down, circumscribed? And dispersed to myriad locations of everyday life? What is the moral climate that informs this restored ending? What could responsibility, choice, decision-making, and the like possibly mean in this new context?*

James Holstein and Jaber Gubrium, *The Self We Live By*

TRADITIONAL SOCIETIES, as well as a good many modern ones, seem to be worlds that are largely moralistic: often raised in the presence of strict moral codes, people are told what to do, and value judgments tend to be absolute. As we move into the new social worlds of postmodernity, however, that old order has started visibly to crumble. Any grand or absolute narratives of a universal morality seem more and more under stress, weakened, besieged. This may well signify a decline in moralism, but it is not necessarily a decline in morality. The weakening of a foundational ethic does not lead us straightaway into a relativistic morass, as many critics charge. Relativism is not the only alternative to authoritative moralism. Although we need to recognize empirically that all ethical principles are indeed relative to specific cultures, we also need a position of "thin" universals—maybe not as strong and firm as in the past, but certainly universals of a kind. If moral relativism is taken to an extreme, it becomes an absolute in itself, one capable of generating its own moral indifference to anything beyond the confines of a local context. To avoid this, we must have a sense of values that help us transcend the local: we must have a broader sense of the good. This chapter turns to such issues.

## Pluralizing the Values:
## Postmodern Ethics and Citizenship

Under the emerging conditions of late modernity, more and more people are now charged with becoming responsible beings in their own right. They have to ask not "What should I do or not do?" but "How should I deal with this?"[1] They have to look to a range of competing claims about how to live a good life, rather than simply following preordained patterns. Citizenship becomes a form of identity that stresses self-determination.[2] And this is hard.

At the broadest level we might sense the tentative arrival of what Zygmunt Bauman has called a "postmodern ethics." For him, a contemporary ethics must recognize ambivalence, nonrationality, the aporetic, and the non-universalizable as necessary features of ethical debate. Contradictions and tensions cannot be overcome—they have to be lived with as part of struggle and disagreement. "Human beings," Bauman says, "are morally ambivalent." Yet this is not a stance of moral relativism, to which he is firmly opposed. For as he says: "The great issues of ethics—like human rights, social justice, balance between peaceful cooperation and personal self-assertion, synchronization of individual conduct and collective welfare—have lost nothing of their topicality. They only need to be seen, and dealt with, in a novel way."[3]

Others, such as John Gibbins and Bo Reimer, have also suggested that the beliefs we hold about what is good and bad, and the way we hold these beliefs, have begun to shift with the advent of the postmodern. In contrast to the ethical orientations of more modernist groups such as second-wave feminists or some environmentalists, the values that younger groups are starting to espouse "allow great variety, eclecticism and personal patterning" while displaying "little fear of abandoning traditional principles." We are fast reaching a stage when society (and its members) will construct their own ever-changing value orientation. "Postmodern value orientations are held together with an ordering system more like a web than a building or a body." Postmodern values will be

> self-fashioned, pooled and permed from a variety of sources. They will be highly differentiated in design, mixing old and new in eclectic forms, and they will be individualized or personalized even when the value orientation is shared by a group. . . . Adherents to postmodern values can mix and match their values in a more or less never-ending set of possible permutations.[4]

Postmodernism, then, may be a self-critical working-through of the problems that modernism brought. In summary, I suggest that this shift in ethics highlights a move from an abstract system of ethics to a relatively more grounded one. The shifts are:

| From | To |
|---|---|
| relying on a given content | learning new ways of thinking (a process) |
| a search for absolutes | a pragmatic approach and a struggle with ambivalence |
| abstract principles and philosophies | actual life stories and other narratives |
| general rules or universals | situated, grounded, local responses |
| principles dictated by authorities | a struggle with the self |

## The Grounding of Everyday Moralities in Lives and Stories

Intimate citizenship is not meant to be an abstract concept but one stuffed full with life. Although academic philosophers are, quite appropriately, prone to abstract debate around moral philosophy, the concept of intimate citizenship does not easily lend itself to this mode of analysis. Rather, its concern is more sociological: discovering how people—all over the world from all kinds of backgrounds—engage with a ceaseless round of moral problems in the course of their daily lives. On the whole, people are not much interested in the abstractions of academic philosophers or social theorists, if indeed they are familiar with them at all. Yet people may be perfectly competent at inspecting their lives, reasoning around problems, and developing their own grounded approaches to dealing with the ethical and political problems that come up.

How, then, should we live? Everywhere we turn—from restaurants and bars to street corners and schools, from churches and the media to the workplace and the home—there is a swirl of human activity and talk around such issues. As George Noblit and his colleagues point out in *The Social Construction of Virtue,* moral debate may well be too important to be left to the philosophers. "Virtue is much more complex than even moral philosophy has imagined," they argue. "It is not so much a product of reason and rational thought as it is a construction in everyday life. Morality may be a subject for moral philosophy, but moral philosophers are not needed for people to be moral." Indeed, moral philosophy, in its search for universal principles, often sets too far aside the messiness of human experience. It can sometimes fail to sense how people really do go about their everyday affairs and engage with their own complex set of moral ideas. In day-to-day life, the grand moral narrative of philosophers "no longer stands over and above the local, but instead is one more body of accounts alongside the many other narratives we use to construct ourselves."[5] While Noblit and his colleagues are primarily concerned with how schools become necessary sites for the construction of moral meaning, all ordinary life situations can be seen as potential sites for moral work. As they recognize, *"people in their everyday lives suggest possibilities for us all to consider."*[6]

In looking at ethics this way, I am suggesting a more sociological approach: that *grounded everyday moralities* may be a key tool in understanding how people conduct their moral lives, one that can help us in seeing dialogues and the possibility of building intimate citizenships. I haven't space to develop a detailed argument here, but, in synoptic form, grounded everyday moralities display the following critical features:

1. *Grounded processes.* Here we are concerned with what specific, real people from widely divergent sets of circumstances say and do about moral issues in their everyday lives. As people experience their "intimate troubles"—a son with HIV, a stepchild who goes astray, a daughter with an eating disorder—they listen to stories of the practical, concrete ways in which others have dealt with such matters and talk about their own concerns. We need to investigate just what these everyday processes of moral learning and talking are.

2. *Life stories, autobiographies, and other narratives.* When people work out their moral stances, they usually draw on particular events in their lives. They tell how they dealt with their infertility, their different sexual experiences, their divorces. They turn their moral concerns into their life stories or the life stories of others. We can ask just how these moral stories come to be told and then become recurring features in people's lives. And how do others learn from them, creating webs of interconnected stories?

3. *The presence of different and multiple voices.* A unitary voice no longer prevails in moral matters. Instead, there is a "relational self" that links

diverse moralities to a range of others, bringing their own tensions.[7] We can look at just what these tensions and differences are.

4. *The importance of the local and the situational.* Again, moral life is rarely abstract but is usually bound up with the very immediate crisis at hand. What are these local contexts in which moral life gets played out?

5. *The importance of "the other" and the significance of sympathy in everyday life.* Crucial to moral matters are an awareness of how we view other people and the kinds of empathy and sympathy we have for them. We need to understand the daily processes of "taking the role of the other," of "sympathy giving," of "sympathy etiquette," of "sympathy biography," of "sympathy margins" and the so-called "micro-hierarchies of sympathy."[8]

6. *Ideas about normalcy.* We base much of our moral discussion on what we think most other people do, which serves as a day-to-day standard for how a life works.[9] We construct social worlds of the normal, and we use these to locate ourselves and our sense of the deviant or the aberrant.

7. *Moral passages.* All of this takes place over time. We thus need to understand moral concerns as having passages, pathways, contingencies, fateful moments, transformations, and epiphanies. Moral passages are emergent, always becoming, never quite arriving. We need to examine the ways in which people handle moral changes.[10]

8. *Embodied emotions, honor, and shame.* Moral debate is rarely simply a matter of purely rational debate but is also bound up with bodies and feelings. Behind much of moral debate may well exist patterns of shame and shaming, of honor gained and honor lost. Viewing ourselves from the standpoint of others, we need to ask how often we project a hidden rage against ourselves onto "others." More generally, we must recognize the ways that emotions can shape our day-to-day ethics.[11]

9. *The creation of moral economies.* Moral economies have been defined as the "popularly shared moral assumptions underlying certain societal practices." They are often linked to economic status—who is entitled or not, and who has the resources for a particular choice of lifestyle.[12]

## The Power of Stories

The above list suggests some of the broadest elements of the grounded moralities of everyday life. Many of these elements have already been recognized, at least to some extent, by a number of political scientists and moral theorists.[13] Increasingly popular has been the view that ethical systems are built around notions of storytelling, that moral life is a web of narratives. Alasdair MacIntyre, for example, sees narrative as the ethical bond that holds the morality of a society together and asks, "How best may I live the narrative unity of my life?" For him, narratives harbor traditions which in turn may shape lives.[14] For Martha Nussbaum, not just stories but the whole of literature becomes a source of moral learning: "Moral philosophy requires attentive and lively novel reading."[15] Likewise, within feminist philosophy, Carol Gilligan's work has shaped the study of narrative, feminism, and empirical research in psychology and ethics. In what has been called "unquestionably one of the most influential books of the 1980s," *In a Different Voice*, Gilligan challenged the idea that moral development is directed by one dominant voice— that of justice (which is usually male and abstract). Advocating instead an attentiveness to the complex tales that people tell about their moral choices, she found a different, relational voice that can allow for a "dialogue between fairness and care."[16]

Richard Rorty also sees stories as the new bases of public life: "the novel, the movie, and the TV program have, gradually but steadily, replaced the sermon and the treatise as the principal vehicles of moral change and progress." He is indeed very disdainful of pure, abstract *systematic* theorizing—favoring *edifying* philosophies which shun grand systematic theorizing for all time and seek instead irony, parody, and satires.[17] For Rorty, edification, which is a way of finding more interesting ways of speaking, becomes a way of providing "social hope, not universal knowledge."[18] He takes an interest in the telling of stories full of imagination, which refuse to engage with stultifying vocabularies that bring closure, and he champions irony as a "reaction against the absoluteness of final vocabularies." For him, people make communities and identities, and through these they become the "generators of new descriptions"—of "something new under the sun."[19] Continuing in the pragmatist tradition, then, we need to hear new stories and anticipate how they might change our lives.

One more example of this trend must suffice. The Mexican political philosopher Maria Pia Lara has also written forcefully, intricately, and extensively about the power of women telling the stories of their lives to shift the boundaries of the public spheres. She seeks to show how "social movements, through their interventions in the public sphere, create and generate solidarity through narratives which demand recognition and, at the same time, aim to redefine the collective understanding of justice and the good life by proposing new visions of institutional transformation."[20] Her particular focus is on women, whom she sees as bringing to the public sphere new kinds of relationships and understanding.

Although she draws heavily on academic philosophy in her discussion, her points are straightforward and important. The telling of stories bridges different worlds and can thus connect the moral, the aesthetic, and the political. Stories and the reaction of their audiences deepen human understanding of moral issues in all these areas. The role of storytelling in moral matters has a long history, of course. The private lives of Saint Augustine and Jean-Jacques Rousseau took on public goals and became linked to moral claims once their lives were turned into public autobiographies or confessions. More recently, however, through the rise of feminism and of social movements more generally, the importance of these stories has come to the forefront of our understanding.

Lara is concerned with showing "how a wide range of different kinds of feminist effort can be understood as constructions of new public narratives which retell the stories of women, interrelating the aesthetic and the moral spheres and redefining the relationship between justice and the good." She identifies what she calls "narrative cultural interweaving," whereby narratives made at one historical moment can transform the experiences of others at a later time.[21] As she says: "In creating a new vocabulary social groups provide for new descriptions that not only illuminate once repressed truths but create possibilities for relationships that were never envisioned before. In their struggles for recognition, women have achieved all these tasks."[22] Important as women's voices are in this process, however, it is a much wider set of vocabularies, descriptions, and struggles for recognition that are both coming into existence and need to come into existence.

Underlying these philosophical discussions is a concern with how one learns about ethics from the stories and narratives of others who tell of living through their own moral dilemmas, including those connected with intimacy. "Stories of intimate citizenship" may thus be the most appropriate mode of communication when it comes to the clarification of ethics and moralities and the settling of conflicts. The concrete stories people are telling about their "new lives," and the difficult decisions that they are having to make around them, seem to be the very stuff of a movement toward intimate citizenship. Full of contradictions and contestations, sufferings and strivings, the stories of others—even those of our "enemies"—have much to tell us. Intimate citizenship ultimately suggests new communities of stories, new ways of storytelling, and new ways of making dialogue. It suggests new ethical strategies that are moving into the public sphere and that are starting to configure the ethical worlds of the future. It is to this we now turn.

## The New Stories of Intimate Citizenship

In two earlier studies, I argued for the importance of stories in social life; suggested how they are socially produced, organized, and heard; and explored their role in moral understanding. Most life stories can be read, among other things, as telling the tale of a moral struggle—either over life in general or over a more specific and focused issue.[23]

To take a very simple example first. As I have suggested at many points in this short book, multifarious shifts are taking place over the family— from "families of choice" to problems posed by the "new reproductive technologies"—and everywhere here are moral issues. Abstract principles cannot provide the only path to moral understanding; indeed, they could just lead to a new kind of moralism. Instead, what is required is both careful telling of and "attentive listening to"[24] the stories told by people in a diverse array of family settings as they struggle to make sense of their daily problems.

A series of studies in Britain have focused on the shifting family patterns of the late modern world: stepparenting, divorce, new "families of choice," and other outcomes of the new reproductive technologies, showing that the decisions taken in these areas are saturated with moral languages. For instance, Carol Smart and Bren Neal, in *Family Fragments*, examine the moral narratives of members of post-divorce families to see how relationships between family members have to be negotiated and renegotiated, and they pay special attention to the impact of new parenting arrangements on the children of the marriage. Through their work, a complex set of post-divorce relationships, processes, phases, and "practices" come into view. New roles start to appear: solo-parenting, co-parenting, custodial parenting. As Smart and Neal point out, parenting is surrounded by a complex interaction between the original parent and the other people, such as grandparents, stepbrothers, and stepsisters— or possibly even step-grandparents. They stand firmly against the moral traditionalist position—of Patricia Morgan, for example, who is cited as saying that divorce law "allies itself with the spouses who want to break up marriages and, in doing so, it rewards *selfishness, egoism and destructiveness* over altruistic commitment."[25] Rather, they focus much more on the daily moral struggles that arise through divorce. They look at the stories of Stella Drew, who tries to keep the father's position valued; of Jessica Hunt, who struggles to prioritize the children; of Bella Tomkins, who struggles with her own errors of judgment; and of Meg Johnson and Ingrid Milton, who strive to provide an "ethic of care." Following

Bauman and Gilligan (as I have, too), they suggest that "what makes people moral agents is not whether they always make the right decision, but whether they reflect upon the decision they take and weigh up the consequences of their actions."[26]

Likewise, in *Parenting and Step-Parenting: Contemporary Moral Tales*, Jane Ribbens McCarthy and her colleagues find that the parents they talked to overwhelmingly agree that "adults must take responsibility for children in their care, and therefore must seek the needs of children first." This viewpoint, they say, "is such a strong moral imperative that it seems to have been impossible for anyone to disagree with it in the accounts we have heard."[27] Moral decision making in families may entail a long process of negotiation, but there are elements of sharedness. It may be the hallmark of (post)modern morality to recognize this process of decision making and to listen to it carefully. We need to examine how people with all their problems that I have linked to intimate citizenship actually go about making their moral decisions. This includes children, who are exposed to a more complex set of relations from an earlier time than perhaps they were in the past, as well as the aging, who, in living longer and longer, are confronted by more and more issues of "how to live life" than any aging group in the past. As life spans increase, new issues of whom to live with, how to handle the body, whether to have sex and what kind, and how to confront the perpetual speeding up of change, all now confront the eighty-, ninety-, even hundred-year-olds.[28]

A further study by Jeffrey Weeks, Brian Heaphy, and Catherine Donovan looks at the stories of non-heterosexuals as they construct friendships and partnerships and raise children. Again, reading their stories I could not help but be struck by their constant concern with the ethical issues of living life, of being moral beings in various ways. In one sense, the gays and lesbians interviewed for the book remain outside of the normal citizenship roles of society. At the same time, they talk about the friendship ethic with its concerns for caring, responsibility, respect, and knowledge. A few voices may help here:[29]

> My standards are about honesty, mutual respect and a mutual sort of caring, and looking after each other.

> I am more aware of people, of feelings. I am more aware of the importance of friendship—of relationships, I am more aware of the need for trust, and being dependable.

> I share. . . . I know they would be there for me . . . with an element of caring that my actual family I don't think would have.[30]

Part of the problem for many of these emerging areas of moral concern about intimacies—from new families to cybersex—is that we have yet to develop a new language that can be accepted into the public sphere and thus allow life stories to be told. For example, with so many changes in families and parenting it is often hard to know how to start to refer to the members of these new families. We do not have a language—let alone a commonly accepted language—that can name all the new relationships. Just finding the right words for the stories, words that perhaps do not yet exist or cannot fully capture the complexities of lived experiences, becomes an issue. Thus, as Elizabeth Silva and Carol Smart put it:

> What is the name for the relationship between a sperm donor (biological father) and a child with whom he does not live but with whom he has a good, companionate relationship? What is the name for the relationship between the children conceived in prior relationships but who live together under one roof because their parents have decided to cohabit (but not to marry)? What is the name of the relationship between a child and the woman who provided the genetic material to her birth mother to allow her to be conceived? It is interesting that a new vocabulary is not in fact emerging to deal with these new relationships. Rather, what seems to be occurring is that the notion of the family is being stretched to cover everything.[31]

Finding these new languages that can recognize new phenomena at work will allow us to gain a sense of the newly emerging and often conflicted roles within families and the moral dilemmas that result. Recent research has provided "stories" about some of these dilemmas and has thus furnished the beginnings of a moral language of the daily, and gendered, practices inside families. This is an area in which additional research should be of considerable value.

## Moral Struggles and Public Identity Narratives

But these "stories of intimate citizenship" are not simply told to researchers or to friends or family members in the privacy of one's room. They are told in the media and have thus become an omnipresent feature of everyday life. Indeed, one of the most apparent consequences of contemporary identity formation and moral debate has been the emergence (over a long time period) of what we may call *public identity narratives.*

As we watch television, read a newspaper or magazine, or buy someone's autobiography, we regularly encounter these narratives. Moral tales are attached to certain concrete people, their stories and their identities. When we say Monica Lewinsky, O. J. Simpson, or even "Roe versus Wade," we evoke symbolically a host of moral issues. A public identity narrative basically tells the story of someone's life, but it is told in some part of the public sphere. The story can be grafted onto a telling public issue, usually one that highlights a moral/political tension that speaks to some wider issue of humanity: a concern about homophobia, a worry about how to raise children, an issue of racism, a sense of justice at work, the meaning of care. Listening to such a narrative, we learn how one person "handles" this problem. But the story is also likely to raise debates over alternative ways to cope with the problem. And ultimately it evokes commentaries from others—often in the media—such that the ethical issues raised in the story are examined from multiple perspectives. In other words, we hear interpretations.

In one sense the great religious heroes of the past provided public identity narratives—Jesus, Buddha, Muhammad, Gandhi. Their stories, however, explicitly spoke of morals and standards—of dharma, precepts, and commandments.[32] Here, however, I am using the term *public identity narrative* to suggest how the mere mention of a name can evoke certain moral debates. Hearing the story of a life told in public—as we do all the time—not only puts into play a range of ethical issues but also illustrates how they can be resolved. To list some of the well-known names is to sense how iconic some have become:

- "O. J. Simpson" speaks of race, violence toward women, power
- "Louise Woodward" speaks of family, child rearing, battered babies
- "Mike Tyson" speaks of rape
- "Anita Hill" and "Clarence Thomas" speak of harassment, race, gender, and power
- "Jeffrey Dahmer" speaks of serial murder, cannibalism, victims of crime
- "Jamie Bulger" speaks of murder, children, social breakdown
- "Baby M" speaks of parenting, children, infertility, new reproduction technologies
- "Bill Clinton" and "Monica Lewinsky" speak of sex, power, harassment, solicitation, gender roles
- "Mary Kay Letourneau" speaks of child sex, age of consent, male and female sexualities

· "Matthew Shepard" speaks of homophobia, fag baiting, hate crimes, teenage gays

· "Michael Jackson" speaks of race, fame, and child abuse[33]

Public identity narratives are likely to fit into a range of political projects. Darnell Hunt, for example, has elegantly illustrated how the enormous flurry of interest in the O. J. Simpson case fed into at least four major "contested" political projects current in the United States. These political projects are linked to major commonsense explanations of what is going on and get reactivated again and again when different stories appear. They help people make sense of the world, but they are also pitted against each other as political disagreements. The first, the celebrity defendant project, raised issues of wealth and fame and how wealthy people can purchase better legal help. The second, largely a feminist issue, used the story as a way to galvanize people into getting concerned about domestic violence. The third project saw Simpson as the "Black Other" and became the discourse in which Simpson and many other blacks could be demonized as potentially violent or dangerous. It is the overtly racist discourse. By contrast, a fourth project—the "Just Us" project—tapped into ways in which blacks were so often discriminated against by police, the courts, and the media—and hence became a major tool for black citizens to critique official practices. Darnell Hunt analyzes these projects in some detail and provides a model for thinking about the ways in which what I have called "public identity narratives" can be slotted into wider patterns of thought.[34]

Likewise, the Clinton-Lewinsky scandal provided a major occasion for people the world over to debate the relationship between private morals and public life—to ask whether Bill Clinton's sex life was at all relevant to his role as a world leader. The scandal was simultaneously a feminist project about harassment, sex in the workplace, and the relationship between gender and power; a moral project about promiscuity and the decline of marital and family values; a culture wars project about how sexual standards have changed; and a postmodern project about what counts as sex—whether "sex" must mean intercourse. On top of all this, it even raised questions about precisely what was the public and what the private.[35]

In every sphere of intimate life, a major mode of engagement involves the telling of these public identity narratives. In thinking about assisted conception, for example, the public is led through a litany of such stories. Thus, in 1978, the story of Louise Brown became the first "test-tube baby" story in Britain; the story of Baby Cotton in 1985 became the first "commercial surrogate baby" story; in the United States the story of Baby M in 1986 raised troubling issues of surrogate contracting and parenting rights. There have been many special "baby issues" of newspapers, and the narratives continue.[36]

As I write this, in early 2001, a story has appeared that brings a number of these elements together. Baby girl twins (of mixed race) were bought over the Internet from their estranged parents, Tranda and Aaron Wecker, who had just split up and were eager to have their children adopted (the "mixed race" story). The children were placed with a California couple—the Allens—by an Internet broker for a fee of $4,000. The Allens were tricked into handing the babies back to the parents a couple of months later (the "multiple parents" story). The children were then sold again via the Internet, this time to a British couple—Judith and Alan Kilshaw—who paid $8,000 for them and brought them to England (the "child custody" story). Previously, in Great Britain, the Kilshaws had been denied the right to adopt children (the "fit parents" story). They traveled to the United States to take speedy custody, but when they returned to England they were greeted by a press furore and public outrage at purchasing babies over the Internet (the "Internet babies" and "global babies" stories). The babies were taken from the Kilshaws and placed in care (the "child custody" story). The Kilshaws then returned to the United States (sans babies), where they told their story on the Oprah Winfrey show, thereby making it an international media event. Meanwhile, the husband of the Allen couple was found to be involved in child sexual abuse (the "abuse" story); and so the saga continued, all the time receiving avid media coverage and raising yet more and more moral issues for the public to digest.[37]

Many such stories exist. Some have gained almost global notoriety ("The Life and Death of Princess Diana") while others are known only locally. Some have a long staying power—Diana, again—while others are transitory (the life story of a guest on a local talk show, for example). Some are major media events and thus achieve a kind of celebrity status; others receive less attention.

As I have been suggesting, there is a need for *grounded moral stories,* and we need as well to be attentive to how people resolve the new intimate troubles they face through the telling of such stories. But a caution is in order. Intimate stories have a tendency (in Western cultures at any rate) to speak a language of individuals, choices, and the personal. Thus, the story of Baby M, the Clinton-Lewinsky scandal, or the trial of O. J. Simpson can be seen as stories of specific individuals that focus on their own individual plights. These stories can reinforce a sense of intense individualization, a sense that the matters they raise are deeply personal. This is a danger—for my argument is that stories of grounded moralities provide shared stories through which we can learn of moral and ethical dilemmas that many people face and perhaps understand that broader issues may be at stake, issues that go beyond an individual set of circumstances. For example, while the Clinton-Lewinsky story was unique and individual, it raised much wider issues of sex in the workplace—who holds the power and how is it negotiated?—and the changing nature of sex—what are the ethics of oral sex? Such stories generate conflicts across groups, and these very conflicts speak to some of the contested issues of our lives. Once again we can see how such stories need to be put into dialogue.

## Candidates for Common Ground, Resources for Grounded Moralities

As I have hinted throughout this book, the idea of intimate citizenship must work from a position of recognizing difference and uniqueness within provisional universals, or what Ruth Lister has called a "differentiated universalism." In building dialogues across opposing groups of people, it tries to find a common ground in the stories of grounded everyday moralities these people tell. It looks at how these tellings can help build local moral orders, out of which people can start to sense shared values and assumptions, even while much remains in conflict.

Dialogues, grounded moral tales, and public identity narratives see the surrounding social worlds as resources at hand in the construction of more general systems. Part of this world of resources does have to do with the moral systems laid out by theologians and philosophers, past or present. But since everyday life is seldom concerned with the relatively esoteric debates generated within philosophy and theology, people draw upon other, local resources—the media, everyday talk, friends—to help make sense of their own moral worlds.

When students in several of my graduate classes (including students from Japan, Hong Kong, Southeast Asia, Canada, Germany, and Greece) were asked to list any "key" values they thought to be found in the world at large, they came up with lists that included equality, freedom, justice, respect for others, decency, altruism, peace and harmony, individual autonomy, mutuality, and tolerance—a list that sounds very much like classic liberal values. One similarly international group came up with specific precepts, such as "Do not kill," "Do not steal," "Do not deliberately hurt someone." (And indeed they remarked that their list looked like a latter-day Ten Commandments.) A class in California—in the wake of 9/11—seemed much more skeptical about the existence of universal human values, but struggled with the idea that there must be some fundamental human rights.

Social scientists often come up with lists of virtues and values, too. Jeffrey Weeks, arguing that we should not stick to the old values that haunted sex and that allowed us to invent perversions and castigate all kinds of sexual outlaws, suggests instead that we develop an "ethic of love" and a radical humanism to serve as major guidelines in evaluating personal life. Four virtues should guide us: care, responsibility, respect, and knowledge. Mary Lyndon Shanley, looking at a series of case studies concerning new reproductive ideas from in vitro fertilization to surrogacy, suggests that decisions in these areas should be informed by a "cluster of values for family life": liberty, equality, relationships, and care. Anthony Giddens, in setting out his agenda for a "third way," outlines third-way values such as equality, protection for the vulnerable, freedom as autonomy, cosmopolitan pluralism, and "no rights without responsibility." And Rosalind Petchesky, in looking for a more positive vision of sexual rights, suggests five broad ethical principles—sexual diversity, habitational diversity, health, autonomy in decision making, and gender equality—as a backdrop to decision making.[38]

Finally, we find that some school districts in the United States have created laws that put certain values forward as mandatory. Typical of these, perhaps, are the following:

1. trustworthiness, including honesty, reliability, and loyalty
2. respect, including . . . tolerance and courtesy
3. responsibility, including accountability, diligence, perseverance, and self-control
4. fairness, including justice and freedom from prejudice
5. caring, including kindness, empathy, compassion, consideration, generosity, and charity
6. citizenship, including concern for the common good, respect for authority and law, and community-mindedness.[39]

The detailed contents of these lists need not delay us here. What matters is the general idea that a postmodern ethics, wherein individuals struggle to find their grounded moralities, also entails negotiating with the problem of universal values. We learn from the stories of the virtue of others, but these need to be linked to broader debates that people across the world engage in and intuitively build on. I am not saying that we will all agree on certain values, but we do sense that there must be something universal. Thus, on a somewhat grander scale, studies of world value systems often do come up with many values held in common.[40] Philosophers like Martha Nussbaum[41] have argued strongly for universalism, an acknowledgment of universal potentials and capacities that in effect define what it means to be a human being. Nussbaum certainly recognizes some of the pitfalls in a quest for universals—that it is wrong to criticize another culture unless one's own house is in order, that we can sometimes fail to understand the ethos of another culture, and so forth. And in presenting a list of universal human capacities, she is well aware that they are to some degree problematic and open to change. Nevertheless, she argues that certain universals must exist, an argument she pursues with reference specifically to female genital mutilation, which she cannot condone in any culture. She begins by asking, "What activities characteristically performed by human beings are so central that they seem definitive of a life that is truly human? In other words, what are the functions without which . . . we would regard life as not, or not fully, human?"[42] For her there are ten main capabilities: to live a full life span, to enjoy bodily health, to possess bodily integrity, to draw on one's senses, imagination, and thought, to experience emotions, to employ practical reason, to pursue affiliation (a respectful relation to self and others), to have concern for other species, to be able to play, and to exert political and material control over one's environment (see Figure 5).

It is hard, I think, to comprehend the rejection of any one of these principles once they have been broadly articulated. Certainly we in the West often take them for granted in everyday life. Constructive dialogue between people who hold opposing views may well require the tacit acceptance of something like this list as a basic precondition for discussion. The right to exercise basic capabilities such as these is fundamental to human life: what price abortion if the child is to die within a few weeks of birth from malnutrition.

Knowing that this is a fool's exercise, let me quickly sketch some possible universal standards that people might draw upon in engaging in dialogues and in formulating their own situated moralities. Of course, people's actions do not always conform to the universal ideals they in principle uphold. Although we commonly believe that one cannot hold incompatible positions, in everyday life people are not so theoretically minded: they muddle along in their practical affairs, seizing on fragments of general ideas as need be, with little regard for their consistency. People talk of the right to speak freely and then seek to stop others from talking. They declare that "all people are equal" and then pursue policies that enhance the quality of their own lives by exploiting others. They acknowledge that it is good to care for others and then proceed to devalue the caretakers by minimizing the importance of their tasks and paying them poorly for their work. They claim to want "rights for all" and are soon restricting or even denying the rights of others. In short, we live in a mess of contradictions.

Nevertheless, there are rough general guidelines that many people at least pay lip service to and sometimes try to follow. Among them, I would include the need to promote democratic policies; to enlarge areas of autonomy, choice, and freedom; to extend the spheres of justice and equality to all; to designate a common program of human rights; and to minimize harm.[43] This could be a longer list, but I will treat just four more in a little more detail.

First, and underpinning the search for basic human rights, is the need to *acknowledge minimal human functional capabilities.* Human beings have certain life capacities—and, while we are not required to draw up some grand model of human self-actualization, these capacities do need to be met. At the most basic level, people know that any society in which some people lack food or shelter must be problematic. If we look at the most basic of Nussbaum's functional capabilities, we can immediately see that many people the world over cannot expect to live out a full life span or to enjoy bodily health. But that does not make such a situation right.

Second is the need to *recognize others*—or what has been called the struggle for a *politics of recognition.* It has been championed especially by Charles Taylor and Axel Honneth, who claim that:

> The discourse of recognition has become familiar to us on two levels:
> First, in the intimate spheres, where we understand the formation of
> identity and the self as taking place in a continuing dialogue and strug-
> gle with significant others. And then in the public sphere, where a pol-
> itics of equal recognition has come to play a bigger and bigger role.[44]

This, then, is a potentially universalist ethic that attempts to inculcate a commonly shared sense of awareness of others—both the specific and the generalized, those in one's company and those without. The politics of recognition relies upon a basic and universal principle—that people are able to see themselves from the viewpoint of others. And seeing oneself in this way necessarily starts to build a bridge of empathy, sympathy, and respect for other points of view. To fail to appreciate the

1. *Life.* Being able to live to the end of a human life of normal length; not dying prematurely or before one's life is so reduced as to be not worth living.

2. *Bodily health.* Being able to have good health, including reproductive health; being adequately nourished; being able to have adequate shelter.

3. *Bodily integrity.* Being able to move freely from place to place; having one's bodily boundaries treated as sovereign, i.e., being able to be secure against assault, including sexual assault, marital rape, and domestic violence; having opportunities for sexual satisfaction and for choice in matters of reproduction.

4. *Senses, imagination, and thought.* Being able to use the senses; being able to imagine, to think, and to reason—and to do these things in a "truly human" way, a way informed and cultivated by an adequate education, including, but by no means limited to, literacy and basic mathematical and scientific training; being able to use imagination and thought in connection with experiencing and producing expressive works and events of one's own choice (religious, literary, musical, etc.); being able to use one's mind in ways protected by guarantees of freedom of expression with respect to both political and artistic speech and freedom of religious exercise; being able to have pleasurable experiences and to avoid unnecessary pain.

5. *Emotions.* Being able to have attachments to things and persons outside ourselves; being able to love those who love and care for us; being able to grieve at their absence; in general being able to love, to grieve, to experience longing, gratitude, and justified anger; not having one's emotional development blighted by overwhelming fear or anxiety, or by traumatic events of abuse or neglect. (Supporting this capability means supporting forms of human association that can be shown to be crucial in the development of emotions.)

FIGURE 5. *Martha Nussbaum's Central Human Functional Capabilities*

6. *Practical reason.* Being able to form a conception of the good and to engage in critical reflection about the planning of one's own life. (This entails protection for the liberty of conscience.)

7. *Affiliation.* (a) Being able to live for and in relation to others, to recognize and show concern for other human beings, to engage in various forms of social interaction; being able to imagine the situation of another and to have compassion for the situation; having the capability for both justice and friendship. (Protecting this capability means, once again, protecting institutions that constitute such forms of affiliation, and also protecting the freedoms of assembly and political speech.) (b) Having the social bases of self-respect and nonhumiliation; being able to be treated as a dignified being whose worth is equal to that of others. (This entails provisions of nondiscrimination on the basis of race, sex, sexual orientation, religion, caste, ethnicity, or national origin.)

8. *Other species.* Being able to live with concern for and in relation to animals, plants, and the world of nature.

9. *Play.* Being able to laugh, to play, to enjoy recreational activities.

10. *Control over one's environment.* (a) Political: being able to participate effectively in political choices that govern one's life; having the rights of political participation, free speech, and freedom of association. (b) Material: being able to hold property (both land and movable goods); having the right to seek employment on an equal basis with others; having the freedom from unwarranted search and seizure; in work, being able to work as a human being, exercising practical reason and entering into meaningful relationships of mutual recognition with other workers.

---

Adapted from Martha Nussbuam, *Sex and Social Justice* (Oxford: Oxford University Press, 1999), pp. 41–42, and *Women and Development* (Cambridge: Cambridge University Press, 2000), pp. 78–80.

FIGURE 5 *continued*

perspective of the other (and this can be quite common) is one starting point for the breakdown of relationships and ethics. At the level of intimacies, it can contribute to everything from minor squabbles to bitter, lifelong rifts between friends or family members. In the public sphere, however, it can cause immeasurably greater damage. All kinds of atrocities can come about if this process of due recognition is not brought into play.[45]

Closely linked is the universal injunction to *promote daily caring for others,* a position recently advocated and consolidated by many feminists as *an ethics of care.* For feminist theorist Joan Tronto, and likewise for Berenice Fisher, care refers to "everything we do to maintain, continue and repair our world so that we can live in it is as well as possible."[46] It assumes four core values of attentiveness, responsibility, competence, and responsiveness. Indeed, this position has much in common with what I am calling a grounded ethics, insofar as it moves away from broad and abstract principles. As Selma Sevenhuijsen says:

> An ethics of care involves different moral concepts: responsibilities and relationships rather than rules and rights. Second, it is bound to concrete situations rather than [being] formal and abstract. And thirdly, the ethics of care can be described as a moral activity, "the activity of caring," rather than a set of principles which can be simply followed. The central question in the ethics of care—how to deal with dependency and responsibility—differs radically from that of rights ethics—what are the highest normative principles and rights in the situations of moral conduct.[47]

In developing her ideas of care, Tronto does however note just how far ideas of care are often devalued in society.[48] "Carers" tend to be placed somewhere near the bottom of the hierarchy. Caregivers are unpaid (mothers, for example), underpaid, devalued, and often marginalized. Put like this, it ironically comes to appear that care really may not be one of the core assumptions on which we can agree. Who cares about the shift workers? Who cares about the carers? But I agree with Tronto that care is a value worth striving for. It is a value that merits more recognition and requires being placed more firmly on our agenda.

Finally, there is a need to *sponsor an ethic of love.* Love is a good thing! Fred Twine's discussion of citizenship makes this an important issue. In our closest relationships we establish a "life course interdependence," and society demands this in order to reproduce itself. Twine compiles a valuable list of some of the key features of love: trust, reciprocity, altruism, commitment, sacrifice, tolerance, understanding, concern, solidarity, interdependence.[49] Again, to me these seem pretty good values on which to base living a life.

## Toward "Moral Freedom"

The need to listen to the stories of everyday folk confronting their daily dilemmas in all the spheres of intimate life is the central message of this chapter. Such stories can be found scattered throughout society, but one way of finding them is through research. As I have suggested—through the works of Jeffrey Weeks, Carol Smart, and others—it is indeed a task for social scientists to gather intimate stories and to find the ways in which people make their grounded ethical choices and often evolve a "common ground" with others.

The sociologist Alan Wolfe has embarked upon a series of investigations about the moral state of the American nation. Just as I have suggested in this chapter, he finds that "there is moral talk aplenty in America." Indeed, he says, "if talk about morality were only a measure of morality, we would be hearing about a moral surplus, not a moral deficit." Through intensive interviews, he finds what we have been depicting: a plethora of moral views on every issue. Some are born-again Christians who worry about homosexuality; some are intellectuals who worry about Christianity; some see the breakdown of loyalty and trust; some see a new moral progress. But Wolfe also finds commonalities. At the heart of this is the newfound American belief in "moral freedom": whatever the issue, people need to decide for themselves on how to live the ethical life. Of course, for many this means consulting traditional sources of moral wisdom.[50] As he says:

> Our respondents mentioned in passing not only popular television programs and self-help books, but also the example of Jesus Christ; philosophers from Plato and Aristotle to Kant and William James; novelists such as F. Scott Fitzgerald, Jane Austen, and Alexander Solzhenitsyn; theologians including Teilhard de Chardin and the Rabbi Hillel; historical figures from Winston Churchill to Dorothy Day; and films ranging the gamut from *Saving Private Ryan* to *The Thin Blue Line*. Some of them sought pastoral guidance from ministers, priests, and rabbis, while others relied on counselors and therapists. Many appreciated the wisdom of their elders and told of being inspired by great teachers. But for nearly all of them, when a moral decision had to be made, they looked

into themselves—at their own interests, desires, needs, sensibilities, identities and inclinations—before they chose the right course of action.[51]

My own life and times reflect this. I came of age in the late 1960s and
had then to confront my own homosexuality. Moral, legal, and scientific
responses to this dreadfully illegal sin and sickness meant that I was
trapped initially in a world of moral absolutes. I could have, like so many
before me, lived with these absolutes: undergone therapy, repressed my
sexuality, married, shuddered in the closet, denied all. If I had been brave,
I could even have had a homosexual relationship and suffered the bitter
consequences: living a life of sin, being blackmailed, going to prison,
undergoing taunts and jeers, being the victim of hate crimes, and getting my just deserts on the final judgment day. None of this was a pretty
prospect.

But precisely because I was born at the cusp of postmodern times,
when intimacies were being refashioned and taking new forms, when new
grounded moralities and new public narratives about intimacy were in
the making, I did have the opportunity to fashion my own moral life.
Slowly I heard the stories of others and learned that it was not homosexuality that was the problem, but the unethical responses of the con-
demners, those full of loathing and hatred. Slowly, too, I heard stories
of gay men and lesbians who perhaps after struggles could come to terms
with their lives. And slowly I heard the good news: gays, lesbians, queers,
transgendered, bisexual, sadomasochistic, fetishistic people can and do
lead moral and ethical lives. They had to fashion their own moralities,
which is the "moral work" that lies at the heart of this chapter.

But it comes in a new time and is not necessarily to be found across
any one country, let alone the world. It is to these wider issues of relevance in the global scheme of things that I now turn.

# 8

# Globalizing Intimate Citizenship

*These days, the personal is global.*

   Arlie Hochschild, *"Global Care Chains and Emotional Surplus Value"*

*From now on, nothing that happens on our planet is only a limited local event.*

   Ulrich Beck

*There are few countries in the world where there isn't intense discussion about sexual equality, the regulations of sexuality and the future of the family. . . . The transformations affecting the personal and emotional spheres go far beyond the borders of any particular country.*

   Anthony Giddens, *Runaway World*

IT IS DIFFICULT these days to write a book in the social sciences without paying homage in various ways to the idea of globalization. The term became a buzzword during the 1990s, but its precise meaning remains far from clear. Indeed, the very existence of globalization is sometimes contested. Most generally, globalization suggests "a runaway world becoming one place." Specifically, it directs us to major economic and market convergences within liberal capitalism (usually associated with widening economic disparities), to the spread of the new media and new information technologies, including their networks (heavily concentrated in the hands of certain powerful groups), and to the weakening of what has traditionally been perceived as the autonomous nation-state, alongside the growth of major transnational corporations with greater power and more economic assets than many small countries. It suggests the rise of new "trading blocs," the growth of global "megacities," the collapse of tradition and of local communities, the increase of "risk," and a subsequent massive reordering of our sense of time and space. Although much of this is not wholly new,[1] in the late modern world such developments are exerting more and more influence: *they occur more deeply, more rapidly, more widely, and more pervasively than in earlier times.* Globalization is everywhere.[2] In this chapter I want to locate some of the arguments developed earlier in the book within the context of globalization and to look at a few of the ways in which intimacies are becoming globalized.

By and large, of course, I have been talking about how intimate relationships are changing in the wealthier, more privileged parts of the world, for it is here that these changes are most conspicuous. It is here that gender roles are most obviously being redrawn, that new "families of choice" are in the making, that sexualities are increasingly likely to be divorced from reproduction. But in much of the world, marriages are still arranged, gender roles are strictly circumscribed by religious custom, and sexuality is tightly regulated.

And yet it is not hard to see that changes around intimacies are afoot in every part of the globe. And they cover an enormous range: from controversies over the one-child-per-family policy in China to the appearance of "childless families" in Japan; from the catastrophic spread of HIV and AIDS in sub-Saharan Africa to the United Nations support of reproductive rights; from the spread of sex markets in East Asia and Eastern Europe to religious fundamentalists striving to preserve traditional views of women and the family; from indigenous transvestite lives to a wider transnational politics of transgenderism; from the search for ways to promote fertility through new reproductive technologies to the efforts to restrict fertility through encouraging the use of birth control; and from the sale of body parts in low-incomes countries to their consumption in wealthier ones. In short, it would be foolish to think that shifts in intimacies could be neatly isolated in one country or one part of the world.

But once we move into discussions of intimacy in the non-Western world, we are, in the main, considering countries where the basic economic conditions of life make the sort of intimate relationships we have been addressing seem like a cruel joke—an example of elite Western self-indulgence. It is hard to discuss the legitimacy of "choices" around lesbian and gay marriages in societies in which most of the population lives on the breadline. It is hard to discuss the "contested bodies" of the rich when the bodies of the poor are dirty, disease-ridden, and dying in the millions.

Consider the case of child marriage. Many children across the world get "married," and the custom is pervasive in parts of Africa and South Asia. In some countries over half of all girls are married by the time they reach age eighteen.[3] In 2000, the figure was 74 percent in the Democratic Republic of the Congo, 70 percent in Niger, and around 50 percent in Bangladesh and Afghanistan. Child marriage may well place major restrictions on the lives of the girls. It can have a serious impact on their health, it can cut off educational opportunities. And it will almost certainly mean premature pregnancy—bringing with it higher rates of maternal mortality and the prospect of a lifetime of domestic and sexual subservience. According to a UNICEF report on child spouses, domestic violence is common and causes some girls to run away in desperation. "Those who do so," the report says, "and those who choose a marriage partner against the wishes of their parents, may be punished, or even killed by their families. These girls run the risk of "honor killings" that occur in Bangladesh, Egypt, Jordan, Lebanon, Pakistan, Turkey and elsewhere."[4] In countries like Bangladesh, poverty-stricken parents may be persuaded to part with their daughters through a promise of marriage, or by false marriages, with the girls then sold into prostitution abroad. According to a recent estimate, in fact, at least a million of the earth's children are forced into child prostitution. But since poverty is one of the major factors underpinning child marriage and child prostitution, it is really not a simple matter of being critical or condemnatory, as Western observers often are.

So, simultaneously we have demands for the recognition of lesbian and gay marriages in the well-to-do West, and we have moves to prohibit child marriage and prostitution in low-income societies. Any attempt to establish an evaluative hierarchy—to claim that one issue is more important than the other—would clearly be misguided. *Both* are important for the people involved. Both issues need recognition. Both need to be the subject of dialogues, to be evaluated through a process of debate. And both have global implications. What culture wars do they generate? What are the grounded moral tales to be heard? How might dialogues be built up around these issues? And as we confront such issues in the future—not just locally, but globally—we must also remember to ask just how many stories in many low-income countries are simply not being heard at all.

## The Circulation of Global Intimacies

As we saw in Chapter 2, intimacies circulate around the globe embedded within vast social and cultural "flows." They flow across the world in technologies—through telephones and cyberspace; through representations in the media—films, television, music, books; through major world markets—including those for pornography and sex work; through people—who migrate, travel as tourists, and have friends or partners in different cities worldwide; and through ideas—religious, political, cultural. We thus have finanscapes, ethnoscapes, mediascapes, technoscapes, and ideoscapes in which ideas about intimacy circulate around the world.[5]

Within these flows three critical contrasts are visible. The first is between *the local and the global.* Rivers of economic and cultural change flow across the globe, but they end up in specific local contexts that give them a unique shape. World processes are taken up through local communities and transformed into something that clearly shows signs of a global culture while also assuming a particular form connected to the local culture. Roland Robertson has usefully termed the two processes *globalization* and *glocalization.* In a sense this is a version of the adage Think globally, act locally. The *globalization and glocalization of intimacies* thus suggest processes through which local cultures pick up, and usually transform, the many features of personal life displayed across the globe. The AIDS pandemic, for example, has been of concern for over twenty years. Every country in the world has been touched by it, and major international organizations—from the World Health Organization to the United Nations—have been involved. There are global institutes for monitoring the disease; global conferences that discuss it; global pharmaceutical companies that market HIV drugs to countries that can afford them; and education and health-concern programs in virtually every country in the world. A kind of global AIDS-speak also seems to have developed—a new language of "safer sex," immune systems, and T-cell counts. Yet although AIDS is a global problem, each culture has its own specific concerns and brings its own cultural modifiers to bear on AIDS-related issues. Included here are campaigns for safer sex that often highlight individual stories.[6]

A second, closely linked contrast is between *sameness and diversity.* Here, a major tension arises between tendencies toward homogenization, on the one hand, and tendencies toward diversification, on the other. The McDonaldization thesis, for instance, points to a certain global uniformity: the world becomes predictable, calculable, efficient, and standardized. This phenomenon is apparent, of course, in ubiquitous corporate chains such as McDonald's, Walt Disney, Starbucks, or Nike. But the homogenization of culture—a kind of bland sameness—is visible as well in baby stores, greeting cards, self-help books, and even telephone sex. People buy the same gear for their babies, send the same messages on greeting cards, read the same twelve-step programs in the same self-help books, and are even led into the same catalogues of sexual activity by sex phone lines! By contrast, the hybridization thesis suggests much more a crossover and mixture of cultures, a "global mélange," a creolization. Often the creolization takes place as a direct resistance to the McDonaldization process. The *McDonaldization of intimacies* suggests simultaneously a global trend toward certain stock images of sex, marriage, bodies, and gender roles that are packaged and marketed in efficient and predictable forms. Even self-identities—gay, sex addict, single mom—carry standard expectations. At the same time, a *hybridization of intimacies* comes about in which the choices surrounding private life are increasingly diversified, pluralized, fragmented.[7]

A third contrast highlights the very different impacts that globalization has on different people. Zygmunt Bauman talks of *tourists and vagabonds.* "Nowadays" he says, "we are all on the move," and yet we move in divided ways.[8] New patterns of intimacies create one set of options for tourists, who may be prolific consumers of sex tourism or who may seek out the global markets in pornography, infant children, or brides. They may also have friends or lovers in other countries, or they may travel to international conferences on AIDS, women's issues, the family, and so on. They create quite another set of options for what we might call global vagabonds—the abject poor, who are simply stuck in one place (the favelas, the shanty towns, the street) or are obliged to move from one place to another because of poverty, enforced work, sweatshop labor, or slavery. Selling their bodies (and their body parts) or their babies (and their wombs) makes the intimate lives of the poor a matter of misery, not indulgence.[9]

Thus, at one extreme, tourists can move around the world with ease: their home is the airport lounge. Ulrich Beck has linked this to the "globalization of biography," and writes:

> In the global age, one's own life is no longer sedentary or tied to a particular place. It is a travelling life, both literally and metaphorically, a nomadic life, a life spent in cars, airplanes and trains, on the telephone or the Internet, supported by the mass media, a transnational life stretching across frontiers.[10]

Such a life leads to what he calls "place polygamy"—people now can live in several different places at once and find themselves equally at home in each. It is also more likely to be an experimental life, a reflexive life, a life defined through freedom and choices (even when those freedoms and choices are so regulated).[11] Beck is not talking about the bulk of the world's population, of course, but about an international group made up of relatively well-to-do and well-educated people. By contrast, vagabonds move with difficulty and constantly run the risk of being excluded from civil society. The vast bulk of the world's humanity, far from immediately benefiting from globalization, is entering "the black hole of informational capitalism" of ever-increasing poverty, social breakdown, crime, and ultimately chaos.[12] In a striking passage, Manuel Castells captures the more devastating effects of globalism and the arrival of what he calls the Fourth World:

> Informationalism does create a sharp divide between valuable and nonvaluable people and locales. Globalization proceeds selectively, including and excluding segments of economies and societies in and out of the networks of information, wealth and power that characterize the new dominant system. Individualization of work leaves workers to each one of themselves, to bargain their fate vis-à-vis constantly changing market forces. . . . [Thus, out of a] global whirlwind of accumulation of wealth and diffusion of poverty . . . a new world, the Fourth World, has emerged made up of multiple black holes of social exclusion throughout the planet. [It] comprises large areas of the globe, such as much of sub-Saharan Africa and impoverished rural areas of Latin America and Asia. But it is also present in literally every country and every city in this new geography of social exclusion. It is formed of American inner-city ghettos, Spanish enclaves of mass youth unemployment, French *banlieues* warehousing North Africans, Japanese Yoseba quarters and Asian megacities' shanty towns. And it is populated by millions of homeless, incarcerated, prostituted, brutalized, stigmatized, sick and illiterate persons. . . . Everywhere they are growing in number.[13]

To put it bluntly: some 100 million children work on the streets, and maybe 27 million people live in some kind of slavery. There are early marriages, forced marriages, servile marriages.

## Global Intimacies: A Brief Tour

The globalization of intimacies is evident in many spheres of personal life. Global intimacies are present in *families:* through child care, in families whose members are dispersed across the globe, in family migration patterns, and in intimate partnerships between people living in different parts of the world. They are to be found in changing *sexualities:* through sex tourism, transnational sex scenes, global sex workers and sex markets, global media representations of sex, and the global world of cybersex.[14] They are present in *political and social life:* in worldwide debates over reproductive rights and birth control, in international social movements around sexuality and gender such as the transgender movement and the lesbian, gay, and bisexual movement, and in religious organizations such as the worldwide Metropolitan Community Church. They are literally present in our *bodies,* as an international traffic in body organs—the "new cannibalism"—spreads across the globe and babies born in one culture are sold, turned over to the new parents, and taken to another country in a kind of "procreative tourism." They are present in our *identities* as national identities struggle with more globalized sexual and gender identities—lesbian, sadomasochist, "new man," radical feminist. And they are present in the reworking of gender across the globe. Let me briefly survey a few examples.

First, we can sense a global transformation of personal relations. Families, parenting, children, reproduction, partnering, friendships, all are starting to change their global shape. There have always been migrations, for instance, and with this, people who find themselves at a distance— displaced even—from their loved ones. But nowadays this happens on a very large scale. In 1994, an estimated 120 million people migrated from one country to another.[15] Sometimes migration is a matter of choice— as when work splits partners or family members, who come to live in different parts of the world. Millions of people now conduct their intimate life across countries, becoming transnational families, partners, or children. But sometimes migration is largely coerced—as in the case of refugees, when migration is necessary for survival (and there are upwards of 23 million refugees in the world).[16] Arlie Hochschild speaks of "global care chains," in which "the paid or unpaid work of caring" creates links between people from different parts of the globe. As Hochschild explains: "Just as global capitalism helps create a Third World supply of mothering, so it creates a First World demand for it."[17] Thus it is that women— and it is largely women, although children are heavily involved as well—leave their home countries and their own families to find work in other countries caring for the children of wealthier families—families who nonetheless might not be able to afford child care otherwise. Again, there is nothing new about poorer women looking after the families of richer people except that it now takes place more often and on a global scale. And with the growing availability in the West of child-care workers from the Third World come new and complicated patterns of interfamilial caring or of exploitation and transnational "intimate slavery."[18]

More and more countries are also confronting issues like gay and lesbian registered partnerships, families of choice, or even marriages. Partnership laws currently exist in Denmark (1989, amended in 1999), Norway

*Personal relations and families*
Models of new families across the world
Children being adopted across countries
Issues of migration and the acceptance of partners
Global partnerships
Global intimate friendships
"Global care chains"
The phenomenon that Nin Boyd Krebs has called "edgewalkers"
Global repatterning: trendsetting in newly industrialized countries'
   change in family size, China's policy on birth control
*The global transformation of self-identity*
Hybrid identities
Migrating identities
Globalization of biography
Individualism and individuation transported
*Cyberspace, media, and shifting global intimacies*
Abstract intimacies
Cyber-relations
Virtual relations
Cyberpartners
*The global commodification, commercialization,*
   *and consumption of intimacy*
Selling sex
Sex tourism
Sex work
The selling of infant children
The selling of human body parts
*Social movements and politics*
Global reproductive rights
Gay and lesbian movements
Fundamentalisms and culture wars
Global human rights
Global cities and cultures
Health and AIDS
Science and information

FIGURE 6. *The Globalization of Intimacies*

(1993), Sweden (1994, in force 1995), Iceland (1996), the Netherlands (1997, in force 1998), France (1999), and Germany (2001). Only in the Netherlands, however, are marriage and adoption formally recognized as well. In addition, partnership laws are currently being considered in Finland, Portugal, Switzerland, Luxembourg, Belgium, Spain, and Mexico. Just how far can such a model flow around the globe, and how will it be transformed within countries such as Taiwan or South Africa, where gay populations are increasingly active on their own agendas?

In addition, messages about sex and sexualities are disseminated throughout the world in the media as well as through the vast offerings of mass culture. It has long been recognized that much of pop culture has a latent—if not an explicit—sexual content, but that content is now available in virtually every part of the globe. Rocking around the clock is also rocking around the world, and much of the rocking is highly sexualized. So, too, are stories that focus on intimacies, appearing in everything from films to documentary news programs. Anthony Giddens tells the following anecdote:

> A friend of mine studies village life in central Africa. A few years ago, she paid her first visit to a remote area where she was to carry out her fieldwork. The day she arrived, she was invited to a local home for an evening's entertainment. She expected to find out about the traditional pastimes of the isolated community. Instead, the occasion turned out to be a viewing of *Basic Instinct* on video. The film at that point hadn't even reached the cinemas in London.[19]

It is perhaps not surprising that Giddens's anthropologist friend found herself watching a Hollywood movie set in the middle of Africa. Along with soap operas, sit-coms, music videos, and popular fiction, Hollywood films now roam the newly global world and, in their various ways, present narratives of the intimate life. Media images also promote standards of beauty, as, of course, does the fashion industry—another global concern. Performers such as Madonna, Michael Jackson, or Eminem, all of whom command huge international followings, bring to their performances a plethora of sexual images and a conspicuously sexualized language. Global disco is another site for eroticism. James Farrer has shown how Western disco arrived in Shanghai, where it was regarded as very sexy, and quickly became part of the "elite cosmopolitan culture of modern youth around the world."[20] Nor does it all go one way: Japanese comics, for instance, have entered parts of the U.S. market, turning homosexual images originally meant for heterosexual Japanese schoolgirls into images for gay American men.

Intimacies have also increasingly become part of global consumer markets dominated by the logo.[21] The range of commodities being sold and consumed that are linked to intimacy is truly colossal: underwear and outerwear, face-lifts and weight lifts, breast implants and face jobs. These countless sexual images and messages about intimate life may not be absorbed into all cultures, but they have to be dealt with in some way—even if they are ultimately rejected.

Globalization may also have a special impact on the world's new megacities. Although social scientists have studied the global city fairly extensively, their insights have not been integrated into a growing awareness that the city space is often a sexualized one, as Henning Bech, for example, has argued. And put onto a global level, we can find gay men traveling the world in search of gay scenes, gay tourists, gay parties. Writing about sex "beneath the equator," mainly in Rio de Janeiro, anthropologist Richard Parker can draw complex world maps that illustrate how gay populations flow across countries.[22] He charts, for example, major flows of Brazilian gay men migrating to Japan, San Francisco, Miami, New York, London, Paris, Rome; suggests how a global gay world has become part of the imagined community of men; and also suggests ways in which electronic communities spread through the world, creating common images as well as the means for men to meet other men.

The words "globalization" and "global" are often overworked and may be open to much criticism. But there is a clear sense that, at the start of the twenty-first century, intimate lives for many are changing because of such processes.

## "They Shall Be Sad People": A Dystopian Future?

When we start putting all these global changes together, we can come up with starkly different scenarios of the future, as Figure 7 illustrates. From a utopian perspective, the world is becoming more democratic. Intimacies are guided by an overarching ethic of equality, and there is greater openness and acceptance of differences. According to the dystopian view, however, the world is becoming ever more brutal. Intimacies are subject to continuing patterns of inequality that lead to polarization and bitter disagreements. Globalization also opens new possibilities for exploitation—

| The Dystopian View | The Utopian View |
|---|---|
| Abject intimacies: widening economic disparities and greater world poverty | Luxurious intimacies: a higher standard of living for a growing number of people |
| Violent and / or exploitative intimacies | Democratic intimacies |
| Fragmented intimacies, the balkanization of intimacies | Pluralized intimacies, differences celebrated |
| Impersonal intimacies, a world of strangers | New communities of intimate communication |
| Cyborgs as monsters | Cyborgs as helpers |
| Intimate narcissism and intimate self-centeredness | Intimacies based on mutual concern |
| Intimate *Unsicherheit* | Intimate openness |
| McDonaldization of intimacies | Globalization of intimacies |
| Commercialization and commodification of intimacies | "Real" intimate choices |
| The dumbing-down of intimacy | Enhanced intimate self-awareness |
| Moral decline and a lack of sexual caring or concern | Moral effervescence, intimate citizenship |
| Entrenched hierarchies of sexual exclusion | The democratization of personhood and relationships, intimate dialogue |
| Intimate tribalism | Intimate dialogue |
| Uncertainty, risk, chaos, a world out of control | The chance for a new world order and global human rights |

FIGURE 7. *Intimacies in a Runaway World: Dystopian and Utopian Possibilities*

for damaged lives, for inhumane treatment, for physical and moral degradation. Let us begin by looking at some of the dystopian consequences of globalization for human intimacies.

A key dimension of globalized intimacies, and one that by all accounts is growing in significance, is the global sex business. Again, the sex industry is nothing new: in 1911 Emma Goldman, appalled by the white sex trade, wrote *The Traffic in Women.* But today sex is a huge international business, linked simultaneously to cultures of development, tourism, mass consumption, organized crime, and sex work, while at the same time tapping into the prevailing symbolism and imagery of indigenous cultures. The process of globalization has meant the growth of cross-cultural connections involving sex. There are more sex tourists; and, across the globe, an increasing number of women, men, and even children, all of whom have relatively easy access to one another via the Internet, are doing more things—engaging in telephone sex and cybersex, selling sex videos, performing in live sex acts, working in fetish markets, and the like. Thanks to both local and international organizations of sex workers, they are also becoming politically organized. But while much has been said about these global trends, it is also the case that each culture maintains its own distinctive cultural forms, reworking its experience of globalization to accord with its own history and traditions and to suit its present needs. A recent major study of global sex work contains many stories that suggest ways in which sex work—practices of prostitution, to borrow Wendy Chapkis's phrase—does indeed take on specific meanings and serves specific ends in local communities.[23] Blanket condemnation of sex work may thus be ill advised. For a poverty-stricken child, even life as a child prostitute may be preferable to begging on the streets or to the prospect of dying from disease and malnutrition.

But the sex trade is not the only way in which bodies are for sale. With globalization has come an increased demand for cheap labor. "To whom do the bodies of people belong?" asks an article in the *New Internationalist.* "Who controls the bodies of a row of young men in the gay club in Pattaya, Thailand, who masturbate competitively for a hatful of money donated by an audience of Americans and Japanese? Who owns the eyes and fingers of the women laborers in the electronics factories in the free trade zones? Who commands the energy of the young women in the garment factories of Dhaka?"[24] Much of this labor is provided by women, for whom globalization has brought both new opportunities for employment and the risk of exploitation. Christa Wichterich offers some useful illustrations:

Female textile-workers from Upper Lusatia in Eastern Germany are los-
ing their jobs to women in Bangladesh; Filipinas clean vegetables and
kitchens in Kuwait; Brazilian prostitutes offer their services around
Frankfurt's main railway station; and Polish women look after old people
at rock-bottom prices in various parts of Germany. Women in the
Caribbean key in commercial entries for North American banks.[25]

But if bodies are for sale as labor, they are also for sale as bodies. As Nancy
Scheper-Hughes remarks: "We are now eyeing each other's bodies greed-
ily as a potential source of detachable spare parts with which to extend
our lives." There is a thriving international market in body organs, from
both live and dead donors, sometimes from children, and sometimes
from condemned, or recently executed, prisoners.[26] An international
organization—Organs Watch—has recently been set up to try to expose
many of the problems generated through the traffic in body parts (especially kidneys) across the world. On the agenda are issues such as the
inequalities in acquiring, harvesting, and distributing body organs (abject
poverty drives many people to sell parts of their bodies in order to feed
their families); the role of coercion in coaxing some people to give their
organs; the robbing of mortuaries of organs and tissues; and medically
substantiated allegations of kidney theft during surgery on vulnerable
patients. All of these suggest the dangerous commodification of intimate
body parts.

"Homosexuality" is another one of the many "intimate" issues at the
forefront of this global crisis. Although within the gay movement in many
Western countries, where there is a relatively widespread acceptance of
"queer life," the debates have now shifted more to issues of gay marriage
and registered partnerships; in many countries throughout the world the
situation is radically different. New anti-gay legislation continues to be
enacted in various parts of the world, and many anti-gay atrocities have
been documented by international agencies such as Amnesty International and the International Organization for Gay and Lesbian Rights.
In 2001, the former produced its third major international— country by
country—survey of the persecution of gays and lesbians. More than sev-
enty countries have laws that criminalize homosexual relations. In Iran,
Afghanistan, Saudi Arabia, and Chechnya, gay sex is punishable by the
death penalty. From Europe to Africa to the Americas to Asia, case after
case of ill treatment, including torture, violence, and discrimination
directed against lesbians and gay men, has been documented. In Colombia,
"death squads" routinely target and kill gay men and transvestites as local

authorities promote *limpieza social,* or social cleansing. The death squads operate without fear of prosecution since the gunmen themselves are often police officers and gays are regarded as "disposable people." There are also numerous cases of transgender rights activists—the ultimate gender outlaws—being abused across the world.[27]

Organized religion is often at the global forefront of attacks on gays and lesbians. The Lambeth Conference, for example, which meets every ten years and brings together leaders of the Church of England from around the world, was last held in August 1998 in Great Britain. Although the bishops advocated a compassionate attitude toward homosexuals ("we commit ourselves to listen to the experience of homosexual people"), they rejected "homosexual practice" as being "incompatible with the scriptures." (In the end, 526 Bishops voted for the motion to condemn homosexual practices, 70 opposed it, and 45 abstained.)[28] The dilemma seems irresolvable: to affirm homosexual practice would alienate much of the Church membership, yet to condemn it is to alienate a growing gay movement worldwide. Some adopt an even more extreme stance toward the homosexual issue, arguing that its broad acceptance in the West provides a key to why the church is dying in Europe. Moreover, in Africa and in South and East Asia, there is a growing fundamentalism and rivalry with Islam: to be seen as sympathetic to gays would weaken the position of the Church considerably. Although some radical Western priests view attempts to ban homosexuality as "just one step up from witchcraft," the issue of gay and lesbian rights clearly provides fuel for an ongoing battle between tradition and change, between fundamentalism and new, more progressive attitudes. The debates that currently reign in the West are not to be lightly transposed onto the rest of the world: they can raise volatile issues and generate bitter conflicts.

In 1995, President Robert Mugabe launched an attack on lesbians and gays, which he has continued over the years. Calling them perverts, he accused them of offending against the law of nature and against the moral and religious beliefs of the country:

> If we accept homosexuality as a right, as is being argued by the organization of sodomists and sexual perverts, what moral fiber shall our society ever have to deny organized drug addicts or even those given to bestiality the rights they might claim and allege they possess under the rubrics of individual freedoms and human rights, including the freedom of the press to write and publicize literature on them. . . . Let the Americans keep their sodomy, bestiality, stupid and foolish ways to

themselves, out of Zimbabwe. Let them be gay in the U.S., Europe and elsewhere. They shall be sad people here.[29]

Whatever else, it is clear that the world is still a long way from being a globalized melting pot, in which everything is dissolving into a harmonious whole.

## Rumors of Utopia: The Movement for Human Rights

In contrast to the above, the more optimistic scenario for the future of intimacies looks toward cosmopolitan and diverse cultures located within an active civil society, as well as a thorough "democratizing democracy" that would extend throughout relationships and institutions. As Anthony Giddens writes:

> Democracy is perhaps the most powerful energizing idea of the twentieth century. There are few states in the world today that don't call themselves democratic. . . . Democracy is spreading all over the world, yet in the mature democracies there is widespread disillusionment with democratic processes. In most Western countries, levels of trust in politicians have dropped over past years. . . . What is needed in democratic countries is a deepening of democracy itself. . . . We need to democratize above—as well as below—the level of the nation.[30]

Part of this optimism has to be located both in the emergence of global political organizations and the growing importance attached to one of the key issues of the late twentieth century: a worldwide concern over human rights.[31] Although the argument for human rights has a long history, only recently has the issue become a major topic in common discourse across the globe. Human rights organizations are slowly becoming part of a major international network. There are now over 200 nongovernmental organizations devoted to human rights in the United States, along with a similar number in Great Britain and Europe, and they are swiftly growing. Even countries that are riddled with the denial and corruption of human rights still talk the language of rights. According to the optimistic view, the twenty-first century will bring a critical cosmopolitanism and will witness the consolidation of global human rights and the emergence of true global citizens.[32] World conflicts will increasingly be conducted by dialogic citizens who will take seriously the grounded moralities of everyday life as they are experienced and narrated in all parts of the world and will seek out common grounds.

Benjamin Barber talks of a "world of citizens without frontiers."[33] There are many forms this global citizenry may be taking. Perhaps most conspicuous is a class of affluent and sophisticated global elites, mainly composed of well-to-do men who have few civic responsibilities and can afford to jet around the world. Especially privileged citizens have always existed (see Chapters 4 and 5), but they now enjoy the further advantages of global capital. But there are other forms appearing. In *The Global Age* Martin Albrow talks of a new kind of citizenship—*global citizenship*—that "begins in people's daily lives, is realized in everyday practices and results in collective action up to the level of the globe."[34] He sees the model for a global citizenry in the international working-class movement in the nineteenth century, but now this citizenry is composed of a much more diverse assortment of people who are—as he puts it—"performing the state." Here are global actions at the local level.

Many of the claims to global citizenship now originate with the new social movements—the Green Party of eco-warriors, the gay / lesbian / / queer / transgender movement, the women's movement—and the idea of global citizenship itself is epitomized in what has come to be called the Battle of Seattle. The actions of these would-be global citizens may not dovetail with the goals of national governments and may even run sharply counter to them. Members of these movements argue for the recognition of new key issues, often linked to how people can gain control over their (personal) lives in a "runaway world," to which end they organize global conferences that seek to establish worldwide rights agendas. Crucial to this has been the only very recent establishment of a discourse around human sexual rights and intimate citizenship.[35] Once again, such a discourse raises issues about the meaning of rights and of particular forms of citizenship, of who is included and who excluded, and about how these rights come to be socially constructed and interpreted by particular powerful groups.

A clear illustration of the issues that cluster around global intimate citizenship is found in the debates over reproductive rights. We cannot begin to understand the complexities of this issue by foisting on the world the views of the West: we must develop a sensitivity to the "glocal." Population control programs throughout the world, for example, often involve putting women on the pill, inserting IUDs in women, or sterilizing women. There is a general and indiscriminate targeting of women. Much of this smacks of the imposition of Western values on the rest of the world. Yet the issue of "safe motherhood" arises because in areas where health care and health facilities are poor, large numbers of women die during pregnancy or in childbirth. One woman in 5,000 dies in childbirth in Great Britain, but in some of the poorest countries, 1 in 10 pregnant women will not survive.[36] Likewise, the problem of low fertility rates in the West creates a market for the sale of babies in the East, which can complicate efforts to promote birth control. In short, to be understood properly, the concept of human rights needs to be grounded in concrete cultural locations.

The campaign for reproductive rights may have had a long gestation in the United States and Europe, but action campaigns have now moved around the world. Developing their own analyses of population problems and reproductive issues, these newer indigenous organizations come to develop action programs in countries that were often extremely hostile to their goals. In Africa, there have been campaigns against genital mutilation; in Bangladesh, there has been resistance to attacks from Islamic religious tribunals; in the Philippines, Brazil, and Mexico, there have been struggles against the Catholic Church. One model for handling these kinds of issues on a worldwide scale may well be the International Reproductive Rights Research Action Group (IRRRAG). Building on much earlier work by the women's movement, it was established in 1992 and is now based in seven countries—Brazil, Egypt, Malaysia, Mexico, Nigeria, the Philippines, and the United States. One of IRRRAG's major goals is to move the concept of "sexual and reproductive rights" away from the abstract and into the concrete: to listen to the stories concerning reproductive health told locally by women around the world and to try to appreciate the meanings that attach to these stories.[37] Grounded in a notion of "cultural citizenship" (an idea not that different from what I am calling intimate citizenship), the stories became part of a program to improve women's health and living conditions generally.[38]

But "reproductive rights" is only one area of global intimacy in need of attention. The issue of violence against women has also come to the fore. As Rosalind Petchesky and Karen Judd explain:

> The international human rights vocabulary now includes not only "the basic right of all couples and individuals to decide freely and responsibly the number, spacing and timing of their children and the means to do so" but also freedom from "violence against women and all forms of sexual harassment and exploitation" including "systematic rape, sexual slavery and forced pregnancy"; freedom from genital mutilation; "the right to make decisions concerning reproduction free of discrimination, coercion and violence"; and the right "to have a satisfying and safe sex life."[39]

Petchesky herself was a leading activist at the Beijing women's conference in 1995, and she struggled with many other conference participants over the question of whether a language of "sexual rights" should be included in human rights charters, as Petchesky felt it should.

In an essay titled "Sexual Rights," Petchesky identifies four ethical principles that can guide us toward a positive vision of sexual rights. These are *sexual diversity,* which recognizes that "diverse types of sexual expression are . . . beneficial to a just, humane, culturally pluralistic society"; *habitational diversity,* which acknowledges the "many types of arrangements across the world's societies" that exist for living together and raising children; *health,* which affirms "the right to sexual pleasure as part of basic health"; and the principle of *autonomy or personhood,* which upholds "the right of individuals—children and youth as well as adults— to make their own decisions in matters affecting their bodies and health."[40]

Yet such an idea is nearly always opposed by those who persistently connect any debate on sexual matters to those they generally regard as enemies—those who condone or even support homosexuality, prostitution, pedophilia, incest, adultery, and so on. The full array of the sexual fringe is invoked over and over again in an effort to deny sexual rights generally. The Pope, for example, condemns both reproductive and sexual rights overall by linking them to a "hedonistic mentality unwilling to accept responsibility in matters of sexuality" and "a self-centered concept of freedom."[41]

## The Trouble with Human Rights

The language of citizens and human rights may be the best language we have at the moment in which to formulate a global politics of intimacy. It can perhaps provide a common ground for telling our stories and engaging in dialogue surrounding our concrete, or grounded, moralities. At the same time, it is not without its problems. It is well to be clear what these problems are.

### Differentiated Universalism

First, as we have seen throughout this book, is the claim to universalism. We have been talking in the main about "rights" that are founded on a set of assumptions that, while originating in affluent Western democracies, are taken as universals. When the Universal Declaration of Human Rights was adopted by the United Nations in December 1948, a significant number of the low-income countries of the Third World were still under colonial rule, and even today many remain suspicious of it. Such a platform of rights is often regarded as a universalization of privilege, on top of which concerns over human rights can all too easily furnish an excuse for Western intervention in other countries. Confidence is further eroded when it is noted that the United States—a prime mover behind human rights legislation—notoriously fails to sign up to certain such agreements itself. Moreover, many of the rights claimed in the declaration simply do not make much sense in many parts of the world. The right to a "reasonable limitation of working hours and periodic holidays with pay," for instance, can seem a cruel mockery where sweatshop labor conditions apply. Likewise, as we have seen, talk of women's rights can become a serious problem when these rights clash with cultural and religious expectations around family and gender. In short, the language of human rights can be seen as a vehicle for Enlightenment ideas that are too closely identified with Western democracies—countries that are nonetheless racist, sexist, and shamelessly capitalist. Will Kymlicka's theory of multicultural citizenship and Ruth Lister's notion of a "differentiated universalism," which were examined in Chapter 4, may prove enormously helpful in resolving this tension.

At the same time, it should be remembered that many traditions—not just those of the West—were represented when the United Nations declaration was being drafted. As Michael Ignatieff has remarked, the Chinese, Middle Eastern Christian, Marxist, Hindu, Latin American, or Islamic cultures all "construed their task not as a simple ratification of Western convictions but as an attempt to define a limited range of moral universals from within their very different religious, political, ethnic and philosophic backgrounds."[42] Indeed, it may be a backhanded form of Western arrogance to accept the argument that human-rights values are the prerogative of the West and hence not to be trusted.

## Unenforceability

Another, rather more simple difficulty is the general unenforceability of many rights claims. Many countries across the world sign up for human rights in their various forms but then proceed to ignore them. Human rights standards are frequently violated, not least by liberators as well as oppressors. The actual work of achieving human rights in different countries is often hidden from sight and not public; in such instances, standards become all but unenforceable, even with good will. And in some countries—whose governments may be corrupt in diverse other ways—

they cannot be enforced at all. Still, to acknowledge the problem of enforceability in human rights regimes is not to condemn their arguments. Rather, it signals a need to improve the way in which such regimes work.

## Collective Human Rights

Third, discussions of human rights are sometimes accused of being too oriented toward the individual—as focusing too far on individual rights as opposed to group rights. In the context of intimate citizenship, individual human rights theory necessarily concerns the right of citizens to pursue intimacies of their own choosing. But it must also pay attention to other ethical issues that might place limitations on these rights. Taken too literally, the concept of intimate rights for the individual can just see people doing their own thing—buying babies, selling their own wombs, cheating on their husbands or wives, visiting prostitutes in the Third World who may have been sold into slavery, taking pornographic pictures of children, and so on. Instead, those who uphold such rights also need to recognize the collective solidarity of specific groups—to acknowledge the ways in which some groups are socially excluded, inferiorized, marginalized, or otherwise severely disadvantaged. In other words, individual rights must be viewed within broader frameworks of exclusion and inequality.

Human rights theory has traditionally focused on the rights of the individual, independent of social groups, and advocates for individual human rights mainly seek redress through the nation-state or through intergovernmental structures such as the United Nations. Collective human rights, of course, focus instead on the rights of social groups. Those who support collective rights often seek to create an innovative framework independent of nation-states to enhance and protect these rights.[40] Such rights would crisscross many of the very issues that we have been discussing—the contrast (and potential conflict) among ethnic groups, religious groups, or groups that pursue one sexual lifestyle as opposed to another.

## Universal Capabilities and Ethics

Finally, there remains the very serious problem of "moral condescension" and cultural superiority that has haunted this book. In writing my little list of universal moral guidelines for the close of Chapter 7—the need to acknowledge minimal human functional capabilities, to recognize others, to promote caring for others, and to sponsor an ethics of love—I was struck by how much in Western culture does not begin to match these seemingly benign principles. It is very easy, too easy, to fail to understand what is actually central to local cultures even if disliked by others. As I mentioned earlier, Martha Nussbaum examines the abhorrence Western feminists feel at the practice of female genital mutilation, and she expresses concern about their attempt to intervene by means of special pleading. Is it morally wrong to criticize other cultures, especially when there are so many things wrong with one's own? Yet Nussbaum ultimately argues that certain universal rights provide the grounds for attacking such practices. Customs such as child marriage, female circumcision, or genital mutilation may prevail in certain societies and thus be built into their specific cultural expectations. Perhaps to attack such customs, as Nussbaum does, signals moral condescension on the part of the West. But it may also represent a genuine moral appeal to broader universal values or rights. Sometimes there seems to be no way round this dilemma. At the same time, some commentators suggest that certain basic ideas of human worth, of tolerance, of respect, and the like can be found across many cultures and that customs such as genital mutilation are thus open to critique from within the cultures that practice them.

## A Return to Stories, Common Grounds, and Dialogue

One way to mediate between these opposing views may again be to listen to the stories that people tell of their own experiences, to see what it is that they say about them. To take the case of genital mutilation, how do women and girls feel about the experience? What is their story? And what, too, is the story of their mothers and their families? Do they tell of the shame that will be brought to the family who refuses to engage in such acts? And is there any common ground? Shashi Tharoor, an Anglo-Indian writer and Under-Secretary-General for Communications and Public Information at the United Nations, offers one answer:

> When one hears of the unsuitability or ethnocentrism of human rights, what are the unstated assumptions? What exactly are these human rights that someone in a developing country can do without? Not the right to life, I hope. Freedom from torture? The right not to be enslaved, not to be physically assaulted, not to be arbitrarily arrested, imprisoned, or executed? No one actually advocates in so many words the abridgement of any of these rights. Tolerance and mercy have always and in all cultures been ideals of government rule and human behavior.[43]

## Global Intimate Citizens

I have tried in this chapter to suggest that many of the issues raised in previous chapters now have, or are beginning to have, global implications. Issues such as HIV / AIDS, gay and lesbian studies, the new reproductive technologies, the future of families, the changing meanings of sexual conduct, the sale of body parts, and so on, all raise global concerns. As more and more of our intimacies "go global," so they generate more and more intimate troubles that in turn create more and more contested intimacies on a worldwide scale. The culture wars around intimate citizenship in the West may also have their equivalents in clashes and conflicts across the globe. The search for pluralized public spheres across countries that can generate dialogues and a common moral ground may be an even more daunting task than it originally seemed.

# 9

# The Intimate Citizenship Project

*Human beings have a dignity that deserves respect from laws and social institu-*
*tions. The idea has many origins in many traditions; by now it is at the core of*
*modern liberal democratic thought and practice all over the world. The idea of*
*human dignity is usually taken to involve an idea of equal worth: rich and poor,*
*rural and urban, female and male, all are equally deserving of respect, just in*
*virtue of being human, and this respect should not be abridged on account of a*
*characteristic that is distributed by the whims of fortune. Often, too, this idea of*
*equal worth is connected to an idea of liberty: to respect the equal worth of per-*
*sons is, among other things, to promote their ability to fashion a life in accor-*
*dance with their own view of what is deepest and most important.*

Martha Nussbaum, *Sex and Social Justice*

*We are all familiar with the threats that hang over the world today. . . . We all*
*know what conflicts lie dormant within humanity now that a single global civi-*
*lization is pushing people from different spheres of culture ever closer together,*
*thus inevitably arousing their determination to defend their identity against the*
*pressure towards uniformity. But what are we doing to avert these dangers or con-*
*front them? . . . We have entirely ignored one of the pillars of the European tra-*
*dition: universalism, the commandment to think of everyone, to act as everyone*
*should act, and to look for universally acceptable solutions.*

Václav Havel, *"The Hope for Europe"*

THIS STUDY IS very much a "work in progress"—an initial exploration into what I have called the "intimate citizenship project." It
is grounded in my wider concern with developing a critical humanistic
theory.[1] On the one hand, the present book aims to be a work of descrip-
tive and analytic sociology in which I investigate a whole new arena of
life and talk around the personal that will no doubt continue through
the twenty-first century. On the other, it aims also to be a mini-work of
public policy, one that focuses on the critical arguments about how we
should live our lives that are presently emerging in newly pluralized public spheres. It straddles disciplines, too, owing as much to political theory as it does to sociology. The book will succeed if it can open doors to

some sideways thinking that disregards the traditional boundaries between academic fields.

At the heart of my discussion is a concern with what goes on in intimate worlds and a conviction that intimacies can only be adequately understood in relation to the major changes and conflicts characteristic of the late modern world. Also of key importance is an awareness that arguments originating in one country may soon find themselves being discussed and contested in others. Perhaps above all I have tried to point out that we will ultimately need to find ways through these "intimate troubles" before they lead us into conflicts that might overwhelm and even destroy us.

My initial research interests, some years ago, lay with the largely political conflicts over gay and lesbian lives. From this I was led to an interest in women's lives and sexual violence, which has in turn broadened out to include all matters of intimacy. I use the sensitizing term intimate citizenship to flag all these concerns. In pursuing these topics, I hope to suggest some ways of moving ahead in difficult times.

## The Intimate Citizenship Project: A Paradigm for Analysis

This brief book has opened up a number of avenues for continuing a deeper investigation. Against a backdrop of major global change and conflict, the concept of intimate citizenship suggests pathways into the ongoing debates about intimate life that we, as dialogic citizens, now carry out in increasingly pluralized public spheres. The substance of these debates ranges all the way from teenage sexuality to the rights and obligations of divorced, single, or gay parents to the proliferation of Web sites devoted in one way or another to sex and to the possibility of genetically engineered "designer children." Not surprisingly, most of these debates are steeped in ethical controversy.

Drawing together much of the book, the concerns over "intimate citizenship" can be outlined as follows.

1. *Change and the construction of "new intimacy" debates.* Here we ask: What are the many ways in which people "do intimacies" in the early twenty-first century? How do we "do relationships" or "do emotions" or do bodies or genders or sexualities? What are the major changes taking place in these areas and how deep do these changes go? What consequences are they presently having or are they likely to have? We will

need to clarify the nature of the changes now underway and to explore the debates to which they give rise.

2. *Culture wars and moral conflicts, or cultures of contested intimacies.* Here we ask: What are the key positions on contemporary intimate conflicts within and between social groups, as well as across the world? What views do individuals typically hold, and how do people arrive at these views? How do we navigate among traditionalists, fundamentalists, progressives, social critics, libertarians, dialogists, and others? What are the main features of late modern moral conflicts, and how widespread are such disagreements?

3. *Invention of intimate citizenship.* Here we ask: How are older approaches to citizenship now being reworked so as to accommodate current social changes and political issues? Can we chart the precarious meanings of intimate citizenship that cluster around sexuality, eroticism, the human body, personal and family relationships, and so on? How can we best understand the language and the rhetorical tactics characteristic of the claims now being made about relationships, gender roles, sexualities, bodies, emotions, and what we might call "intimate identities"? We should aim to interrogate these new citizenship debates and, in particular, to examine the new citizens and new identities they bring about and the shifting boundaries they help form.

4. *The new pluralized public spheres.* Here we ask: What changes are occurring in the public spheres in which citizenship debates take place? What are the main arenas of debate, and how are such debates being animated for different groups? How do new public spheres come into being, and to what extent are new voices succeeding in being heard? We will need to look closely at the various new social movements, along with the Web and mainstream media such as television and newspapers, in an effort to understand their role in reworking public spheres and the tensions and contradictions to which they give rise.

5. *The grounded and concrete moralities of everyday life.* Here we ask: How do people, in the course of their everyday lives, work through ethical dilemmas, and what can we learn from their experiences? Can we identify ways in which commonplace moral dilemmas are typically framed or conceptualized? How and why do concrete moralities tend to inhabit stories and narratives—the "stories we live by"? Seeking answers to these questions will require that we collect and analyze an array of everyday narratives that focus on some sort of ethical problem, while also searching for any universals or common grounds that may exist.

6. *Dialogues and stories.* Here we ask: How best can we study and learn

from the narrativization process characteristic of concrete moralities? How can constructive dialogue take place between social groups whose members may have very different stories to tell? How is the notion of dialogue built into newer ideas of citizenship? How can the limits of dialogue be identified and the positive role of conflict acknowledged?

7. *Globalization.* Here we ask: As the various changes outlined above take place in more affluent countries and we grapple with the issues they raise, how do these changes also form part of a globalized discourse around increasingly globalized intimacies and the conflicts they generate? Is a "thin universalism" of intimacies possible?

8. *Evaluation.* Here we ask: What is the positive, or utopian, vision of the outcome of all these changes, and what is the negative, or dystopian, vision? How are these respective viewpoints linked to social inequalities— the patterns of social exclusion organized around wealth, age, ethnicity, and gender? Can (or should) a utopian image prevail?

## Some Potential Difficulties

I am well aware that these basic topics—the building blocks of the intimate citizenship project—are very wide-ranging and tend to raise more questions than they answer. My project overall is, moreover, open to criticism from a number of directions. Let me briefly indicate what these might be.

### The Creeping Return of the Metanarrative

Intimate citizenship could—like earlier accounts of citizenship—be viewed as a rather all-encompassing concept, or metanarrative, that sweeps into a single heap all intimacies, every broad social change, every conflict and its possible resolution, all universal moral landscapes, and even all of globalization. Indeed, if postmodern theories are supposed to be skeptical of grand narratives, then my account could be accused of backsliding, inasmuch as it might seem very grand indeed. I hope it will not, however, for I have in fact been at some pains to rework certain of the classical modernist concepts—public versus private spheres, citizenship, the ethical, the intimate—in order precisely that they become more local and grounded, more in the nature of a pastiche, more pluralized. These are indeed words that crop up on many pages of this book. Far from understanding intimate citizenship as a grand, monolithic concept, I see it as creating a somewhat loose array of mini-concepts that, at least to some degree, share and thus hold together a sprawling common object—the fragmented intimacies of the late modern world and the troubles they can entail. This approach allows me, I hope, to talk about intimacy and citizenship without turning either concept into something all-embracing and inappropriately homogenized.

As I have sought to clarify the meaning of both *intimate* and *citizenship,* it should have become clear that I am using these terms in much broader ways than usual—stretching them to incorporate a range of postmodern ambiguities. For me, as well as many others, this broadening out is a strength. I have tried to show that the classic ideas of citizenship—as bequeathed to us by Marshall and his lineage—have been too restrictive and in some respects biased, and have hence outlived at least some of their usefulness. Pushing out the boundaries of citizenship and likewise of intimacy helps me cut across issues that are often seen as belonging to specific, and usually quite strictly demarcated, fields of study such as, in the case of intimacies, family studies, gay and lesbian studies, the new reproductive politics, gender studies, and the like. In so doing, I am able to pinpoint certain similarities that might otherwise never have been revealed.

## The Need for Detail

This is a short study, and in it I have raised a lot of issues. But as I bring the study to a close it is apparent that some key gaps remain. Notably, I have not been able to include nearly as many examples as I would have liked of concrete moral stories, of how dialogues work, of the widening of the public sphere to encompass all kinds of new media, and so forth. More serious, perhaps, is the lack of detailed attention to the state, to governance, to all manner of the workings of the political at national and international levels. Even though citizenship is an element of civil society, this, too, has barely been touched on, nor has the law received adequate attention. But, as I well know, it is in the details that the workability of an idea emerges most clearly and convincingly, and no doubt the addition of more particulars would considerably enrich my argument. In order to cover as much ground as I have, however, without writing a very long book, I have been obliged to make certain sacrifices. The best I can say here is that, as always, there is more work to be done.

## The Problem with Rights

In the end this study opts for the currently fashionable language of "rights" in expressing its hope for universal justice. I am not unhappy with this, but we must bear in mind that the concept of rights is not without its pitfalls. It can mean all things to all people—few people are against rights in general! Nonetheless, it remains an essentially Western concept that can tend to privilege Europe and North America, if only as the perceived originators of the values with which the theory of human rights is undergirded. In some interpretations the idea of rights is too individualistic, overvaluing access to personal freedoms while failing to take collective suffering sufficiently seriously. Nor can violations of such rights be easily monitored. Despite the activities of organizations such as the Human Rights Commission or Amnesty International, gross crimes against human rights may be committed and yet pass unnoticed. At the same time, if the language of human rights has become popular, this is arguably because it is the best language currently available.

## Utopianism

If I am to be accused of a certain naïve optimism, I would probably have to plead guilty. As I see it, many of the developments characteristic of late modernity could enhance personal life if only we could sit down and talk them through reasonably and with mutual compassion, rather than descending into partisanship and personal preference of all kinds. If only we would accept that we live in an immeasurably aporetic and contradictory world, where voices will never really agree, where significant—at times even enormous—differences will (and should) forever remain. And yet without some slender threads of the universal to bind us together, however loosely, we may be doomed. Many processes are now at work that militate against my (guarded) optimism. There is, for example, the increasing dominance of market relations, which threaten to turn almost every facet of intimacy into a commodity. More seriously still, the growing inequalities of a global world now render billions undernourished, illiterate, and disenfranchised, if not outright oppressed. For those whose lives are so brutally diminished, my talk of choices and new ways of living must sound at best irrelevant, and at worst like an obscene affront. In our desire to find hope for the future, the plight of these people must not be forgotten: it is indeed more important than the story I have been telling.

## Intimate Inequalities

The widening gap between those who have and those who have not leads me to what I might call my core worry. As the book has progressed, I have regularly sensed that something is missing. When I think of how the bodies, and body parts, of the poor are being sold to the relatively wealthy; of the fact that some mothers can choose to have babies via costly new reproductive technologies while others lack the most basic prenatal medical care; of how the voices of many who struggle to talk about their intimate needs are either never heard or massively discredited; of the ways in which some religions—or, rather, the privileged few who speak on behalf of religions—continue to denounce abortion, homosexuality, even divorce—then I sense that the problems are bigger than I have perhaps acknowledged. Intimacies are lodged in worldwide inequalities of class, gender, age, race, and the like. These inequalities structure on a daily basis the debasement and degradation, the patterns of exclusion and marginalization, the sense of powerlessness that, in one way or another, many people experience as the inevitable backdrop of ordinary intimacies. Cutting across my entire book is a persistent need to return to these issues.

## Moving On: Learning to Listen

Despite these concerns and disclaimers, I hope the book charts one possible way to move ahead. My major concerns have been with finding new languages that will enable us to see a different world in the making. An array of very familiar words—citizenship, identity, community, public sphere, morality, ethics—can never be the same as they were in the recent past. For in the past they were "tight words" for a modernist world. They often closed things down, led to a neat order, defined, classified, and established boundaries. Now, in late modern times, they are becoming of necessity more open, polyvocal, flexible, porous, and interwoven; they sensitize rather than define, their meanings are emergent rather than fixed. This is a world in which our intimate lives are lived in the throes of major changes and conflicts. The intimate troubles that beset us are no longer likely to find simple solutions but will more probably reside in some kind of permanently unsettled state. I cannot envisage a future world in which all will more or less agree on the critical question of "how to live life."

This does not mean, nor should it mean, that we must resign ourselves to anarchistic chaos, relativist vacuums, or tribal wars. But we do have to learn to listen to one another's stories of how we make our way through the moral tangles of today—because I do believe that for many people a lot of the time is spent in concerns about ethical issues. As we strive to be good people, we do not grapple with the grand abstractions of moral philosophers but simply the routine worries of daily living—

and the explanations we give for what we do usually arrive through our telling of stories.

Storytelling has always played a prominent role in societies, and it is no different today—except that we do have available to us new means of communication and new (public) spheres within which to tell our stories. Thus, more people are able to hear how other people view intimate problems and how they deal with them. And in this lie some pathways to hope. Of course people will not agree with each other. But they may learn to engage in dialogues. Even where gross inequities in wealth and power exist, people might become willing to award each other some respect, if only out of an awareness of the dangers of creating "evil enemies" to attack. If we can learn how to talk and how to listen, we may begin to sense that in the end there are some common values that hold humanity together.

# Notes

## Preface

1. This phrase was originally uttered by the leading microsociologist of the twentieth century, Erving Goffman.

2. I discuss this idea in *Documents of Life: An Invitation to a Critical Humanism.*

3. Howard S. Becker, *Doing Things Together.*

4. Mills, *The Sociological Imagination,* p. 8.

5. An extremely valuable account of this change is Toulmin's *Cosmopolis.*

6. I first raised versions of these ideas in *Modern Homosexualities* and more fully in *Telling Sexual Stories.*

## 1. Intimate Troubles

1. I place the word "choice" in quotation marks here to indicate that its meaning is far from straightforward. As should become clear, the act of choosing, insofar as it is linked to autonomous individuals, is deeply social, structured into time and place—as the opening epigrams are meant to suggest.

2. The term "issues culture" is introduced and developed in R. Smith and R. Windes, *Progay / Antigay* and belongs to the general tradition of constructionism on which this book draws. See especially Donileen Loseke, *Thinking About Social Problems,* for a useful introduction.

3. Pedophilia and child sexual abuse have become persistent moral panics of recent times. This panic has drowned out the possibility of debating the nature of childhood sexualities. One major exception to this is Judith Levine's *Harmful to Minors: The Perils of Protecting Children from Sex.*

4. Polyamory is another relatively new word and idea, which focuses on relationships where there is multiple love.

5. For the term "practice," see Pierre Bourdieu, *Outline of a Theory of Practice.* See also David Morgan, who applies the term to families in his *Family Connections.* I prefer the more general idea of "doing intimacies."

6. On the history of homosexual marriage, see John Boswell, *The Marriage of Likeness: Same-Sex Unions in Pre-Modern Europe.*

7. See Gertrude Himmelfarb, *One Nation, Two Cultures,* p. 3, who draws on the work of Adam Smith; and Elaine Showalter, *Sexual Anarchy,* chap. 1, esp. p. 4.

8. Ulrich Beck, for example, distinguishes between a "first modernity," signaled by collective, full employment and the existence of both nation states and welfare states, as well as by the exploitation of nature, and a "second moder-

nity," in which increased individualization, gender revolution, globalization, the decline of paid employment, and ecological crises come about. "Normal biographies" cease, and there is a "revolution of side effects." The future is likely to become "more open"—full of new possibilities but at the same time more uncertain—and to bring with it both hope and despair. He suggests too the evolution of a "risk regime" of globalization, ecologization, digitalization, individualization, and the politicization of work. See Ulrich Beck, *Brave New World of Work,* pp. 18–19, 72.

9. On the shift to postmodern values across the world, see Lawrence Harrison and Samuel Huntington, eds., *Culture Matters: How Values Shape Human Progress*—especially the essay by Ronald Inglehart on the World Values Survey.

10. Fukuyama provides four case studies of strongly familistic societies (China, France, Italy, and South Korea) and talks about the centrality of trust in such societies and the common social capital their members share.

11. See Kendrik, *The Erotic Museum.*

12. Cees Hamelink, *The Ethics of Cyberspace,* p. 39. Ironically, Hamelink later outlines suggestions for a Ten Commandments for Computer Ethics (p. 42).

13. Zeldin, *An Intimate History of Humanity,* p. 324.

14. See West and Zimmerman, "Doing Gender"; Shilling, *Social Theory and the Body;* and Arlie Hochschild, *The Managed Heart.*

15. For a discussion of the problem of postmodern values, see Francesca Klug, *Values for a Godless Age.*

16. See Will Van den Hoonaard, *Working with Sensitising Concepts: Analytical Field Research.*

17. Ken Plummer, *Telling Sexual Stories: Power, Change and Social Worlds,* p. 151.

## 2. Postmodern Intimacies

Some of the ideas in this chapter were explored in a more preliminary fashion in my article "Intimate Choices," in *Theory and Society: Understanding the Present,* ed. Gary Browning, Abbey Halcli, and Frank Webster.

1. Many of the key issues in this reproductive revolution are discussed, pessimistically, by Francis Fukuyama in his *The Posthuman Future.*

2. See Peter Berger and William Eerdmans, *The Desecularization of the World.* Berger is a Catholic sociologist who finds religion everywhere on the increase—except in Europe and among academics. He is also a key theorist of the "plausibility structures" described in the previous section: see Peter Berger et al., *The Homeless Mind.*

3. Thus, for instance, Robert Connell identifies what he calls hegemonic masculinities, along with an array of subordinated masculinities. See Connell, *Masculinities.*

4. Judith Stacey, *In the Name of the Family,* p. 37.

5. See Manuel Castells, *The Power of Identity,* p. 235.

6. See William Simon, *Postmodern Sexualities,* for a useful overview of the shifts taking place around sex.

7. The latest world figures can be found at http://www.global-reach.biz/globstats/evol.html

8. See Sadie Plant, "Coming Across the Future" (1998). It is one of a useful series of articles on cybersex contained in Bell and Kennedy's *The Cybercultures Reader,* pp. 460–70.

9. See Alberto Melucci, *The Playing Self,* p. 117. For an insightful discussion of "the age of assisted conception," see also Jeanette Edwards et al., *Technologies of Procreation.*

10. On the possibility of a post-human age, key studies include Donna Harraway, *Simians, Cyborgs, and Women;* Patrick Hopkins, ed., *Sex / Machine;* Gray, *The Cyborg Citizen;* and Hales, *How We Became Posthuman.*

11. Alberto Melluci, *The Playing Self,* p. 118.

12. For a brief and clear statement of globalization, see Anthony Giddens's 1999 Reith Lectures published as *Runaway World: How Globalisation Is Shaping Our Lives;* and for the most apocalyptic vision of all, see Jean Baudrillard's *The Vital Illusion.*

13. Sex tourism involves vacations and travels undertaken in order to engage in some kind of sexual activity. Some of this will involve sex workers and has been widely documented as frequently exploitative and degrading in Third World contexts.

14. Isaiah Berlin, *Four Essays on Liberty,* p. 131.

15. Ulrich Beck and Elizabeth Beck-Gernsheim, *The Normal Chaos of Love,* pp. 5, 6.

16. Beck, *Risk Society,* p. 92; and Beck, *The Reinvention of Politics,* p. 95.

17. Anthony Giddens, *Modernity and Self-Identity,* p. 5.

18. Lynn Jamieson, *Intimacy,* p. 158.

19. Peter Clecack, *America's Quest for the Ideal Self;* Francesca Cancian, *Love in America.*

20. See Giddens, *Runaway World,* pp. 62–63; see also Giddens, *The Transformation of Intimacy.*

21. See Zygmunt Bauman, *In Search of Politics,* p. 5. Bauman develops the concept of *Unsicherheit* in *Liquid Society.*

22. Bauman, *In Search of Politics,* p. 5.

23. See Cohen and Taylor, *Escape Attempts.*

24. George Ritzer, *Enchanting a Disenchanted World,* p. 2.

25. For a brief account of but one segment of the commodification of sex, the porn industry—which is estimated to be worth some $56 billion a year—see Micklethwait and Wooldridge, *A Future Perfect.*

26. An interesting account of telephone sex is Amy Flowers's *The Fantasy Factory.*

27. See "The Second Sexual Revolution," *New York Times Magazine,* Feb. 20, 2000.

28. See Sadie Plant, "Coming Across the Future." It is one of a useful series of articles on cybersex contained in Bell and Kennedy's *The Cybercultures Reader.*

29. The latest figures can be found at http://www.unaids.org.

30. Giddens, quoted in Beck, *World Risk Society,* p. 112.

31. See the classic discussion of different kinds of individualism and their emergence in Steven Lukes, *Individualism.*

32. UNFPA, *The State of the World Population 2000,* p. 11.

33. See "Rwandan Sorrow," *Time,* Apr. 17, 2000. For a compelling look at rape and genocide, see Beverly Allen, *Rape Warfare: The Hidden Genocide in Bosnia-Herzegovina and Croatia.*

34. UNFPA, p. 25.

35. Jeffrey Weeks, *Making Sexual History,* p. 212.

## 3. Culture Wars and Contested Intimacies

1. On global conflict, see Samuel Huntington, *The Clash of Civilizations and the Remaking of the World Order,* and Barber, *Jihad vs. McWorld: How Globalism and Tribalism Are Reshaping the World.* On dissension within the women's movement, see Carole Vance, ed., *Pleasure and Danger.*

2. See Christian Smith et al., "The Myth of the Culture Wars: The Case of American Protestantism," in Rhys Williams, ed., *Cultural Wars in American Politics: Critical Reviews of a Popular Myth,* pp. 175–95. This book suggests that culture wars function as popular myths.

3. The phrase "variant sexuality issues" comes from R. Smith and R. Windes, *Progay / Antigay: The Rhetorical War over Sexuality* (p. xv), which provides a valuable account of the arrival of this new, sexually pluralistic culture, as well as of the ways in which it depends upon a culture of opposition to keep it alive. Smith and Windes's study is a model of the kind of work that needs to be done on various other, sometimes bitter, social conflicts, such as those surrounding abortion, pornography, or "the family."

4. Smith and Windes, *Progay / Antigay,* p. 61.

5. For an illuminating look at the history of contraception, see Linda Gordon, *Woman's Body, Women's Right.*

6. Janice Raymond, *Women as Wombs: Reproductive Technologies and the Battle over Women's Freedom,* p. 30

7. See Leon Kass, "Preventing a Brave New World: Why We Should Ban Human Cloning Now," *New Republic,* May 5, 2001.

8. On the sex wars of the 1970s and 1980s, see Echols, *Daring to Be Bad;* Ann Ferguson, "Sex War: The Debate Between Radical and Libertarian Feminists," *Signs* 10 (1984):106–12; Dorchen Leidholdt and Janice Raymond, *The Sexual*

*Liberals and the Attack on Feminism;* Lisa Duggan and Nan Hunter, *Sex Wars: Sexual Dissent and Political Culture.*

9. Kathleen Barry, *The Prostitution of Sexuality,* pp. 51, 53; Kamala Kempadoo, "Introduction," in Kamala Kempadoo and Jo Doezema, eds., *Global Sex Workers: Rights, Resistance and Redefinition,* p. 11, citing also Chandra Talpade Mohanty.

10. Shulamith Firestone, *The Dialectic of Sex,* p. 198.

11. Andrea Dworkin, *Right-Wing Women: The Politics of Domesticated Females,* p. 188.

12. Gena Corea, *The Mother Machine,* p. 85.

13. Raymond, *Women as Wombs,* p. 103.

14. Michael Bronski, *The Pleasure Principle: Sex, Backlash, and the Struggle for Sexual Freedom,* pp. 8–9.

15. Ibid., pp. 11, 25.

16. See François Peraldi, "Polysexuality," *Semiotext(e)* no. 10 (1981).

17. On the normalizing trend within gay cultures, see Kirk and Madsen, *After the Ball,* which lays out a code of conduct for gays; Andrew Sullivan, *Virtually Normal: An Argument About Homosexuality;* and Bawer, *A Place at the Table.* For a critique of this development, see Warner, *The Trouble with Normal: Sex, Politics, and the Ethics of Queer Life.*

18. In a vast literature, see Valerie Lehr, *Queer Family Values: Debunking the Myth of the Nuclear Family.*

19. Michael Kimmel, *The Gendered Society,* p. 144.

20. See Ken Plummer, "The Gay and Lesbian Movement in Britain."

21. See Wells's introduction to Margaret Sanger's *The Pivot of Civilization.* I came across this while reading Kathryn Pyne Addelson, *Moral Passages: Toward a Collectivist Moral Theory,* p. 10.

22. Hunter, *Culture Wars,* pp. 44, 45.

23. In *Telling Sexual Stories,* I identified three such modes of argument; two more—metacriticism and dialogism—are now added here.

24. I draw here from the key essays collected in Martin E. Marty and R. Scott Appleby, eds., *Fundamentalisms Comprehended.* I quote especially from Gabriel A. Almond, Emmanuel Sivan, and R. Scott Appleby, "Fundamentalism: Genus and Species," pp. 405–8.

25. William Connolly, *The Ethos of Pluralization,* pp. xii, 405–7.

26. Ibid., pp. xii, xvi, 105–6.

27. See Amitai Etzioni, *The New Golden Rule: Community and Morality in a Democratic Society.*

28. See Jürgen Habermas, *Justification and Application: Remarks on Discourse Ethics.*

## 4. The New Theories of Citizenship

1. Engin F. Isin and Patricia K. Wood, *Citizenship and Identity,* p. 20.

2. On cybercitizens, see Gray, *The Cyborg Citizen.* The new bio-techno iden-

tities are raised by Marilyn Strathern in "Enabling Identity: Biology, Choice and the New Reproductive Technologies," in Hall and du Gay, *Questions of Cultural Identity*.

3. See Ronald Beiner, ed., *Theorizing Citizenship*, and Thomas Janoski, *Citizenship and Civil Society: A Framework of Rights and Obligations in Liberal, Traditional, and Social Democratic Regimes*.

4. Janoski, *Citizenship and Civil Society*, p. 7.

5. Martin Bulmer and Anthony M. Rees, eds., *Citizenship Today*, p. 3.

6. T. H. Marshall, *Citizenship and Social Class and Other Essays*, pp. 28–29.

7. Marshall, *Sociology at the Crossroads*, p. 74.

8. Nick Ellison, "Towards a New Social Politics: Citizenship and Reflexivity in Late Modernity," *Sociology* 31, no. 4 (Nov. 1997): 697, 708. Ellison's full discussion is important, but I focus on only part of it here. His wider argument suggests a more complex range of different models of citizens—state-centered, pluralist, and poststructuralist—and he argues for a new "reflexive citizenship." Here I am ignoring the pluralist model, which is critical of universalist state-centered discourses.

9. Iris Marion Young, "Polity and Group Difference: A Critique of the Ideal of Universal Citizenship," *Ethics* 99 (Jan. 1989): 259.

10. Will Kymlicka, *Multicultural Citizenship*, p. 175.

11. Ruth Lister, *Citizenship: Feminist Perspectives*, pp. 66, 90. Lister draws significantly on the important work of Iris Marion Young, Jane Flax, and David Harvey, among others.

12. In Kate Bornstein, *My Gender Workbook*, p. 271.

13. Bornstein, *Gender Outlaw*, p. 68.

14. Alan Wolfe, "Democracy Versus Sociology: Boundaries and Their Consequences," in *Cultivating Differences*, ed. M. Lamont and M. Fournier, p. 323.

15. Ibid., pp. 311–12.

16. The expression "pluralization ethos" is William Connolly's. As Connolly remarks, "The drives towards pluralization and fundamentalism condition each other" and "any drive to pluralization can itself become fundamentalized" (*The Ethos of Pluralization*, p. xii).

17. On the idea of a "countervailing civic culture," see T. Bridges, *The Culture of Citizenship: Inventing Postmodern Civic Culture*, p. 20. David Bell and Jon Binnie also discuss dissident citizenship in *The Sexual Citizen: Queer Politics and Beyond*.

18. A now classic collection of essays on the way in which the modern gay identity was invented can be found in Ken Plummer, ed., *The Making of the Modern Homosexual*.

19. Rickie Solinger has shown how issues of choice over life style and intimate politics (such as abortion rights and adoption) are clouded deeply by issues of inequalities. See her *Beggars and Choosers*.

20. Questions drawn from Iris Marion Young, *Justice and the Politics of Difference,* pp. 53, 57, 59.

21. Ibid., p. 61. See also Young's *Inclusion and Democracy.*

22. Janoski, *Citizenship and Civil Society,* p. 55.

23. The classic statement of the evolution of the modern conception of identity and self in the Western tradition can be found in Charles Taylor, *Sources of the Self.*

24. The word entered the language around 1570. The quality or condition of being the same; absolute or essential sameness; oneness; individuality, personality (1638).

25. See Isin and Wood, *Citizenship and Identity,* p. 14.

26. Useful studies of citizenship and gender abound, but see especially Beiner, *Theorizing Citizenship;* Ellison, "Towards a New Social Politics: Citizenship and Reflexivity in Late Modernity"; Isin and Wood, *Citizenship and Identity;* and Lister, *Citizenship: Feminist Perspectives* (all cited earlier in the notes to this chapter); David Evans, *Sexual Citizenship;* Diane Richardson, "Sexuality and Citizenship," *Sociology* 32, no. 1 (1998): 83–100; "Constructing Sexual Citizenship: Theorizing Sexual Rights," *Critical Social Policy* 20, no. 1 (2000): 105–35; and Jeffrey Weeks, "The Sexual Citizen," *Theory, Culture and Society* 15, nos. 3–4 (1998): 35–52. See also Jock Young, *The Exclusive Society,* 1999; Sylvia Walby, "Is Citizenship Gendered?" *Sociology* 28 (1994): 379–45; and Rian Voet, *Feminism and Citizenship.*

27. Evans, *Sexual Citizenship,* p. 9.

28. Ibid., p. 64. In formulating his concept of sexual citizenship, Evans draws on Marshall's work as well as on that of John Rawls.

29. Jeffrey Weeks, *Invented Moralities,* p. 118.

30. See Jeffrey Weeks "The Sexual Citizen," *Theory, Culture and Society* 15, nos. 3–4 (1998): 35–52. In a more recent work coauthored with Brian Heaphy and Catherine Donovan, *Same Sex Intimacies,* Weeks turns more and more to the term *intimate citizenship,* recognizing, as I do, some of the limitations of the term *sexual citizenship. Same Sex Intimacies* appeared just as I was finishing this book.

31. Diane Richardson, *Rethinking Sexuality,* p. 9.

32. Ibid., p. 75. For Richardson's discussion of sexual rights, see esp. chap. 6.

33. David Bell and Jon Binnie, *The Sexual Citizen: Queer Politics and Beyond.* In addition, see the comparably radical case made by Shane Phelan in *Sexual Strangers.*

34. Bell and Binnie, *The Sexual Citizen,* p. 3.

35. Holloway Sparks, "Dissident Citizenship," pp. 74–110.

36. On redistribution and recognition, see Nancy Fraser's classic essay "From Redistribution to Recognition," in her *Justice Interruptus,* pp. 11–40.

37. The idea of "differentiated universalism" strikes me as a very important one in attempting to bridge the universal with difference. See Kymlicka, *Multicultural Citizenship,* and Lister, *Citizenship: Feminist Perspectives.* Kymlicka

has used the idea to talk about rival ethnic factions in the nation-state, but Lister has usefully broadened the concept.

38. Controversial as this may be, I would argue that pedophilia needs to be included in the debates about intimacy because it raises so many issues—of childhood sexualities, of consent and coercion, of affection and abuse—that tread on the taboos surrounding children.

## 5. Public Intimacies, Private Citizens

1. Jürgen Habermas, *The Structural Transformation of the Public Sphere,* p. 1. For examples of the commentary the book generated, see the essays collected in *Habermas and the Public Sphere,* ed. Craig Calhoun.

2. Habermas's initial formulation has since been somewhat modified, as he has considered the contemporary role of the media in modernity and public life and the nature of a "deliberative democracy." It seems to me to be somewhat less pessimistic. See Habermas, *Between Fact and Norms.*

3. While certainly influenced by Habermas, Seyla Benhabib, Nancy Fraser, Iris Marion Young, and others have in various ways taken his ideas a step further. See the essays in Joan B. Landes, ed., *Feminism: The Public and the Private.*

4. Fraser, "Rethinking the Public Sphere," pp. 75, 81, 81–82.

5. A good example of outsider discourses encouraging the dominant discourse to stretch its boundaries can be found by comparing Andrew Sullivan's *Virtually Normal: An Argument About Homosexuality* and Michael Warner's *The Trouble with Normal: Sex, Politics, and the Ethics of Queer Life.*

6. The title of a book by William Connolly.

7. See, for example, Sara Diamond, *Facing the Wrath;* John Gallagher and Chris Bull, *Perfect Enemies;* or the discussions by John Green and Didi Herman in *The Politics of Gay Rights,* ed. Craig A. Rimmerman, Kenneth Wald, and Clyde Wilcox.

8. See especially the strong cases made by Alan Wolfe, *Marginalized in the Middle,* and Jeffrey Goldfarb, *Civility and Subversion.* In Britain some of the key figures to highlight the public role of the intellectual are Anthony Giddens—in numerous well-known books and in his Reith lectures, published as *Runaway World*—and Stuart Hall, especially through his formative role at the Open University. Although Giddens and Hall adopt the role, British intellectuals have generally been much more low-key.

9. A number of critics have drawn attention to alternative ways in which the private life can be discussed publicly. Perhaps most famously, Carole Gilligan contrasted what she called moral reasoning with the more rationalist approach of Lawrence Kohlberg. In so doing, Gilligan identified a mode of speech often found among women that is relatively more grounded, more particular, more concrete (that is, more focused on actual life situations), and at the same time more ambiguous and more prone to storytelling. Likewise, Deborah Tannen has

suggested that much of our public talk depends upon a combative imagery: we must argue, take sides, take a stance, criticize our enemies—and in this adversarial process men are often able to dominate women.

10. Putnam, *Bowling Alone: The Collapse and Revival of American Community*, p. 180.

11. See, for example, William A. Gamson, *Talking Politics;* Pippa Norris, *Critical Citizens;* Nina Eliasoph, *Avoiding Politics: How Americans Produce Apathy in Everyday Life.* Community studies also suggest involvements: see, among others, Arlene Stein, *The Stranger Next Door.*

12. See Ulrich Beck, *The Reinvention of Politics*, especially chap. 3.

13. Dineh M. Davis, "Women on the Net: Implications of Informal International Networking Surrounding the Fourth World Conference on Women," in *Digital Democracy: Policy and Politics in the Wired World,* ed. Cynthia Alexander and Leslie A. Pal, pp. 90–91.

14. See, for example, the essays collected in Kamala Kempadoo and Jo Doezema, eds., *Global Sex Workers: Rights, Resistance and Redefinition,* which conveys a fine sense of the emergence of a global public sphere of sex workers. On the globalization of sexualities more generally, see chap. 8.

15. Andrea Press and Elizabeth Cole, *Speaking of Abortion: Television and Authority in the Lives of Women,* pp. 125–26.

16. See Jane M. Shattuck, *The Talking Cure: TV Talk Shows and Women.*

17. Josh Gamson, *Freaks Talk Back,* p. 13.

18. Patricia Joyner Priest, *Public Intimacies: Talk Show Participants and Tell-All TV,* p. 105.

19. Elayne Rapping, quoted in J. Gamson, *Freaks Talk Back,* p. 13. On the so-called Oprahfication of America, see also Patricia Priest, *Public Intimacies,* and Kathleen S. Lowney, *Baring Our Souls: TV Talk Shows and the Religion of Recovery.* The former is good at locating the different kinds of contestants—such as marginalized people or promoters of various products—who go on talk shows; the latter suggests that far from being dens of iniquity, these shows do indeed offer a new kind of American civil religion, providing meaning to people's confused lives.

20. *Guardian,* March 14, 2001, citing data obtained from Linx (the London Internet Exchange), a nonprofit organization.

21. And, of course, sites are often international. It is interesting to compare approaches to artificial reproduction. The largest British Web site (http://www.hfea.gov.uk) is that maintained by the government; its language is very formal, as are the rules that regulate artificial reproduction in Britain. In contrast, there are numerous American Web sites that offer information about artificial reproduction, most of which are commercial (see, e.g., http://www.surrogacy.com).

22. I am very grateful to Jody O'Brien for a personal communication in which she shared some of her ideas about digital communication.

23. Eric O. Clarke, *Virtuous Vice: Homoeroticism in the Public Sphere*, p. 1. For another lively discussion of the public sphere and its relation to gay life, see Michael Warner, *Publics and Counterpublics.*

24. See the listings in any issue of *Gay Times*, the long-running British gay magazine, from which my examples were culled. But any gay newspaper in any big city is likely to provide comparable listings.

25. On "Ivory Closets," see Jeffrey Escoffier's "Inside the Ivory Closet: The Challenge Facing Lesbian and Gay Studies," in his *American Homo.* The concept of "social worlds" is much wider than community and group and points to fragmenting and changing wider reference groups across the globe with which people identify. The term is developed in the work of Anselm Strauss; see his "A Social World Perspective" and *Continual Permutations of Action.*

26. I am reminded here of the classic race-relations–cycle model of Robert Park and others—in the shared elements of conflict, adjustment, and ultimately assimilation.

27. Stephen O. Murray has suggested that what is distinctive about the modern gay experience is the way it combines four characteristics: It is, as he says, "the combination of (1) a consciousness of group distinctiveness, (2) separate institutions and culture (deassimilation) based on the possibilities of (3) egalitarian (not gender-role bound or involving the submission of the young) and of (4) exclusive (not bisexual) same-sex relations" (*American Gay*, p. 2).

28. See the interesting case study of Los Angeles by Moira Rachel Kenney, *Mapping Gay L.A.*

29. The idea of looking at the contributions of gay culture to the culture at large was suggested by the epilogue to Richard Parker's *Beneath the Equator: Cultures of Desire, Male Homosexuality and Emerging Gay Communities in Brazil.* The terms "safe sex" and "safer sex" were introduced into the gay community (through Gay Men's Health Crisis in New York) as early as 1982. Subsequently, they have been adopted worldwide and by major organizations such as the United Nations. See Jeff Escoffier, "The Invention of Safer Sex," 1999.

30. Plummer, *Telling Sexual Stories: Power, Change and Social Worlds*, p. 126.

31. Todd Gitlin, "From Universality to Difference: Notes on the Fragmentation of the Idea of the Left," in *Social Theory and the Politics of Identity*, ed. Craig Calhoun, p. 152.

32. An early, important, and still influential articulation of the need for a gay consciousness is found in Steve Epstein, "Gay Politics, Ethnic Identity", *Socialist Review* 17, nos. 3–4 (May–August 1987).

33. Shane Phelan, *Identity Politics: Lesbian Feminism and the Limits of Community*, p. 136. Identity theory is now littered with such terms, as is evident in the work of scholars like Stuart Hall, Iris Marion Young, Paul Gilroy, Steve Seidman, Jeffrey Weeks, and Kath Woodward. See, for instance, Kath Woodward, ed., *Identity and Difference;* Steven Seidman, *Difference Troubles: Queering Social Theory and Sexual Politics;* and Steven Seidman, ed., *Queer Theory / Sociology.*

34. See Jeffrey Weeks, Brian Heaphy, and Catherine Donovan, *Same Sex Intimacies*, pp. 89–90.

## 6. Dialogic Citizenship

1. See Mary Kaldor, *New and Old Wars*.

2. See the discussions in Rickie Solinger, *Beggars and Choosers*.

3. According to *The Observer*, Apr. 22, 2001: "Damned If You Do," p. 1.

4. Taylor, "The Politics of Recognition," pp. 32–33.

5. Dean, *Solidarity of Strangers*; quotes are from pages 3 and 29.

6. See Duggan, *Sex Wars*; and Berger, *The War over the Family*.

7. Tannen, *The Argument Culture*. The material presented here is largely derived from Tannen's chap. 1; short quotes are from pages 5, 6, and 10.

8. Hunter, *Culture Wars*, p. 42.

9. See John Green, "Varieties of Opposition to Gay Rights," in Rimmerman et al., *The Politics of Gay Rights*, pp. 121–38; Didi Herman, "The Gay Agenda Is the Devil's Agenda: The Christian Right's Vision and the Role of the State," in Rimmerman, *The Politics of Gay Rights*, pp. 139–60.

10. For a recent important discussion of the links between the emotional and political and the need to bring a modestly cautious therapeutic approach to all political debate, see Samuels, *Politics on the Couch*.

11. Ackerman, "Why dialogue?" p. 5.

12. In my more pessimistic moments, I seriously doubt that there will be a future. The twentieth century was arguably the most inhumane in history, and the twenty-first has gotten off to a very poor start, too. As I write this, the date is September 11, 2001. I will not comment, except to say that lying close to me is a book by Jonathan Glover called *Humanity: A Moral History of the Twentieth Century*.

13. Davis, "Women on the Net," p. 99.

14. W. Barnett Pearce and Stephen Littlejohn, *Moral Conflict*, chap. 8.

15. I draw heavily here on Casparty, *Dewey on Democracy*, pp. 148–51, and on Ginsburg, *Contested Lives*.

16. The classic statement of this is Lewis Coser's *The Functions of Social Conflict*.

17. Barber, *Conquest of Politics*, p. 51.

## 7. Stories and the Grounded Moralities of Everyday Life

1. I develop this idea later. Much of this distinction is derived from Selma Sevenhuijsen, *Citizenship and the Ethics of Care*, as well as the work of Jane Ribbens McCarthy and others. I thank Carol Smart for leading me to these issues.

2. Thomas Franck, *The Empowered Self*, p. 61.

3. Bauman, *Post-Modern Ethics*, p. 10.

4. I draw from the work of John Gibbins and Bo Reimer, *The Politics of Postmodernity*; quotes are on pp. 98, 99, 100, 102, respectively. They suggest that

these values can now be found among a small but growing group of Europeans, especially among the young and educated and in Holland and Sweden. Likewise, I draw from Ronald Inglehart's "World Values" study, which looks at a wider range of countries and sees postmodern values appearing in many societies. See his *Modernization and Postmodernization,* and updates on the World Values Web site.

5. James Holstein and Jaber Gubrium, *The Self We Live By,* p. 215.

6. Citations from *The Social Construction of Virtue* are all from page 185 (italics are mine). But see also the now neglected work of Jack Douglas, especially *American Social Order,* for a strong treatment of everyday moralities (e.g., p. 149).

7. See Carol Gilligan, *In a Different Voice;* Lyn Brown and Carol Gilligan, *Meeting at the Crossroads;* and Susan Hekman, *Moral Voices, Moral Selves.*

8. Candace Clark, *Misery and Company,* p. 274. Clark introduces her major discussion of sympathy in everyday life through an array of mini-concepts, such as "sympathy etiquette" and "sympathy giving."

9. Gay Becker *The Elusive Embryo,* chap 2.

10. Kathryn Addelson, *Moral Passages.*

11. This is linked to a major argument developed by Tom Scheff. See Tom Scheff and Suzanne M. Retzinger, *Emotions and Violence.*

12. For a fuller analysis, see Booth, "On the Idea of the Moral Economy."

13. As diverse as Alisdair MacIntyre, Richard Rorty, Seyla Benhabib, Benjamin Barber, Iris Marion Young, Kathryn Pyne Addelson, and Hannah Arendt.

14. MacIntyre, *After Virtue,* p. 201.

15. Martha Nussbaum, *Love's Knowledge,* p. 95.

16. Gilligan, *In a Different Voice,* p. 174

17. Rorty, *Contingency, Irony and Solidarity,* p. xvi.

18. Rorty, "Posties," p. 12.

19. Rorty, *Philosophy and the Mirror of Nature,* pp. 370, 378.

20. Maria Pia Lara, *Moral Textures,* p. 1.

21. Ibid., p. 18. "Moral identities (are) products of performative narratives between social groups and civil society that simultaneously create and reconfigure the symbolic order" (p. 24).

22. Ibid., p. 171.

23. See Plummer, *Telling Sexual Stories;* Plummer, *Documents of Life,* p. 2. See also "The Role of Public Ethnography at Century's End" and "The Call of Stories."

24. The phrase is Martha Nussbaum's.

25. Smart and Neal, *Family Fragments,* p. 32 (my italics); Morgan is quoted on p. 112.

26. Smart and Neal, *Family Fragments,* p. 114. For details of the stories mentioned here, see ibid., chap. 6.

27. McCarthy et al., *Parenting and Step-Parenting,* p. 16.

28. For an enlightening series of moral stories about aging, see Jaber Gubrium, *Speaking of Life: Horizons of Meaning for Nursing Home Residents.*

29. The quotes from Weeks et al., *Same Sex Intimacies,* are on pages 62, 75, and 60, respectively.

30. I think also of Peter Nardi, *Gay Friendships,* and Chris Carrington, *No Place Like Home,* along with Smart and Neal's "Negotiating Parenthood" Project; see also Judith Stacey's *Brave New Families,* and Gillian Dunne, *The Lesbian Household Project.*

31. Smart and Neal, *Family Fragments,* p. 10.

32. See Robert Coles, *Lives of Moral Leadership.*

33. For the uninitiated, the controversies around most of these names can be found quite easily on Web sites. Quite frequently they have also become the topics of books or films.

34. For a fuller discussion of this insightful study, see Hunt, *O. J. Simpson,* esp. chap. 2.

35. See ibid.; Stein et al., "A Symposium on the Clinton-Lewinsky Affair," pp. 247–66; and Lull and Hinerman, eds., *Media Scandals.* Hollway and Jefferson, "A Kiss Is Just a Kiss," provides an example of using these cases for a full-scale analysis.

36. Richardson, ed., *On the Problem of Surrogate Parenthood: Analysing the Baby M Case;* Chesler, *Sacred Bond: The Legacy of Baby M.*

37. Details of the Kilshaw story are taken from *The Independent,* Jan. 23, 2001; *The Guardian,* March 2 and Apr. 10, 2001; and Guardian.co.uk/twins.

38. See Weeks, *Invented Moralities;* Shanley, *Making Babies, Making Families;* Giddens, *The Third Way;* Petchesky, "Sexual Rights."

39. James Hunter, *The Death of Character,* p. 209.

40. See Norris, ed., *Critical Citizens.*

41. But most notably, for me, Nussbaum's *Sex and Social Justice.*

42. Nussbaum, *Sex and Social Justice,* p. 39.

43. Once again I find myself producing a synoptical listing from a huge literature and debate. I can only defend myself by saying that this was always meant to be a short book that only opened up issues. These issues are far too grand to be developed here.

44. Taylor, "The Politics of Recognition," p. 37. See also Honneth, *The Struggle for Recognition: The Moral Grammar of Social Conflicts.*

45. An important lead here must be the work of G. H. Mead and the idea of generalized other: *Mind, Self and Society.* See also Stanley Cohen's moving *States of Denial* on the problems of relating to others who torture and destroy your loved ones.

46. Tronto, *Moral Boundaries,* p. 103

47. Selma Sevenhuijsen, *Citizenship and the Ethics of Care,* p. 107

48. Tronto, *Moral Boundaries,* especially pp. 111–24.

49. Twine, *Citizenship and Social Rights,* p. 32.

50. Wolfe discusses all of this in two books: *One Nation, After All* and *Moral Freedom.*

51. Wolfe, *Moral Freedom,* pp. 196–97.

## 8. Globalizing Intimate Citizenship

1. See Roland Robertson's *Globalisation* for a history of the flows between nations since at least the 1500s.

2. Giddens, *Runaway World;* Beck, *What Is Globalization?,* p 19.

3. The United Nations Children's Fund, March 2001, press release.

4. *Early Marriages, Child Spouses.* UNICEF Report, March 2001.

5. The idea of global flows was first put forward by Arjun Appadurai, "Disjuncture and Difference in the Global Culture Economy," 1990.

6. For a quick introduction and overview, look at the United Nations Web site on AIDS: http://www.unaids.

7. Ideas of creolization and hybridization are borrowed from Jan Pieterse, "Globalization as Hybridization," 1995.

8. Bauman, *Globalization,* chap. 4.

9. For a key recent discussion of modern slavery and enforced work, see Kevin Bale, *Disposable People: New Slavery in the Global Economy.*

10. Beck, "Living Your Own Life in a Runaway World," p. 168

11. Beck outlines fifteen propositions for the globalized personal life in "Living Your Own Life in a Runaway World"; I draw on them freely here. He clearly believes it is true of all the world, citing Indian taxi drivers.

12. Castells, *End of Millennium,* esp. chap. 3 (vol. 3 of *The Information Age*).

13. Ibid., pp. 61–65.

14. Altman, *Global Sex.*

15. See Arlie Russell Hochschild, "Global Care Chains," p. 131. She draws notably on the work of Rhacel Parrenas, *The Global Servants* (forthcoming).

16. UNHCR, *The State of the World's Refugees,* p. 11.

17. Hochschild, "Global Care Chains," p. 140.

18. For an extended discussion of all this, see Barbara Ehrenreich and Arlie Russell Hochschild, *Global Woman: Nannies, Maids and Sex Workers in the New Economy,* 2002.

19. Giddens, *Runaway World,* p. 6.

20. See Farrer, "Disco Super Culture," p. 157.

21. For a strong, persuasive, and popular critique, see Naomi Klein's *No Logo.*

22. Bech, *When Men Meet Men;* Parker, *Beneath the Equator.*

23. See Chapkis, *Live Sex Acts: Women Performing Erotic Labor.*

24. *New Internationalist,* Apr. 1998, p. 29.

25. Christa Wichterich, *The Globalized Woman: Reports from a Future of Inequality,* pp. vii–ix.

26. Nancy Scheper-Hughes, "The Global Traffic in Human Organs" and "Commodity Fetishism in Organs Trafficking." I draw heavily in the text from the latter, pp. 34–36. There is also a Web site for Organs Watch based at the University of California at Berkeley.

27. Amnesty International, *Crimes of Hate, Conspiracy of Silence*. See also Vanessa Bird, *The No-Nonsense Guide to Sexual Diversity*.

28. Cited in *The Guardian*, Aug. 6, 1998, p. 10.

29. Margaret Aarmo, "How Homosexuality Became Un-African: The Case of Zimbabwe."

30. Giddens, *Runaway World*, pp. 68, 71, 75. It is Giddens who speaks of "democratizing democracy."

31. Some of the key documents of this period—from the United Nations Universal Declaration of Human Rights 1948 to the Beijing Declaration on Women's Global Rights 1995—have been usefully gathered in Ishay's *The Human Rights Reader*. Early days involved founding the Charter of the World Health Organization (1946), the Universal Declaration of Human Rights (1948), which became the International Bill of Human Rights. Complete texts of most of these are also on Web sites.

32. See, in particular, the account of cosmopolitanism provided by Ulrich Beck in *World Risk Society*, chaps. 1 and 2.

33. Held et al., op cit., pp. 65–70; Barber, *Jihad vs McWorld*, p. 277.

34. Albrow, *Global Age*, p. 177.

35. Rosalind Petchesky suggests that sexual rights are "the newest kid on the block in international debates about the meanings and practices of human rights" in Parker et al., *Framing the Sexual Subject*, p. 13.

36. See Hartman, "The Population Control Movement." She argues that "the myth of overpopulation is one of the most pervasive myths in Western society, so deeply ingrained in the culture that it profoundly shapes the culture's world view" (p. 4).

37. Rosalind Petchesky and Karen Judd, *Negotiating Reproductive Rights*, p. 1. They draw upon the Vienna Declaration and Programme of Action (1993), the ICPD Programme of Action (1994), and the FWCW Declaration and Platform for Action (1995).

38. It is part of the Women's Global Network for Reproductive Rights (WGNFRR).

39. Petchesky and Judd, *Negotiating Reproductive Rights*, p. 10.

40. Ibid., pp. 91–94.

41. Cited in Petchesky, "Sexual Rights," p. 87.

42. Ignatieff, *Human Rights as Politics and Idolatry*, p. 64.

43. Felice, *Taking Suffering Seriously*, p. 18.

44. Shashi Tharoor, "Are Human Rights Universal?," *New Internationalist*, no. 332 (March 2001), pp. 332–33.

## 9. The Intimate Citizenship Project

1. Here I suggest that the recent critical attacks on "humanism" made by post-structural, postcolonial, and feminist thinkers do not necessitate a rejection of the term, but highlight the need for a reworking of it. Humanism is in fact a very old tradition and does not necessarily imply the autonomous "unencumbered" self that philosophers of the Western liberal tradition often imply. The humanism I would like to see developed would encourage a view of human beings as an "embedded," dialogic, contingent, embodied, universal self with a moral (and political) character. They are open to changes. A useful starting point for this rethinking would come from Mead, James, Dewey, and what has been called the symbolic interactionist tradition.

# Bibliography

Aarmo, Margaret. "How Homosexuality Became Un-African: The Case of Zim-babwe." In *Female Desires: Transgender Practices Across Cultures,* ed. Evelyn Blackwood and Saskia E. Wieringa, pp. 255–79. New York: Columbia University Press, 1999.

Ackerman, Bruce. "Why Dialogue?" *Journal of Philosophy* 86 (1989): 5–22.

Adam, Barry, J. W. Duyvendak, and A. Krouwel, eds. *The Global Emergence of Gay and Lesbian Politics.* Philadelphia: Temple University Press, 1998.

Addelson, Kathryn Pyne. *Moral Passages: Toward a Collectivist Moral Theory.* London: Routledge, 1994.

Albrow, Martin. "Globalization: Myths and Realities." Inaugural Lecture, Roehampton Institute, London, Nov. 28, 1994.

———. *The Global Age: State and Society Beyond Modernity.* Cambridge: Polity Press, 1996.

Alexander, Cynthia J., and Leslie A. Pal, eds. *Digital Democracy: Policy and Politics in the Wired World.* New York: Oxford University Press, 1998.

Allen, Beverley. *Rape Warfare: The Hidden Genocide in Bosnia-Herzegovina and Croatia.* Minneapolis: University of Minnesota Press, 1996.

Altman, Dennis. "Global Gays / Global Gaze." *GLQ* 3 (1997): 417–36.

———. *Global Sex.* Chicago: University of Chicago Press, 2001.

Amnesty International. *Crimes of Hate, Conspiracy of Silence: Torture and Ill Treatment Based on Sexual Identity.* London: Amnesty International, 2001.

Appadurai, Arjun. "Disjuncture and Difference in the Global Cultural Economy." In *Global Culture: Nationalism, Globalization and Modernity,* ed. Mike Featherstone, pp. 295–310. London: Sage, 1990.

Bale, Kevin. *Disposable People: New Slavery in the Global Economy.* Berkeley: University of California Press, 1999.

Barber, Benjamin. *Strong Democracy: Participatory Politics for a New Age.* Berkeley: University of California Press, 1984.

———. *The Conquest of Politics: Liberal Philosophy in Democratic Times.* Princeton, N.J.: Princeton University Press, 1988.

———. *Jihad vs. McWorld: How Globalism and Tribalism Are Reshaping the World.* New York: Random House, 1995.

Barret, Robert L., and Bryan E. Robinson. *Gay Fathers: Encouraging the Hearts of Gay Dads and Their Families.* Rev. ed. San Francisco: Jossey-Bass, 2000.

Barry, Kathleen. *The Prostitution of Sexuality: The Global Exploitation of Women.* New York: New York University Press, 1995.

Baudrillard, Jean. *The Vital Illusion.* New York: Columbia University Press, 2000.

Bauman, Zygmunt. *Post-Modern Ethics.* Cambridge: Polity Press, 1993.

———. *Postmodernity and Its Discontents.* Cambridge: Polity Press, 1997.

————. *Globalization: The Human Consequences.* Cambridge: Polity Press, 1998.

————. *In Search of Politics.* Cambridge: Polity Press, 1999.

————. *Liquid Society.* Cambridge: Polity Press, 2000.

————. *The Individualized Society.* Cambridge: Polity Press, 2001.

Bawer, Bruce. *A Place at the Table: The Gay Individual in American Society.* New York: Simon and Schuster, 1994.

Bech, Henning. *When Men Meet Men: Homosexuality and Modernity.* Cambridge: Polity Press, 1997.

Beck, Ulrich. *The Reinvention of Politics: Rethinking Modernity in the Global Social Order.* Cambridge: Polity Press, 1997.

————. *World Risk Society.* Cambridge: Polity Press, 1999.

————. *Brave New World of Work.* Cambridge: Polity Press, 2000.

————. "Living Your Own Life in a Runaway World: Individualization, Globalization and Politics." In *On the Edge: Living with Global Capitalism,* ed. Will Hutton and Anthony Giddens, pp. 164–74. London: Cape, 2000.

————. *What Is Globalization?* Cambridge: Polity Press, 2000.

Beck, Ulrich, and Elizabeth Beck-Gernsheim. *The Normal Chaos of Love.* Cambridge: Polity Press, 1995.

Beck, Ulrich, Anthony Giddens, and Scott Lash, eds. *Reflexive Modernization: Politics, Tradition and Aesthetics in the Modern Social Order.* Cambridge: Polity Press, 1994.

Becker, Gay. *The Elusive Embryo: How Women and Men Approach New Reproductive Technologies.* Berkeley: University of California Press, 2000.

Becker, Howard S. *Doing Things Together: Selected Papers.* Evanston, Ill.: Northwestern University Press, 1986.

Beck-Gernsheim, Elizabeth. *The Social Implications of Bioengineering.* Atlantic Highlands, N.J.: Humanities Press, 1995.

Beiner, Ronald, ed. *Theorizing Citizenship.* Albany, N.Y.: SUNY Press, 1995.

Bell, David, and Jon Binnie. *The Sexual Citizen: Queer Politics and Beyond.* Cambridge: Polity Press, 2000.

Bell, David, and Barbara M. Kennedy. *The Cybercultures Reader.* London: Routledge, 2000.

Berger, Peter, Brigitte Berger, and Hansfried Kellner. *The Homeless Mind: Modernization and Consciousness.* New York: Random House, 1973.

Berger, Peter, and William Eerdmans, eds. *The Desecularization of the World: Resurgent Religion and World Politics.* Washington, D.C.: Ethics and Public Policy Center; Grand Rapids, Mich.: Eerdmans Pub., c. 1999.

Berlin, Isaiah. *Four Essays on Liberty.* London: Oxford University Press, 1969.

Best, Joel. *Threatened Children: Rhetoric and Concern about Child Victims.* Chicago: University of Chicago Press, 1990.

Billig, Michael. *Arguing and Thinking: A Rhetorical Approach to Social Psychology.* Cambridge: Cambridge University Press, 1987.

Bishop, Ryan, and Lillian Robinson. *Night Market: Sexual Cultures and the Thai Economic Miracle.* London: Routledge, 1998.

Blanchard, Dallas A. *The Anti-Abortion Movement and the Rise of the Religious Right: From Polite to Fiery Protest.* New York: Twayne, 1994.

Bly, Robert. *Iron John: A Book About Men.* Longmead, Dorset: Element Books, 1990.

Booth, William James. "On the Ideas of the Moral Economy." *American Political Science Review* 88 (1994): 653–58.

Bornstein, Kate. *Gender Outlaw: On Men, Women, and the Rest of Us.* New York: Routledge, 1994.

————. *My Gender Workbook.* New York: Routledge, 1998.

Boswell, John. *The Marriage of Likeness: Same-Sex Unions in Pre-Modern Europe.* London: Fontana Press, 1994.

Bourdieu, Pierre. *Outline of a Theory of Practice.* Cambridge: Cambridge University Press, 1997.

————. *The Weight of the World: Social Suffering in Contemporary Society.* Cambridge: Polity Press, 1999.

Bridges, Thomas. *The Culture of Citizenship: Inventing Postmodern Civic Culture,* Albany, N.Y.: SUNY Press, 1994.

Bronski, Michael. *The Pleasure Principle: Sex, Backlash, and the Struggle for Sexual Freedom.* New York: St. Martin's Press, 1998.

Brown, Lyn Mikel, and Carol Gilligan. *Meeting at the Crossroads: Women's Psychology and Girls' Development.* Cambridge, Mass.: Harvard University Press, 1992.

Browning, Gary, Abbey Halcli, and Frank Webster, eds. *Theory and Society: Understanding the Present.* London: Sage, 2000.

Bulmer, Martin, and Anthony M. Rees, eds. *Citizenship Today: The Contemporary Relevance of T. H. Marshall.* London: UCL Press, 1996.

Calhoun, Craig, ed. *Habermas and the Public Sphere.* Cambridge, Mass.: MIT Press, 1992.

————, ed. *Social Theory and the Politics of Identity.* Oxford: Blackwell, 1994.

Califia, Pat. *Public Sex: The Culture of Radical Sex.* San Francisco: Cleis Press, 1994.

Cancian, Francesca. *Love in America: Gender and Self-Development.* Cambridge: Cambridge University Press, 1987.

Carignano, Paul, Robin Andersen, Stanley Aronwitz, and William Difazo. "Chatter in the Age of Electronic Reproduction: Talk, Television and the Public Mind." *Sociotext* 25/26 (1990): 33–55.

Caspary, William R. *Dewey on Democracy.* Ithaca: Cornell University Press, 2000.

Castells, Manuel. *The Information Age.* 3 vols. (Vol. 1: *The Rise of the Network Society* [1996]; Vol. 2: *The Power of Identity* [1997]; Vol. 3: *End of Millennium* [1998]). Oxford: Blackwell.

Chadwick, Ruth. *Ethics, Reproduction and Genetic Control.* Rev. ed. London: Routledge, 1992.

Chancer, Lynn. *Reconcilable Differences: Confronting Beauty, Pornography, and the Future of Feminism.* Berkeley: University of California Press, 1998.

Chapkis, Wendy. *Live Sex Acts: Women Performing Erotic Labor.* New York: Routledge, 1997.

Chesler, Phyllis. *Sacred Bond: The Legacy of Baby M.* New York: Time Books, 1988.

Clark, Candace. *Misery and Company: Sympathy in Everyday Life.* Chicago: University of Chicago Press, 1997.

Clarke, Adele. *Disciplining Reproduction: Modernity, American Life Sciences, and the Problem of Sex.* Berkeley: University of California Press, 1998.

Clarke, Eric O. *Virtuous Vice: Homoeroticism and the Public Sphere.* Durham, N.C.: Duke University Press, 2000.

Clecak, Peter. *America's Quest for the Ideal Self.* New York: Oxford University Press, 1983.

Cohen, Stanley. *States of Denial: Knowing about Atrocities and Suffering.* Cambridge: Polity Press, 2000.

Cohen, Stanley, and Laurie Taylor, *Escape Attempts: The Theory and Practice of Resistance to Everyday Life.* 2d ed. New York: Routledge, 1991.

Coles, Robert. *Lives of Moral Leadership: Men and Women Who Have Made a Difference.* New York: Random House, 2001.

Connell, Robert. *Masculinities.* Cambridge: Polity Press, 1996.

Connolly, William. *The Ethos of Pluralization.* Minneapolis: University of Minnesota Press, 1995.

Conrad, Peter, and Joseph Schneider. *Medicalization and Deviance.* 2d ed. Philadelphia: Temple University Press, 1992.

Corea, Gena. *The Mother Machine.* New York: Harper and Row, 1985.

Coser, Lewis. *The Functions of Social Conflict.* London: Routledge and Kegan Paul, 1962.

Davis, Dineh M. "Women on the Net: Implications of Informal International Networking Surrounding the Fourth World Conference on Women." In *Digital Democracy: Policy and Politics in the Wired World,* ed. Cynthia Alexander and Leslie A. Pal, pp. 88–104. New York: Oxford University Press, 1998.

Dean, Jodi. *Solidarity of Strangers: Feminism after Identity Politics.* Berkeley: University of California Press, 1996.

Dewey, John. *Freedom and Culture.* New York: G. P. Putnam and Sons, 1939.

———. *The Public and Its Problems.* Chicago: Swallow Press, 1954.

———. *Human Nature and Conduct.* New York: Modern Library, 1992.

Diamond, Sara. *Roads to Dominion: Right Wing Movements and Political Power in the United States.* New York: Guilford Press, 1995.

———. *Facing the Wrath: Confronting the Right in Dangerous Times.* Monroe, Maine: Common Courage Press, 1996.

Douglas, Jack. *American Social Order: Social Rules in a Pluralistic Society.* New York: Free Press, 1971.

Duggan, Lisa, and Nan D. Hunter. *Sex Wars: Sexual Dissent and Political Culture.* New York: Routledge, 1995.

Dunham, Martin. *The Christian Right, the Far Right and the Boundaries of American Conservatism.* Manchester: Manchester University Press, 2000.

Dworkin, Andrea. *Right-Wing Women: The Politics of Domesticated Females.* London: Women's Press, 1983.

Echols, Alice. *Daring to Be Bad: Radical Feminism in America, 1967–1975.* Minneapolis: University of Minnesota Press, 1989.

Edwards, Jeanette, et al., eds. *Technologies of Procreation: Kinship in the Age of Assisted Conception.* 2d ed. London: Routledge, 1999.

Ehrenreich, Barbara, and Arlie Russell Hochschild, eds. *Global Woman: Nannies, Maids and Sex Workers in the New Economy.* New York: Metropolitan Books, 2002.

Eisenstein, Zillah. *Global Obscenities: Patriarchy, Capitalism, and the Lure of Cyberfantasy.* New York: New York University Press, 1998.

Elias, Norbert. *The Civilizing Process.* Trans. Edmund Jephcott. Oxford: Blackwell, 1978.

Eliasoph, Nina. *Avoiding Politics: How Americans Produce Apathy in Everyday Life.* Cambridge: Cambridge University Press, 1998.

Ellison, Nick. "Towards a New Social Politics: Citizenship and Reflexivity in Late Modernity." *Sociology* 31, no. 4 (Nov. 1997): 697–717.

Epstein, Steve. "Gay Politics, Ethnic Identity." *Socialist Review* 17, nos. 3–4 (May–Aug. 1987).

Escoffier, Jeffrey. "The Invention of Safer Sex." Berkeley *Journal of Sociology,* 43 (1999): 1–30.

Etzioni, Amitai. *The New Golden Rule: Community and Morality in a Democratic Society.* London: Profile, 1997.

———. *Next: The Road to the Good Society.* New York: Basic Books, 2001.

Evans, David. *Sexual Citizenship: The Material Construction of Sexualities.* London: Routledge, 1993.

Farrer, James. "Disco 'Super-Culture': Consuming Foreign Sex in the Chinese Disco." *Sexualities* 2, no. 2 (May 1999): 147–65.

Featherstone, Mike, ed. *Global Culture: Nationalism, Globalization and Modernity.* A Theory, Culture & Society special issue. London: Sage, 1990.

Felice, William E. *Taking Suffering Seriously: The Importance of Collective Human Rights.* Albany, N.Y.: SUNY Press, 1996.

Ferguson, Ann. "Sex War: The Debate Between Radical and Libertarian Feminists." *Signs* 10 (1984): 106–12.

Firestone, Shulamith. *The Dialectic of Sex: The Case for Feminist Revolution*. New York: Morrow, 1979.

Franck, Thomas M. *The Empowered Self: Law and Society in the Age of Individualism*. Oxford: Oxford University Press, 1999.

Franklin, Sarah. *Embodied Progress: A Cultural Account of Assisted Conception*. London: Routledge, 1997.

Fraser, Nancy. *Justice Interruptus: Critical Reflections on the Postsocialist Condition*. London: Routledge, 1997.

Fukuyama, Francis. *Trust: The Social Virtues and the Creation of Prosperity*. London: Hamish Hamilton, 1985.

———. *The Posthuman Future: Consequences of the Biotechnology Revolution*. London: Profile Books, 2002.

Gallagher, John, and Chris Bull. *Perfect Enemies: The Battle between the Religious Right and the Gay Movement*. 2d ed. 2001. Lanhan, Maryland: Madison Books.

Gamson, Josh. *Freaks Talk Back: Tabloid Talk Shows and Sexual Non-Conformity*. Chicago: University of Chicago Press, 1998.

Gamson, William A. *Talking Politics*. Cambridge: Cambridge University Press, 1992.

Gergen, Ken. *An Invitation to Social Construction*. London: Sage, 1999.

Gibbins, John R., and Bo Reimer. *The Politics of Postmodernity: An Introduction to Contemporary Politics and Culture*. London: Sage, 1999.

Giddens, Anthony. *Modernity and Self-Identity: Self and Society in the Late Modern Age*. Cambridge: Polity Press, 1991.

———. *The Transformation of Intimacy*. Cambridge: Polity Press, 1992.

———. *Beyond Left and Right: The Future of Radical Politics*. Cambridge: Polity Press, 1994.

———. *The Third Way: The Renewal of Social Democracy*. Cambridge: Polity Press, 1998.

———. *Runaway World: How Globalisation Is Shaping Our Lives*. London: Profile Books, 1999.

Gill, Richard T. *Posterity Lost: Progress, Ideology, and the Decline of the American Family*. New York: Rowman and Littlefield, 1997.

Gilligan, Carol. *In a Different Voice: Psychological Theory and Women's Development*. Cambridge, Mass.: Harvard University Press, 1982.

Ginsburg, Faye. *Contested Lives: The Abortion Debate in an American Community*. Updated ed. Berkeley: University of California Press, 1998.

Ginsburg, Faye, and Rayna Rapp, eds. *Conceiving the New World Order: The Global Politics of Reproduction*. Berkeley: University of California Press, 1995.

Gitlin, Todd. "From Universality to Difference: Notes on the Fragmentation of the Idea of the Left." *In Social Theory and the Politics of Identity*, ed. Craig Calhoun, pp. 150–74. Oxford: Blackwell, 1994.

Glover, Jonathan. *Humanity: A Moral History of the Twentieth Century*. New Haven, Conn.: Yale University Press, 2000.

Goldfarb, Jeffrey C. *Civility and Subversion: The Intellectual in Democratic Society.* Cambridge: Cambridge University Press, 1998.

Gordon, Lynda. *Woman's Body, Women's Right: A Social History of Birth Control in America.* New York: Grossman, 1976.

Gray, Chris Hables. *The Cyborg Citizen: Politics in the Posthuman Age.* London: Routledge, 2001.

Gray, Chris Hables, ed. *The Cyborg Handbook.* London: Routledge, 1995.

Gubrium, Jaber F. *Speaking of Life: Horizons of Meaning for Nursing Home Residents.* Hawthorne, N.Y.: Aldine de Gruyter, 1993.

Habermas, Jürgen. *The Structural Transformation of the Public Sphere: An Inquiry into a Category of Bourgeois Society.* Cambridge, Mass.: MIT Press, 1989.

———. *Justification and Application: Remarks on Discourse Ethics.* Cambridge, Mass.: MIT Press, 1993.

———. *Between Facts and Norms: Contributions to a Discourse Theory of Law and Democracy.* Trans. Ciaran Cronin. Cambridge, Mass.: MIT Press, 1993; Cambridge, Eng.: Polity Press, 1996.

Halberstam, Judith. *Female Masculinity.* Durham, N.C.: Duke University Press, 1998.

Halliday, Fred. *The World at 2000.* London: Palgrave, 2001.

Hamelink, Cees J. *The Ethics of Cyberspace.* London: Sage, 2000.

Harrison, Lawrence E., and Samuel P. Huntington, eds. *Culture Matters: How Values Shape Human Progress.* New York: Basic Books, 2000.

Hartmann, Betsy. *Reproductive Rights and Wrongs: The Global Politics of Population Control.* Rev. ed. Cambridge, Mass.: South End Press, 1995.

Havel, Václav. "The Hope for Europe." *New York Review of Books* 63, no. 8 (June 20, 1996): 38–41.

Hekman, Susan J. *Moral Voices, Moral Selves: Carol Gilligan and Feminist Moral Theory.* Cambridge: Polity Press, 1995.

———. *The Future of Differences: Truth and Method in Feminist Theory.* Cambridge: Polity Press, 1999.

Heller, Agnes, and Ferenc Feher. *The Postmodern Political Condition.* Cambridge: Polity Press, 1988.

Heman, Edward S., and Robert McChesney. *The Global Media: The New Missionaries of Global Capitalism.* London: Cassell, 1997.

Henize, Eric. *Sexual Orientation: A Human Right.* Dordrecht: Martinus Nijhoff, 1995.

Herman, Judith Lewis. *Trauma and Recovery.* New York: Basic Books, 1992.

Hill, Mike, and Warren Montag, eds. *Masses, Classes and the Public Sphere.* London: Verso, 2000.

Himmelfarb, Gertrude. *The Demoralization of Society: From Victorian Virtues to Modern Values.* London: Health and Welfare Unit, Institute of Economic Affairs, 1995.

———. *One Nation, Two Cultures.* New York: Vintage Books, 2001.

Hobsbawm, Eric. *Age of Extremes: The Short Twentieth Century, 1914–1991.* London: Michael Joseph, 1994.

Hochschild, Arlie Russell. *The Managed Heart: Commercialization of Human Feeling.* Berkeley: University of California Press, 1983.

———. "Global Care Chains and Emotional Surplus Value." In *On the Edge: Living with Global Capitalism,* ed. Will Hutton and Anthony Giddens, pp. 130–46. London: Cape, 2000.

Hollway, Wendy, and Tony Jefferson. "'A Kiss Is Just a Kiss': Date Rape, Gender, and Subjectivity." *Sexualities* 1 (4) (Nov. 1998): 405–25.

Holstein, James, and Jaber Gubrium. *The Self We Live By: Narrative Identity in a Postmodern World.* Oxford: Oxford University Press, 2000.

Honneth, Axel. *The Struggle for Recognition: The Moral Grammar of Social Conflict.* Cambridge: Polity Press, 1995.

Hopkins, Patrick D., ed. *Sex / Machine: Readings in Culture, Gender, and Technology.* Bloomington: Indiana University Press, 1998.

Hunt, Darnell M. *O. J. Simpson, Facts and Fictions: News Rituals in the Construction of Reality.* Cambridge: Cambridge University Press, 1999.

Hunter, James Davison. *Culture Wars: The Struggle to Define America.* New York: Basic Books, 1991.

———. *Before the Shooting Begins: Searching for Democracy in America's Culture War.* New York: Free Press, 1994.

———. *The Death of Character: Moral Education in an Age Without Good or Evil.* New York: Basic Books, 2000.

Huntington, Samuel P. *The Clash of Civilizations and the Remaking of the World Order.* New York: Simon and Schuster, 1996.

Hutton, Will, and Anthony Giddens, eds. *On the Edge: Living with Global Capitalism.* London: Cape, 2000.

Ignatieff, Michael. *Human Rights as Politics and Idolatry.* Edited, with intro. by Amy Gutmann. Princeton, N.J.: Princeton University Press, 2001.

Inglehart, Ronald. *Modernization and Postmodernization: Cultural and Economic Change in Forty-Three Societies.* Princeton, N.J.: Princeton University Press, 1997.

Irvine, Janice. *Discourses of Desire: Sex and Gender in Modern American Sexology.* Philadelphia: Temple University Press, 1990.

Ishay, Micheline, ed. *The Human Rights Reader,* New York: Routledge, 1997.

Isin, Engin F., and Bryan S. Turner, eds. *Handbook of Citizenship Studies.* London: Sage, 2002.

Isin, Engin F., and Patricia K. Wood. *Citizenship and Identity.* London: Sage, 1999.

Iyer, Pico. *The Global Soul.* London: Bloomsbury, 2000.

Jackson, Stevi. *Heterosexuality in Question.* London: Sage, 1999.

Jacoby, Russell. *Social Amnesia: A Critique of Conformist Psychology from Adler to Laing.* Boston: Beacon Press, 1977.

Jamieson, Lynn. *Intimacy: Personal Relationships in Modern Society.* Cambridge: Polity Press, 1998.

Janoski, Thomas. *Citizenship and Civil Society: A Framework of Rights and Obligations in Liberal, Traditional and Social Democratic Regimes.* Cambridge: Cambridge University Press, 1998.

Jordan, Tim. *Cyberpower: The Culture and Politics of Cyberspace and the Internet.* London: Routledge, 1999.

Kaldor, Mary. *New and Old Wars: Organized Violence in a Global Era.* Cambridge: Polity Press, 1990.

Kass, Leon R. "Preventing a Brave New World: Why We Should Ban Human Cloning Now." *New Republic,* May 5, 2001.

Kempadoo, Kamala, and Jo Doezema, eds. *Global Sex Workers: Rights, Resistance and Redefinition.* London: Routledge, 1998.

Kendrik, Walter. *The Erotic Museum: Pornography in Modern Culture.* New York: Viking Penguin, 1999.

Kenney, Moira Rachel. *Mapping Gay L.A.* Philadelphia: Temple University Press, 2001.

Kimmel, Michael S. *The Gendered Society.* Oxford: Oxford University Press, 2000.

Kirk, Marshall, and Hunter Madsen. *After the Ball: How America Will Conquer Its Hatred and Fear of Homosexuals in the '90s.* New York: Doubleday, 1989.

Klein, Naomi. *No Logo.* London: Flamingo, 2001.

Klug, Francesca. *Values for a Godless Age: The Story of the United Kingdom Bill of Rights.* Harmondsworth, Eng.: Penguin Books, 2000.

Kymlicka, Will. *Multicultural Citizenship.* Oxford: Clarendon Press, 1997.

Lakoff, George. *Moral Politics: What Conservatives Know that Liberals Don't.* Chicago: University of Chicago Press, 1996.

Landes, Joan B., ed. *Feminism: The Public and the Private.* Oxford: Oxford University Press, 1998.

Lara, Maria Pia. *Moral Textures: Feminist Narratives in the Public Sphere.* Cambridge: Polity Press, 1998.

Lasch, Christopher. *Haven in a Heartless World: The Family Beseiged.* New York: Basic Books, 1977.

Lash, Scott. "Reflexivity and Its Doubles." In *Reflexive Modernization: Politics, Tradition and Aesthetics in the Modern Social Order,* ed. Ulrich Beck, Anthony Gidden, and Scott Lash. Cambridge: Polity Press, 1994.

Lehr, Valerie. *Queer Family Values: Debunking the Myth of the Nuclear Family.* Philadelphia: Temple University Press, 1999.

Leidholdt, Dorchen, and Janice Raymond, eds. *The Sexual Liberals and the Attack on Feminism.* New York: Pergamon Press, 1999.

Levine, Judith. *Harmful to Minors: The Perils of Protecting Children from Sex.* Minneapolis: University of Minnesota Press, 2003.

Lienesch, Michael. *Redeeming America: Piety and Politics in the New Christian Right.* Chapel Hill: University of North Carolina Press, 1993.

Lister, Ruth. *Citizenship: Feminist Perspectives.* London: Macmillan, 1997.

Loseke, Donileen R. *Thinking about Social Problems.* New York: Aldine de Gruyter, 1999.

Lowney, Kathleen S. *Baring Our Souls: TV Talk Shows and the Religion of Recovery.* New York: Aldine de Gruyter, 1999.

Luker, Kristin. *Abortion and the Politics of Motherhood.* Berkeley: University of California Press, 1984.

Lukes, Steven. *Individualism.* Oxford: Basil Blackwell, 1973.

Lull, James, and Stephen Hinerman, eds. *Media Scandals: Morality and Desire in the Public Marketplace.* Cambridge: Polity Press, 1997.

Lupton, Deborah. *The Emotional Self: A Sociocultural Exploration.* London: Sage, 1998.

Lyon, David. *The Surveillance Society: Monitoring Everyday Life.* Buckingham, UK: Open University Press, 2001.

MacIntyre, Alisdair. *After Virtue.* 2d ed. Notre Dame, Ill.: University of Notre Dame Press, 1997.

Marshall, T. H. *Citizenship and Social Class and Other Essays.* Cambridge: Cambridge University Press, 1950.

————. *Sociology at the Crossroads, and Other Essays.* London: Heinemann, 1963.

Marty, Martin E., and R. Scott Appleby, eds. *Fundamentalisms Comprehended.* Vol. 5 of the Fundamentalism Project. Chicago: University of Chicago Press, 1995.

McCarthy, Jane Ribbens, Rosalind Edwards, and Val Gillies. *Parenting and Step-Parenting: Contemporary Moral Tales.* Occasional Paper no. 4. Oxford: Centre for Family and Household Research, Brookes University, 2000.

Mead, George Herbert. *Mind, Self, and Society.* Chicago: University of Chicago Press, 1933.

Melucci, Alberto. *The Playing Self: Person and Meaning in the Planetary Society.* Cambridge: Cambridge University Press, 1996.

Micklethwait, John, and Adrian Wooldridge. *A Future Perfect: The Challenge and Hidden Promise of Globalism.* London: Heinemann, 2000.

Mills, Charles Wright. *The Sociological Imagination.* New York: Oxford University Press, 1959.

Mohanty, Chandra Talpade, Ann Russo, and Lourdes Torres, eds. *Third World Women and the Politics of Feminism.* Bloomington: Indiana University Press, 1991.

Morgan, David H. J. *Family Connections: An Introduction to Family Studies.* Cambridge: Polity Press, 1996.

Morone, James A. "The Corrosive Politics of Virtue." *American Prospect,* June 1996.

Mount, Ferdinand. *The Subversive Family: An Alternative History of Love and Marriage.* London: Cape, 1982.

Mulkay, Michael. *The Embryo Research Debate.* Cambridge: Cambridge University Press, 1997.

Murray, Stephen O. *American Gay.* Chicago: University of Chicago Press, 1996.

Nardi, Peter M. *Gay Men's Friendships: Invincible Communities.* Chicago: University of Chicago Press, 1999.

Nardi, Peter M., and Beth Schneider, eds. *Social Perspectives in Lesbian and Gay Studies.* London: Routledge, 1998.

Noblit, George W., Van O. Dempsey, Belmira Bueno, and Peter Hessling. *The Social Construction of Virtue: The Moral Life of Schools.* Albany, N.Y.: SUNY Press, 1996.

Norris, Pippa, ed. *Critical Citizens: Global Support for Democratic Governance.* Oxford: Oxford University Press, 1999.

Nussbaum, Martha C. *Love's Knowledge: Essays on Philosophy and Literature.* New York: Oxford University Press, 1990.

———. *Sex and Social Justice.* Oxford: Oxford University Press, 1999.

———. *Women and Development.* Cambridge: Cambridge University Press, 2000.

———. *The Fragility of Goodness: Luck and Ethics in Greek Tragedy and Philosophy.* Updated edition. Cambridge: Cambridge University Press, 2001.

Okin, Susan Moller, with respondents. *Is Multiculturalism Bad for Women?* Princeton, N.J.: Princeton University Press, 1999.

O'Neill, Onora. *Autonomy and Trust in Bioethics.* The Gifford Lectures. Cambridge: Cambridge University Press, 2002.

———. *A Question of Trust.* The BBC Reith Lectures. Cambridge: Cambridge University Press, 2002.

Ong, Aihwa. *Flexible Citizenship: The Cultural Logics of Transnationality.* Durham, N.C.: Duke University Press, 1999.

Parker, Richard. *Beneath the Equator: Cultures of Desire, Male Homosexuality and Emerging Gay Communities in Brazil.* London: Routledge, 1999.

Parker, Richard, Regina Maria Barbosa, and Peter Aggleton, eds. *Framing the Sexual Subject: The Politics of Gender, Sexuality, and Power.* Berkeley: University of California Press, 2000.

Pearce, W. Barnett, and Stephen W. Littlejohn. *Moral Conflict: When Social Worlds Collide.* London: Sage, 1997.

Peraldi, François. *Polysexuality.* No. 10 of *Semiotext(e).* New York: Columbia University Press, 1981.

Petchesky, Rosalind. 2000. "Sexual Rights: Inventing a Concept, Mapping an International Practice." In *Framing the Sexual Subject: The Politics of Gender, Sexuality, and Power,* ed. Richard Parker, Regina Maria Barbosa, and Peter Aggleton, pp. 81–103. Berkeley: University of California Press, 2000.

Petchesky, Rosalind, and Karen Judd. *Negotiating Reproductive Rights.* London: Zed Books, 1998.

Phelan, Shane. *Identity Politics: Lesbian Feminism and the Limits of Community.* Philadelphia: Temple University Press, 1989.

————. *Getting Specific: Postmodern Lesbian Politics.* Minneapolis: University of Minnesota Press, 1994.

————. *Sexual Strangers: Gays, Lesbians, and Dilemmas of Citizenship.* Philadelphia: Temple University Press, 2001.

Pieterse, Jan Nederveen. "Globalization as Hybridization." In *Global Modernities,* ed. M. Featherstone. London: Sage, 1995.

Plummer, Ken. *Modern Homosexualities: Fragments of Lesbian and Gay Experience.* London: Routledge, 1992.

————. *Telling Sexual Stories: Power, Change and Social Worlds.* London: Routledge, 1995.

————. "The Gay and Lesbian Movement in Britain, 1965–1995: Schisms, Solidarities, and Social Worlds." In *The Global Emergence of Gay and Lesbian Politics,* ed. Barry Adam, J. W. Duyvendak, and A. Kruwel, pp. 133–57. Philadelphia: Temple University Press, 1999.

————. "The 'Ethnographic Society' at Century's End." *Journal of Contemporary Ethnography* 28 (December 1999).

————. "Intimate Choices." In *Theory and Society: Understanding the Present,* ed. Gary Browning, Abbey Halcli, and Frank Webster. London: Sage, 2000.

————. *Documents of Life: An Invitation to a Critical Humanism.* 2d ed. London: Sage, 2001.

————. "Gay Cultures / Straight Borders." In *British Cultural Studies,* ed. David Morley and Kevin Robbins, pp. 387–98. Oxford: Oxford University Press, 2001.

————. "The Call of Life Stories in Ethnographic Research." In *Handbook of Ethnography,* ed. Paul Atkinson et al., pp. 395–406. London: Sage, 2001.

Plummer, Ken, ed. *The Making of the Modern Homosexual.* London: Hutchinson, 1981.

————. *Sexualities: Critical Assessments.* 4 vols. London: Routledge, 2002.

Press, Andrea, and Elizabeth Cole. *Speaking of Abortion: Television and Authority in the Lives of Women.* Chicago: University of Chicago Press, 1999.

Priest, Patricia Joyner. *Public Intimacies: Talk Show Participants and Tell-All TV.* Cresskill, N.J.: Hampton Press, 1995.

Putnam, Robert D. *Bowling Alone: The Collapse and Revival of American Community.* New York: Simon and Schuster, 2000.

Rawls, John. *A Theory of Justice.* Oxford: Oxford University Press, 1971.

Raymond, Janice. *Women as Wombs: Reproductive Technologies and the Battle over Women's Freedom.* New York: HarperCollins, 1994.

Richardson, Diane. "Sexuality and Citizenship." *Sociology* 32, no. 1 (Feb. 1998): 83–100.

————. "Constructing Sexual Citizenship: Theorizing Sexual Rights." *Critical Social Policy* 20, no. 1 (2000): 105–35.

————. *Rethinking Sexuality.* London: Sage, 2000.

Richardson, Diane, ed. *Theorizing Heterosexuality.* Buckingham, UK: Open University, 1996.

Richardson, Herbert, ed. *On the Problem of Surrogate Parenthood: Analysing the Baby M Case*. Lewiston, N.Y.: Edwin Mellen Press, 1987.

Rimmerman, Craig A., Kenneth Wald, and Clyde Wilcox, eds. *The Politics of Gay Rights*. Chicago: University of Chicago Press, 2000.

Ritzer, George. *Enchanting a Disenchanted World: Revolutionizing the Means of Consumption*. Thousand Oaks, Calif.: Pine Forge Press, 1999.

———. *The McDonaldization of Society*. London: Sage, 2000.

Robertson, Roland. *Globalisation: Social Theory and Global Culture*. London: Sage, 1992.

Rorty, Richard. *Philosophy and the Mirror of Nature*. Princeton, N.J.: Princeton University Press, 1979.

———. "Posties." *London Review of Books*, p. 12, Sept. 3, 1987.

———. *Contingency, Irony and Solidarity*. Cambridge: Cambridge University Press, 1989.

Samuels, Andrew. *Politics of the Couch: Citizenship and the Internal Life*. London: Profile Books, 2001.

Sanger, Margaret. *The Pivot of Civilization*. New York: Brentano, 1922.

Scheff, Tom, and Suzanne M. Retzinger. *Emotions and Violence: Shame and Rage in Destructive Conflicts*. Lexington, Mass., 1992.

Scheper-Hughes, Nancy. "The Global Traffic in Human Organs." *Current Anthropology* 41, no. 2 (Apr. 2000): 22.

———. "Commodity Fetishism in Organs Trafficking," *Body and Society* 7, nos. 2/3: 31–62.

Seabrook, Jeremy. *In the Cities of the South*. London: Verso, 1996.

Seidman, Steven. *Difference Troubles: Queering Social Theory and Sexual Politics*. Cambridge: Cambridge University Press, 1997.

Seidman, Steven, ed. *Queer Theory / Sociology*. Oxford: Blackwell, 1996.

Sevenhuijsen, Selma. *Citizenship and the Ethics of Care: Feminist Considerations about Justice, Morality and Politics*. London: Routledge, 1998.

Shanley, Mary Lyndon. *Making Babies, Making Families: What Matters Most in an Age of Reproductive Technologies, Surrogacy, Adoption, and Same-Sex and Unwed Parents*. Boston: Beacon Press, 2001.

Shattuck, Jane M. *The Talking Cure: TV Talk Shows and Women*. London: Routledge, 1997.

Shilling, Chris. *Social Theory and the Body*. London: Sage, 1993.

Showalter, Elaine. *Sexual Anarchy: Gender and Culture at the Fin de Siècle*. London: Bloomsbury, 1990.

Silver, Lee M. *Remaking Eden: Cloning, Genetic Engineering and the Future of Humankind*. London: Phoenix Giant, 1999.

Simon, William. *Postmodern Sexualities*. London: Routledge, 1996.

Skrobanek, Siriporn, Nataya Boonpakdee, and Chutima Jatateero, eds. *The Traffic in Women: Human Realities of the International Sex Trade*. London: Zed Books, 1997.

Smart, Carol, and Bren Neale. *Family Fragments.* Cambridge: Polity Press, 1999.

Smith, Barbara Herrnstein. *Belief and Resistance: Dynamics of Contemporary Intellectual Controversy.* Cambridge, Mass.: Harvard University Press, 1997.

Smith, Ralph R., and Russel R. Windes. *Progay / Antigay: The Rhetorical War over Sexuality.* London: Sage, 2000.

Solinger, Rickie. *Beggars and Choosers.* New York: Hill & Wang, 2001.

Sparks, Holloway. "Dissident Citizenship: Democratic Theory, Political Courage and Activist Women." *Hypatia* 12 (1997): 74–110.

Stacey, Judith. *Brave New Families: Stories of Domestic Upheaval in Late Twentieth-Century America.* Berkeley: University of California Press, 1990.

———. *In the Name of the Family: Rethinking Family Values in the Postmodern Age.* Boston: Beacon Press, 1996.

Stein, Arlene. *The Stranger Next Door: The Story of a Small Community's Battle over Sex, Faith, and Civil Rights.* Boston: Beacon Press, 2001.

Stein, Arlene, et al. "Symposium on the Clinton-Lewinsky Affair." *Sexualities* 2, no. 2 (May 1999): 247–60.

Steiner, Wendy. *The Scandal of Pleasure: Art in an Age of Fundamentalism.* Chicago: University of Chicago Press, 1995.

Stinchcombe, Arthur. "Social Structure and Politics." In *Handbook of Political Science,* ed. Nelson W. Polsby and Fred I. Greenstein, vol. 3, pp. 557–622. Reading, Mass.: Addison-Wesley, 1975.

Strauss, Anselm. "A Social Worlds Perspective." In *Studies in Symbolic Interaction,* ed. Norman K. Denzin, vol. 1, pp. 119–28. Greenwich, Conn.: JAI Press, 1978.

———. *Continual Permutations of Action.* New York: Aldine de Gruyter, 1993.

Stychin, Carl F. *A Nation by Rights: National Cultures, Sexual Identity Politics, and the Discourse of Rights.* Philadelphia: Temple University Press, 1998.

Sullivan, Andrew. *Virtually Normal: An Argument about Homosexuality.* New York: Knopf, 1995.

Tannen, Deborah. *The Argument Culture: Stopping America's War of Words.* New York: Random House, 1998.

Taylor, Charles. *Sources of the Self: The Making of the Modern Identity.* Cambridge: Cambridge University Press, 1989.

———. "The Politics of Recognition." In *Multiculturalism: The Politics of Recognition,* ed., with commentary, by Amy Gutmann, pp. 25–74. Princeton, N.J.: Princeton University Press, 1992.

Tharoor, Shashi. "Are Human Rights Universal?" *New Internationalist* 332 (March 2001): 34–35.

Toulmin, Stephen. *Cosmopolis: The Hidden Agenda of Modernity.* Chicago: University of Chicago Press, 1990.

Tronto, Joan C. *Moral Boundaries: A Political Argument for an Ethic of Care.* London: Routledge, 1993.

Turner, Bryan. *Citizenship and Social Theory.* London: Sage, 1993.

Twine, Fred. *Citizenship and Social Rights*. London: Sage, 1994.

UNFPA (United Nations Population Fund). *The State of the World Population: 2000*. New York, 2000.

United Nations Development Programme (UNDP). *Human Development Report*. New York: Oxford University Press, 2000.

United Nations High Commissioner for Refugees. *The State of the World's Refugees*. Oxford: Oxford University Press, 2000.

Vance, Carole S., ed. *Pleasure and Danger: Exploring Female Sexuality*. New York: Routledge, 1984.

Van den Hoonaard, Will C. *Working with Sensitising Concepts: Analytical Field Research*. London: Sage, 1997.

Vattimo, Gianni. *The Transparent Society*. Cambridge, Polity Press, 1992.

Voet, Rian. *Feminism and Citizenship*. London: Sage, 1998.

Walby, Sylvia. "Is Citizenship Gendered?" *Sociology* 28, no. 2 (May 1994): 379–95.

Wallerstein, Judith, Julia Lewis, and Sandra Blakeslee, eds. *The Unexpected Legacy of Divorce: A 25-Year Landmark Study*. New York: Hyperion Books, 2000.

Waltzer, Michael. *Spheres of Justice: A Defense of Pluralism and Democracy*. New York: Basic Books, 1983.

Warner, Michael. *The Trouble with Normal: Sex, Politics, and the Ethics of Queer Life*. Cambridge, Mass.: Harvard University Press, 1999.

———. *Publics and Counterpublics*. New York: Zone Books, 2002.

Watney, Simon. *Policing Desire: Pornography, AIDS and the Media*. London: Methuen, 1987.

Weeks, Jeffrey. *Invented Moralities: Sexual Values in an Age of Uncertainty*. Cambridge: Polity Press, 1995.

———. "The Sexual Citizen." *Theory, Culture and Society* 15, nos. 3/4 (1998): 35–52.

———. *Making Sexual History*. Cambridge: Polity Press, 2000.

Weeks, Jeffrey, Brian Heaphy, and Catherine Donovan. *Same Sex Intimacies: Families of Choice and Other Life Experiments*. London: Routledge, 2001.

Weston, Kath. *Families We Choose: Lesbians, Gays, Kinship*. New York: Columbia University Press, 1991.

Wichterich, Christa. *The Globalized Woman: Reports from a Future of Inequality*. Trans. Patrick Camiller. London: Zed Books, 2000.

Wilcox, Clyde. *Onward Christian Soldiers: The Christian Right in American Politics*. Boulder, Colo.: Westview Press, 1996.

Williams, Rhys, ed. *Cultural Wars in American Politics: Critical Reviews of a Popular Myth*. New York: Aldine de Gruyter, 1997.

Wilton, Tamsin. *EnGendering AIDS: Deconstructing Sex, Text and Epidemic*. London: Sage, 1997.

Wintermute, Robert. *Sexual Orientation and Human Rights*. Oxford: Clarendon Press, 1995.

Wolfe, Alan. "Democracy Versus Sociology: Boundaries and Their Consequences."

In *Cultivating Differences: Symbolic Boundaries and the Making of Inequality,* ed. Michelle Lamont and Marcel Fournier, pp. 309–26. Chicago: University of Chicago Press, 1992.

———. *Marginalized in the Middle.* Chicago: University of Chicago Press, 1996.

———. *One Nation, After All: What Americans Really Think About God, Country, Family, Racism, Welfare, Immigration, Homosexuality, Work, The Right, The Left and Each Other.* New York: Penguin, 1999.

———. *Moral Freedom: The Search for Virtue in a World of Choice.* New York: W. W. Norton, 2001.

Woodward, Kath, ed. *Identity and Difference.* Milton Keynes, Eng.: Open University Press, 1996.

Young, Iris Marion. *Justice and the Politics of Difference.* Princeton, N.J.: Princeton University Press, 1990.

———. "Polity and Group Difference: A Critique of the Ideal of Universal Citizenship." *Ethics* 99 (Jan. 1989): 250–74.

———. *Inclusion and Democracy.* Oxford: Oxford University Press, 2000.

Young, Jock. *The Exclusive Society.* London: Sage, 1999

Yuval-Davis, Nira. *Gender and Nation.* London: Sage, 1997.

Zeldin, Theodore. *An Intimate History of Humanity.* New York: HarperCollins, 1995.

# Index of Names

# Subject Index